BRONSON

This book is to be
the last date st...

CHARLES BRONSON

BRONSON

I FEAR NO-ONE.
VIOLENCE JUST MAKES ME
MADDER AND STRONGER.

JOHN BLAKE

Published by John Blake Publishing Ltd,
3 Bramber Court, 2 Bramber Road,
London W14 9PB, England

www.johnblakepublishing.co.uk

First published in paperback in 2008

ISBN 978 1 84454 655 8

British Library Cataloguing-in-Publication Data:

A catalogue record for this book is available from the British Library.

Design by www.envydesign.co.uk

Printed in the UK by CPI Bookmarque, Croydon, CR0 4TD

7 9 10 8 6

Papers used by John Blake Publishing are natural, recyclable
products made from wood grown in sustainable forests.
The manufacturing processes conform to the environmental
regulations of the country of origin.

Every attempt has been made to contact the relevant copyright-
holders, but some were unobtainable. We would be grateful if the
appropriate people could contact us.

I've no regrets – only for hurting my beautiful mother, Eira. This book is for Mum – with love and respect.

CHARLES BRONSON

ACKNOWLEDGEMENTS

Charlie Bronson would like to thank his many friends, including: Joe Pyle, Roy Shaw, Charlie and Eddie Richardson, Reece Huxford, Simon and Karen, Jan, Andy, Lyn and Chris, Eddie Whicker, Sharon and Steve and Ed Clinton.

Rob Ackroyd thanks his loyal family, and his friends, particularly: Julia, Gerard, Eran, Jane, Graham, Diane, Paul, Olive, Kevin, Janet, and Padraic.

'I'll tell you now Ronnie, that book will outsell the Bible.'

A Word from Reg Kray before his death in October 2000

Charlie Bronson and I have been friends
for many years. My opinion is he would be
more benefit to society helping kids than
wasting any more time in prison.
He has a lot of talent which is going to waste.

God Bless

REG KRAY

INTRODUCTION

There is so much more to Charles Bronson than meets the eye. You may know of him as the strongest man in the prison system, Britain's Number 1 psycho, or the man responsible for more hostage-takings than any other inmate.

Yes, he has been locked in a cage like the fictional Hannibal Lecter because of his extreme danger. And yes, Lecter-style, he did, infamously, threaten to eat a hostage unless he was given a cup of tea. But the Charlie Bronson I know is a man of great humour and warmth; a talented raconteur and artist. In adversity, a man of real insight.

Charlie is genuinely hilarious. 'I'm not Hannibal

bloody Hector,' he says, deliberately mispronouncing the name. 'He eats people. I've never eaten anyone! I'm no more Hannibal Hector than Maggie Thatcher was.'

Charlie is a lost soul, a man from a different age. Ten thousand years ago he would have been the strongest man in the jungle; two thousand years ago, in Roman times, he would have been the unbeaten gladiator; two hundred years ago he would have been a circus strong-man. As I write, he is locked up 23 hours a day in a cell without so much as a window to open, with little natural light, no breeze on his face. His furniture – a chair and table – is made of compressed cardboard. His bed is a concrete plinth with a fire-proof mattress on top. When he is unlocked for his one hour's exercise, in a razor wire-topped pen, he is accompanied by up to a dozen prison officers, sometimes with dogs and often in riot gear.

Charlie has few visitors. Charlie has been locked up, bar 140 days, for 28 years. Most of that time, almost 24 years, has been spent in solitary. His only creature comforts are a battery-operated radio (he doesn't watch television) and paper, pens and pencils for his art work. He has, he says, 'eaten more porridge than Goldilocks and the three bears'. He knows more about the sharp end of prison life than any dozen governors you might nominate. He commands respect from other convicts. Many people fear him; few really know him.

It has been my privilege over recent years to get to know the real Charlie Bronson, to find out what makes him tick, and to work with him on this book. It has not always been easy. He can be very supportive, but also very demanding. I have lost count of the number of lawyers, authors and even members of his own family he has 'blown out' over the years. At one point, I would read only the first and last lines of his letters to me, to gauge his mood, and then put them to one side for a day or two. I really liked the guy, but I could get seriously pissed off with him. I dreaded the words 'I'm not happy, Robin' or 'I've got serious mind problems.'

But his humour kept me going. Here's a little extract from one of his letters:

> At times it looked very doubtful I'd ever get out. But recently I've become a very understanding guy – more in control. Could be I'm maturing? But it's probably because I want to get out to get my dick sucked. Well, I'm only human! I may go into films! If that prat Vinnie Jones can do it, why can't I?
>
> Right. Howz yourself?
>
> Have you met my brief yet? If not … why not! Have you got all the paperwork? If not … why not! How did your sailing trip go? Sea, sun and sex? If not … why not! My last holiday was on the Isle of Wight … but that was only Parkhurst!

And here's a postscript Charlie added in a letter last summer: 'Oh! Guess who's below me? Lifer! Ex-Broadmoor! Swallows things. (Sometimes calls you up.) And he speaks highly of you. (Well, he ain't got much in life.) A very sad case!'

Cheers, pal!

Charlie knows little about modern life, he has been in jail for so long. He first went inside in 1974, the year that President Nixon resigned over the Watergate scandal. His language is from the '70s – 'brill'; 'wizard'; 'geezer'. He talks of Doris Day and Shirley Bassey. He has fought the system for more than a quarter of a century.

When I first met Charlie in Britain's most secure unit – a jail within a jail – he must have shaken my hand half-a-dozen times. Here was a man denied normal human contact. A generous man, who quite simply cannot control his aggression, as he has proved in spectacular style over the years. Not a murderer, but a man who went inside originally for an armed robbery during which no shots were fired. His seven-year sentence doubled because he was uncontrollable in jail, and then, in his first brief taste of freedom, he went to work as an unlicensed boxer. Soon he robbed a jeweller's in his home town of Luton, Bedfordshire. He had lasted just 69 days on the outside.

Sitting opposite me during that first visit was a broad-shouldered man in a green-and-yellow cotton jump-suit, 'HM Prison' emblazoned in big black letters on the back. Charlie was smiling, broken-toothed, through a fearsome black and grey beard. His head was shaven and his eyes were alight behind his small, oval sunglasses.

We had an hour together. I had gone through the most rigorous security checks to visit Britain's most violent inmate: police vetting; forms to fill in; mug-shots. I was frisked twice at HMP Woodhill, on the outskirts of Milton Keynes in Buckinghamshire. An electronic device was used to take a fingerprint, to ensure I was the same person going in and out. A video-grab of my face was taken for a similar comparison. I went through two metal detectors, like the ones you see at airports, and was checked again with a hand-held detector. My shoes had to be taken off to be X-rayed, the inside of my mouth was checked for contraband, as was my hair and my belt buckle. All my possessions, except loose change, had to be put in a locker.

After walking through air-lock doors, I entered the reception area for visitors, clutching a yellow visiting slip in a hand which had been stamped with a fluorescent code. There were about a dozen other visitors, including solicitors. None of them was going to 'House Unit Six' in the new Close Supervision Centre, a maximum security block well away from 'normal' Category A inmates.

'Oh, a yellow slip?' said a friendly prison officer. 'House Unit Six?' Clearly, not many visitors went there. He looked at the form. 'Come to see Charlie? We'll have to escort you.'

I was the first civilian visitor, apart from his solicitor, to see Charles Bronson since he had staged the longest prison siege in living memory, holding an education worker hostage for 44 hours.

Two friendly female warders led me first through barred doors and then across a yard – where, as only Milton Keynes can, there were several life-size concrete sheep on a patch of grass – to the secure block, bounded by razor wire and thick mesh fencing. Down a stark corridor, and under the watchful presence of closed-circuit TV cameras, we finally entered a secure room where I was allowed to use my loose change to buy chocolate bars and fizzy drinks in plastic bottles from two machines. Charlie had signed a form requesting half a dozen bars; I bought eight. The rest of my money was bagged and sealed. I was allowed to take in not a penny, not a scrap of paper – nothing.

And there was Charlie, alone in the brightly lit visiting area – alone apart from six screws and the cameras – pacing up and down like a caged bear.

'Good to see you! Come on, sit down, over here,' he urged me.

Time was precious. This was his monthly hour; two visits rolled into one. He was animated, alive. We joked as we sat opposite one another, across a narrow table, on metal seats screwed to the floor. Charlie crammed chocolate into his mouth as we talked. We were like old friends, pen-pals meeting for the first time. The screws kept their distance.

'Come on, Charlie,' I said within a few minutes of us meeting. 'I don't believe you're as tough as they make out! Let's have an arm wrestle.' We did, and I lasted barely three seconds, my wrist turning white under the pressure. 'No one's ever beaten me,' growled Charlie.

'I will one day,' I told him. 'Just need a bit of practice.'

'No,' he said firmly. 'No one will ever beat me.'

Towards the end of the visit, he turned sideways on his bolted chair, half-eyeing me out of the corner of his sunglasses. It was as if he wanted to liven the hour by showing me another side.

'You know, Robin, I've got no regrets.'

I heard what he was saying, but I found it hard to believe. Prison is tough and, for Charlie, a lonely existence. The thing is, it is virtually all he knows. One little thing really brought home how stuck in a different age Charlie is. In an almost fatherly way, and showing genuine interest, he asked me what sort of car I drove.

'Oh, just an old Jetta,' I said. He looked blank. 'A VW Jetta,' I added. 'You know, a Volkswagen.' I was getting embarrassed. He was wanting to talk, man to man, about something on the outside – and he was lost. I repeated, 'A Volkswagen.'

His eyes lit up. 'Ah! I know! One of them with the engine in the boot!'

I smiled back, reassuringly.

Charlie wrote to me after that visit:

> *So good to see you after so long! You looked fit and well. I bloody enjoyed it, I really did! My brother Mark looks like you. My other brother*

John is out in Australia – lovely man, ex-Royal Marine. Not seen him since 1985, the year I pulled Liverpool Jail roof off! Now, that was a good roof! Summer time … three glorious days up there. I pulled it to bits. Yes, lovely memories! Oh, a terrible beating afterwards. But it was worth it (and the 12 months extra!). A good jail, the old school – not like the nurseries today. The screws were hard, but fair. Some would fight you alone. Nowadays they get a button torn off and they are six months on the sick. How can you respect that?

They are a different breed today (or am I a dinosaur?). Maybe it's time I got out and put it all behind me. Personally, I enjoyed the good old days – piss-pots, slopping out, porridge six times a week. Now it's poxy sugar fucking puffs. We rarely get porridge, and when we do it's not good porridge. Porridge is 'bird'. Sugar puffs! Do me a favour! Is it real, or what? Next they'll be whipping us with lettuce leaves! Or hanging us with elastic!

He added, 'Hey! Did you see the concrete sheep outside the unit? Even Broadmoor ain't that insane!'

That's Charles Bronson, and this is his own story, which I hope you will find exciting, sometimes funny and also deeply sad. I hope you will find it ultimately uplifting. After all, Charlie is one of life's survivors. Has the system created Charles Bronson as much as he has created himself? Does he want to get out, even if he is eventually given the chance? Make up your own mind after reading this book.

Robin Ackroyd

FOREWORD

I've eaten more porridge than Goldilocks and the three bears! Twenty-six years of porridge would fill a swimming pool and I'm sick of it. Now, after all that's happened, I'm facing more years. It's like there's no tomorrow, as if I am meant to be in a cage. Maybe I am.

A friend once described me as being a lost soul. How right that is.

The world left me behind more than a quarter of a century ago. I'm a lost man – what more can be said? Over the past two decades I've had every convenient label, every badge: Mad Man, Danger Man, Violent Man, Disruptive Man and Disturbed Man! I've been on a mission of madness, a mission of destruction, within the prison system.

Sure, I've given them hell. But I've ended up in a living hell. There are roughly 60,000 cons in jail. How many have seen a Hannibal Cage, let alone been locked up in one? I'll tell you – not very many. You can count on the fingers of one hand the men who've been banged up in such max secure conditions. All killers. Danger men. But I've never killed. I fight with my fists. I'm not a gangster. I work on my own, and it has left me facing life on my own.

I've done it all, seen it all, had it all. Prison created what I am today, and what I'll be until I die. A legend within the system.

It's no big deal. It's really been a waste of life – but it has been my life and I'm still a proud man.

So fuck anyone who says it's no life! I've made it exciting!

This story I'm about to tell is a true account of life behind bars. It's not a life as it should be, it's an existence. It's senseless, it's a waste, but it's my life and it's all I know.

I say to all youngsters who are thinking about becoming criminals, 'Stop and think now. Don't be foolish. It's not worth it. You'll break your family's hearts and destroy your own.'

If you do decide to become a criminal, even after reading my story, remember this one thing: there are no tough guys behind these doors. We all search for our souls. It's a truly empty world – believe it!

I've spent my years in most of the top-security prisons, as I've always been a high-risk inmate. My time is always under secure conditions. Being observed, monitored, analysed, assessed.

You'll never understand the true sense of freedom – until you lose it.

To be able to go in and out of doors when you like, to walk in the rain, to walk under the stars. To go to the toilet, to wear nice clothes and to eat nice food, all when you want. And, most importantly, to be loved and wanted.

In jail, they are watching me every day, like a buzzard watches its prey and a mongoose watches a cobra. Like a spider watches a fly. I'm trapped, caught up in the web. I'm a strong believer in fate. I truly believe everything is meant to be. Obviously, certain things we can change but basically it's all planned for us. From our birth to our death, life is a test of our strength and ability – mental, physical and even spiritual.

Some of us end up in a cage like some birds, lions or elephants end up caged. Prison is the human zoo, a cage of man. After 28 years of looking through the bars and searching myself, I am now convinced it's all been my test in life. Even now, as I tell you my story, I face more years caged up.

Maybe this book is the very reason for my existence on earth? I'm not going to preach, or ram goodness down anyone's neck. Just read how it's been and *think*. That's all I ask.

This is a journey through the penal system, the dungeons of hell: beatings; drug control; isolation; asylums; roof-top protests; hostages; violence; hunger strikes. Fate has been cruel and I'm still fighting for a happy ending. But in my heart of hearts I know I'll probably die fighting. I've been labelled Britain's most violent prisoner. To get a label like that doesn't come overnight; it is years of agony, pain and a lot of emptiness.

For every punch you throw in prison you take a dozen back. The system caters for everyone. Where one screw is needed for one prisoner, six will look after another – and the alarm bell will bring 60 more. I've been throwing punches from the day I entered prison. I've actually lost count of all the screws I've punched and they've probably lost count of the times they've punched me. But there is really only one loser. You may as well punch a door or nut a wall – better still, work it out in the gym, because every punch you throw is losing you a big part of your life.

As I tell you this story, remember that, in spite of everything, I'm a born survivor. I lower my eyes to no man. I'm still strong, despite my years. My whiskers may be greying, my skin may be pale after decades with little natural light. But I'm fitter and stronger than men half my 47 years. Maybe I'll never get out, except in a body bag. Maybe I'll have creaky bones, a walking stick and a white 'tash when I finally walk out of here. Who knows?

But I tell you what – right now I'm king of the press-ups and sit-ups. I train alone in solitary; I have done for over 20 years. How else can I keep hold of my sanity? I recently smashed the press-up record by 250. I completed 1,727 in one hour! Yeah, and I still kept some back, just in case I have to make a comeback. I'm an old fox, see. A good poker player! I play to win. I once did 25 press-ups with two men on my back. Show me another man who can do that.

You can be too big, too strong, but you can never be too fit. My strength has caused me a lot of trouble inside, and kept me caged for so long, but I still feel lucky. I have my lows, but I have to keep strong and stay training otherwise I'd just die. I tell all the guys who take drugs or smoke, 'Hey, there's only one drug. It's already in your body. Adrenalin. It works and it's natural. So get it pumping around your veins and feel good! If you wanna be a fat, lazy, useless slob, if you're happy with your fags and drugs, then enjoy it. It's your life. But don't ever bring them near me! Why? Because I don't bloody like it, that's why!'

Right. Before I take you back to the start of my journey, I've got to end here for the moment – as I've got 500 sit-ups to polish off before lights out. Nice 'n' easy!

CHAPTER ONE

'Now I've got you. Take your last fucking breath because this knife is going in you. You're the bastard that slagged my cartoon off.

'Right. You keep quiet now, because most people want to keep quiet for a time before they die. If I don't get what I want, they can carry us both out in body bags.'

Charlie was making loud noises ... shouting, swearing and cursing. He was making monkey-like noises. He was acting like a crazed madman. I passed out, I think from fear and adrenalin. I kept drifting in and out of consciousness ...

'*Charlie, where are you?*'

'Speak when you're fucking spoken to. You talk too much.'

Charlie re-tied me in a different way. He tied my left arm to my body and to the chair, and then tied my wrists together. I was still convinced that I was going to die.

Charlie found a snooker cue and then with a bandage he began to bind the handle of the knife to the end of the cue. The result was a spear. Charlie held the spear by his side and then began marching up and down like a soldier. It was as if he was in some sort of trance.

I thought I was going to be sacrificed on the snooker table. I felt that I had to keep a rapport going with Charlie to try and save myself. He tied one end of the skipping rope around my neck and held on to the other end.

'Dance!'

I started marching and doing silly steps to keep Charlie amused. Every minute felt like an eternity. Charlie then began to sing 'I'll Never Walk Alone'.

I felt like I was being treated like a dog on a lead. Then Charlie said something to me.

'You've been my best hostage. This is the big one. You are also one of the few who hasn't physically shit himself.'

★ ★ ★

1 February 1999 is a day that will live with that man for the rest of his life. It was the day he must have prayed to God that I would not kill him.

The skipping rope went around his skinny ostrich neck and the knife went up to his face.

'You're mine, you faggot!'

The longest British prison siege in living memory

had started. Hull max secure unit was mine. I was the governor.

There is no turning back the clock, but now I'm going back to the beginning. The beginning of the journey which saw me fall into the pit of no hope, trussed up like a chicken in the modern equivalent of a strait-jacket, crawling like a worm across a concrete floor to eat food out of the plastic dish left for me. Being transferred from high-security jail to high-security jail at no notice. Strapped up, stark bollock naked, in a 'body-belt', hands cuffed in medieval-style metal hoops by my sides. Slipped out of the back of one prison into the back of another.

A seemingly endless journey. Sometimes in a wheelchair, like Hannibal Lecter. Not because I'm disabled, but because they wanted to keep me under control. Because I had earned the unenviable reputation as the most violent prisoner in British penal history.

Charles Bronson. Danger man. Serial hostage-taker. One-man army. Double dangerous. Twelve screws plus dogs needed to unlock him. And all looking 'hard', chewing their gum and staring. Big, tough guys. Jangling their keys. I'd like to see their faces if I met them on the outside, without their batons, without their closed-circuit TV.

Don't get me wrong. There are screws I respect, and governors, too. Fair men. Men who have given me a chance. It's been a long journey and I've met the good, the bad – and all of them ugly. Likewise, there are cons I admire, and some I despise. It may seem strange to you, but there's a strong moral code in prison. I've never killed. I hate wife-beaters and paedophiles. My crimes are armed robberies and violence, urges I've been struggling to overcome for more than a quarter of a century. If you're my friend, I'll be loyal until the end. If you mug me off or try to pick a fight, I'll bash your crust in. You'll get no warning. You'll be in hospital; I'll be having a nice cup of tea.

The reason for my length of time in prison is simply my crimes on the inside. The violence, the hostage-takings. But I've never really hurt a hostage – and when I slap a paedophile, am I not doing what most of you would really wish to do? Ask yourself, in your heart of hearts. I love kids. I'd nut a moving train to help a child. That's why so many of my feats of strength – my world-record attempts at lifting weights and doing press-ups – have raised hundreds of pounds for children's hospices. All the lads chip in, even if they only get £2.50 a week in prison wages.

Anyway! I was a lovely baby myself once. My mum says so. So who can argue with that?

I came in at 21. I was in the prime of my life. It was 1974, the year the Three Degrees had their Number 1 hit 'When Will I See You Again?' There's a lot of people I've never seen since that day. A lot of people who will be nothing more than vague memories. It was the year I slung everything away – my car, my home and, most importantly of all, my beautiful wife Irene and my lovely son Michael.

I'd held down a few jobs. I'd tried my best. But my violent urges overcame me. One day I turned to major crime; I got myself a gun, sawed down the barrel, and went to work as an armed robber. The outcome was a prison cell.

In one week of madness, I robbed a post office, a garage and a Tudor mansion. I had committed serious violence. My head was flipped. I even stuck the shotgun up a bloke's arse and was a fraction away from committing a murder. This was not me. But I can't blame anyone except me. I've got no real excuses. Drugs and drink were not the reason. There is no answer but excitement. It was a complete week of insanity. Violence took me over and the courts had no choice but to remand me. It was a miracle I hadn't killed anyone.

I pitched up in Risley Remand Centre, Cheshire. Now, you may not remember, but this jail was at the time the Number 1 prison for suicides – mostly youngsters. It was really gloomy and depressing.

There was a lot of bullying going on – screws intimidating and threatening. This prison was nicknamed 'Grisly Risley', and I hated every stinking day of it.

For a jail that was built in the mid-'60s, it was a disgrace. The cells were designed for one inmate. An 8ft sq cube – and they were doubling inmates up. It really was inhumane. Some guys woke up to find their cellmate hanging.

Most of the deaths seemed to be in the hospital wing, and some of those deaths were mysterious to say the least. The whole fucking place stank of despair.

At night, cons would shit in a newspaper and sling it out of the cell window. What else could we do? Who wants to sit in a cell all night looking at a piss-pot full of shit?

There were rats in Risley as big as cats ... vicious fuckers! I've sat at my window watching them carry away food, bits of fruit, bread and even the shit parcels. I hate rats. I've watched a dog handler do his rounds and seen the alsatian tear a rat to pieces. The shriek went right through me.

The real horror came one night when I woke up to see a rat sitting on my window-sill inside my cell. The fucker was staring at me with eyes as black as coal! As I moved to grab my shoe, it leapt out of the window. I never forgot to close my window after that.

Cockroaches were another type of vermin we had to put up with. These things would come into our cells throughout the night – under the door, through the air vents, the cracks in the walls. They scavenge for bits of food. I've found them in my socks, in my jersey, in my shoes, even in my body hair.

The main thing, though, was who you got in your cell to share your life.

Another human being is forced into your world. You don't know him, he doesn't know you. He could be anyone! I soon found out that I wasn't going to like being in jail. Days were long, weeks felt like months, months felt like years. I was on the edge of madness.

Risley is in Warrington. Most of the cons there were either Liverpool lads or country yokels. Football is the northern lads' religion. Liverpool were the cream, Man United their worst enemies. Risley was a war zone for Scousers and Mancunians. And then there was me – supporting Spurs and coming from Luton. It never made me too popular on a Saturday!

I happen to know a lot of Scousers – and a lot respect me. But to get respect you must earn it. It's not something you can buy. I earned mine in more ways than one, both inside and out. My motto in life has always been 'It's nice to be nice'. But, sadly, it's not always possible. Some guys will take kindness as a show of weakness.

Prison breeds violence. Whenever men are herded together, violent incidents will always occur; black against white, Protestant against Catholic, Muslim against Jew, Hell's Angel against skinhead – and so on. Men stand up and fight for their beliefs. Prison is a fucking powder keg.

My cell was no exception. I got my share of idiots, snorers, moaners, liars, smelly feet, farting and faggots. Some lasted a day, some lasted weeks. Some became life-long pals, some became punch-bags. Risley for me was hell.

At this time, all visits, except legal ones, were closed – without human contact. Closed visits took place in a big room with little boxed cubicles. Our visitors were behind a sheet of unbreakable glass, with a steel vent to talk through. It was frustrating, degrading and inhuman. During my entire stay in Risley, I refused to see my son and my wife Irene. Obviously, I wrote to her and she wrote to me, but I could not see them behind a sheet of glass. Never.

It was bad enough seeing my parents and family like that. No way could I see my three-year-old boy. How the fuck can you accept it? Your own flesh and blood looking at you in a filthy fucking box – and not being able to touch him. I wanted to hold my boy, not watch him! I still feel bitter and hateful, more than 25 years later, over these visits. I still shake with rage. This was the beginning of me losing my sanity.

I next saw Irene and my son when I appeared at Chester Crown Court. My mum Eira was there, too, and my Auntie Eileen. I pleaded guilty to all charges as I was bang to rights. There was no way out of it. I received a total of 28 years, fortunately to run concurrently.

Seven years for all I had done.

Some would say that was a good result – the shotgun alone, the post office, the violence – but I saw it as far too long. I was 21 years old, in the prime of my life. Three years would have been fair. A short sharp shock – it might have worked! But it was seven whole years. With remission, I should serve four years and eight months. With bad behaviour, I would serve seven. Both seemed an eternity for me, my wife and my son.

Little did I know then, I would not be freed for thirteen-and-a-half years. If I had known, I might well have cut my own throat that very night.

Irene was so upset she ran out of the courtroom clutching Michael. My mother and her sister were allowed to come down to the cells to see me.

Chester Crown Court is in an old castle, beneath which is a dungeon. In some of the cells there were rusty rings where the chains used to pass through. There were cast-iron gates, and the walls and floor were made up of big slabs of stone.

It was cold, damp and empty. Mum's eyes were tearful; Eileen was upset, too. They told me Irene had got a taxi home. She was devastated.

I told them seven years would soon go. Be strong!

I gave my mum a big hug. 'I'll be out of here before you know it.'

My mum was 43, a beautiful woman, loved and respected by many. She would be 57 when I next got out. I would be 35, my wife would be 38, my son 17 and my father 64. I'm just glad I never knew my fate then. Hell was just around the corner.

★   ★   ★

I came into this world as Michael Gordon Peterson on 6 December 1952, the year George VI died.

I'll go out of this world as Charles Bronson – my fighting name.

I've lived in two towns during my life on the outside – Luton and Ellesmere Port in Cheshire. But since I've been banged up, I've almost lost count of the places I've been – and never seen.

They call it 'ghosting' – moving high-risk inmates at no notice from jail to jail. From east to west; from the far northern reaches of England like Frankland Prison, County Durham, to the furthest tip of the country – Parkhurst jail on the Isle of Wight. Often, I had no idea where I was going; I was always in the back of a prison van.

Cuffed or strapped up, I've travelled the country more than any other con – and more than most folk on the outside.

But it was in Luton where I grew up. My family are law-abiding – there's nothing in their nature I can put my madness down to. We had a loving upbringing, me and my brothers.

My angel of a mother, Eira, is still alive. Joe, my dear dad, has passed away. I've pretty much lost contact with my brothers. John was 19 months older than me and emigrated to Perth, Australia. Sadly, he died of brain cancer on 3 March last year. Mark is younger, and I sadly fell out with him some years ago. He was born eight years after me, in 1960, and was only seven when I left school to find a job. My cousin Loraine – my mum's sister, Auntie Eileen's daughter – has always been a source of strength. I've turned to her in my hours of deepest need and although I've not always treated her right – mainly because of the way I've been treated on the inside – I still love her dearly. She's always been there for me in the background, and I know that she will be there in my mind when I finally slip out of this world. Hers will be the last face I see on this earth.

I don't know why I'm so close to Loraine. Perhaps it's because my mother had a little daughter – my sister – who died at birth. I've often called Loraine my 'sister'. Perhaps she was meant to take the place of the little girl I never knew.

We are like twins, me and Loraine. One smile, one touch and I light up. Her laughter is contagious – and I love to laugh! Sometimes, I fear she no longer believes in me but, hell, 40 years can't just be swept away.

Prison can destroy families. Not just me and my lovely ex-wife Irene, and the lost years with my son Michael. But also with close relatives like Loraine.

Years of my life have been spent in jails up north – how can working-class families get to visit? It's almost as if the system has tried to make it difficult for me. In fact, I'm sure it has. Letters 'disappear', they deny you your weekly phone call, you're moved to another jail just when your family is planning to visit the one you were in before. So the rift begins.

Just think back to my first days on remand. Not yet convicted, and I was asked to speak through glass to my beautiful wife and baby son. The rot, my hatred for the system, set in at an early stage. If I was a different person, maybe I could have coped, knuckled down. As it was, I felt thrown to the wolves – and I came out fighting. I've been fighting ever since.

My dear old dad, Joe, was a strict man. Never violent, but I knew I could never put a foot wrong. If we had to be in at a certain time as kids, then we were in at that time. He wouldn't stand any cheek. He had a strong moral code, and hundreds respected him for it. Joe was good-looking and powerfully built. He had served in Africa and India from 1942 to 1947 as an aircraft mechanic in the Fleet Air Arm – and he became a Royal Navy boxing champion.

Dad was born in Northampton on 12 July 1924, one of three boys and two girls. He was English but had partly foreign roots. His mum, Dorothy – my grandma – was from Northamptonshire. But his dad, who was called Jack, had a German father and a Swedish mum who had run a bakery in east London. Jack was born over here and when his parents died within weeks of each other, he was brought up in a Dr Barnardo's children's home in London with his four brothers and sisters.

Jack grew up to become a skilled craftsman who used to put gold leaf on horse-drawn carriages and trains. My grandfather Jack's real surname was a German one – Wolerstein. But that caused difficulties for him during the First World War. He was trying to join the British Army, so he changed it to his mother's Swedish maiden name – Petersen. It was only when Jack died that the family found out from the birth records Jack's real name. Later, we changed our surname from Petersen to Peterson.

My mum, Eira, was born in Aberystwyth but left for south Wales aged eight, and then came with her family to Luton in Bedfordshire. She met Dad in Luton just after the Second World War. They got married there in 1949. Mum was 18, Dad was 25.

I remember very little up to the age of eight, but I know Mum and Dad did everything they could to make our lives happy. Some kids went short, but we never did. We weren't rich; we lived in a three-bed council house on the Runfold estate in Luton – number 24, Leyburne Road. But the house was spotless and me and John always wore dickie bows to go to school. We always went somewhere special on Sundays, and we had holidays at the seaside every year. My granny Martha – Mum's mum – had a neighbour with a static caravan at Caister-on-Sea, near Yarmouth in Norfolk. We'd go there for a week in the summer and play on the beach with our buckets and spades. I'd take a friend and so would John. We went there for about six years on the trot, then we would go on caravan holidays to Boscombe near Bournemouth. Dad bought me and John fishing rods, and every evening we'd all sit around playing cards for hours – usually Pontoon.

Mum used to cook a lot at home. Her apple pies were a special treat. I still love an apple pie! Dad was a proud man. He spent hours in the garden, tending to his flowers and shrubs. That garden was the envy of a lot of people on the estate. People waiting at the bus stop nearby used to stand and gaze at it in admiration. You'd never see my old man without a shirt and tie on. He was always immaculate. He never owned a pair of jeans in his life.

I do remember one thing, from when I was about five or six. We used to play on the edge of some big woods at the back of our house – all the kids did. One day some teenage lads grabbed me, John and some girls and boys we were playing with. They took us into the woods and started to interfere with the girls. I was the youngest and I screamed and kicked my way out and ran all the way home crying. They never touched me, but I saw them touch the girls. I told Mum. I can't remember much more, but I do know that three teenagers were sent to Borstal for it. I sometimes wonder if that incident scarred me.

Then, when I was about eight, I remember being hit on the head by my lovely mum. I adored her; she never meant it. She was looking after some neighbour's kids, a boy and a girl who were younger than me. Their mum was at work and my mum used to take care of them for an hour or two after school. I was playing up, showing off, and Mum was trying to make the tea.

'Michael,' she said. 'Michael, for God's sake be quiet!' She spun around with a bottle in her hand. It hit me bang on the head.

★ ★ ★

John and I went to the same schools. He was OK, but I hated it. My brother and I grew up together, but we were so different in so many ways. He was always cool, relaxed, contented … easy come, easy go. He always seemed to be reading something. I was more introverted and less academic. I was never one for team sports but I used to enjoy swimming at school, even though it affected my ears. I found it hard to mix and it took some time to overcome my shyness. I had a great fear of the dark as a youngster and would have frequent nightmares. I couldn't fully control my bladder until I was 10.

When I was eight, my younger brother Mark was born at home. I can still remember Mum's cries of pain in the bedroom. That upset me; I couldn't understand it. Then I heard the crying of a child. I'm still sorry there is so much of an age gap between me and Mark; we never really grew up together. He was only seven when I left school and went out to work.

One day, something strange came over me. I was about 13 and I had my first urge to kill. No one in particular, just anyone.

Maybe this was the start of my fucked-up life. Who knows?

I hung around by a big tree near my home. I had an empty bottle in my hand – a milk bottle. I was ready to bash anyone who came past.

No one came.

I smashed the bottle over my own head until blood trickled down my forehead into my eyes.

★ ★ ★

By about the age of 13, I had a nice little gang together. The four of us would go shoplifting every Saturday. Our hits were mostly big stores; we'd get pens, diaries, purses and jewellery and stash it all away before we sold it here and there. There was no real sense in it – just excitement.

Unfortunately, one of our little team was caught by a store detective, and the police were soon knocking on Mum and Dad's door. That upset my family a lot. I was up before the juvenile court and had to go to an attendance centre for two hours every Saturday morning. That went on for 12 weeks and I hated the regimented discipline of it. I learnt a lot through that episode, mainly about disloyalty.

What had hurt the most was that I'd been grassed on.

By this time, John was in the school brass band and had started going out with girls. But I wanted none of it. I was always trying to be different.

We were in an all-boys school and I had no interest in girls at that age. I got my kicks out of wanting to be Number 1 all the time ... showing off.

I was never a bully, but while my mates would be happy firing their airguns at the birds in the trees, I would want to hit some stranger in the backside. We mucked about on old motorbikes, went camping and had the odd scrap. But I was always pushing things to the limit. So while the other lads were content to ride a motorbike up and down a dirt track, I was the one who had to go on the road. If somebody did 50mph, I had to do 60. If they had £10, I wanted £20.

Then there was a big change in my life. John joined the Royal Marine band. He wasn't even 15 – he did the rest of his schooling in the Marines. I hadn't realised how close we were. I really missed him. Dad was proud to see him in uniform, and so was I. But from then on, even though we'd see him when he came home, something was missing. I knew Dad would have liked to see me join up. But I've always believed in self-discipline, not being forced into it. I hated being told off.

All John's mates asked about him – his pals, his girlfriends, the teachers at school, the neighbours. After a while, I got fed up of hearing about the Marines. Then another big change happened. My school became mixed. I hated being in a mixed class.

I was incredibly shy at first, then I opened up a little. I became very fond of a girl called Shirley – my first girlfriend. I wanted to tell her things but I could never really find the words. I always felt a bit embarrassed. This was about the time I started getting into all sorts of scrapes. God knows why, but I sure wasn't on my own. I'd go out with my mates, stealing motorbikes – just for the joy-ride. I'll never know how I didn't kill myself! We'd often get chased by a police car.

I moved from school to school as I kept getting expelled for fighting. I wasn't evil, but I was sick of school. I would always respect my elders and give up my seat for an old person or a lady on the bus. And I loved animals, so there was definitely a good side to me! We had boxer dogs at home, and Dad used to keep budgies. A few years earlier, when I was about ten, I even had my own little zoo. I kept frogs and mice in the garden shed and used to charge the younger kids a penny or two to come in and see them.

I was coming up to 15, the age I could finally leave school, and I was getting into music … the Beatles, the Stones, the Small Faces. There were Mods, Rockers and Flower People. I was a Mod.

I took pride in my appearance, just like my dad. But I soon went seriously off the rails and ran away from home. I didn't have any idea where to head for, so, with a haversack on my back, I ended up thumbing lifts all over. I decided to go to see my brother John, who was now based at Deal in Kent.

I remember it so well, and for good reason! I was on my way to Deal when I was dropped off by a lorry driver in a little village. It was a hot summer's day and I was thirsty and hungry, so I bought a bottle of orange and put it in my haversack. I thought I'd get out of the village and find somewhere quiet to drink my orange and eat the few sandwiches I had with me. I was just getting out of the built-up area when I saw an orchard. I was over the fence in no time, filling up my bag with apples and pears. Then I came to a dual carriageway and just flaked out in the sun.

On the other side of the road was a girl walking towards where I'd just come from. She was some girl! She was older than me but somehow we got chatting. Anyway, to cut a long story short, we ended up in the fields.

I smiled all the way to Deal. I'd got plenty of fruit that day – more than my apples and pears!

That night, I ended up sleeping in an old barn. I was cold, I felt lost, but that girl had done something to me. I wanted so much to go back and be with her.

I made it to see John the next day. I saw his mates and told them all about my travelling plans. But I was just kidding myself – dreaming. John told me to go home. He was a real man in his Royal Marine uniform. I wasn't. We said farewell and I hung around for a while, watching the Marines going in and out of the gate. They were smart, no doubt about it, but I knew it could never be for me. I knew I couldn't stand the discipline.

I headed to London, and then back home to Luton. I was dirty, tired and hungry, but it was great to be back. I had learnt a lot, but Mum and Dad had been heart-broken.

I had a few months left of school, but I was playing truant so much I was hardly ever there. I just wanted to go out and get some good money. That eliminated an apprenticeship for me. I really started courting Shirley at that stage. I felt good with her, and my family liked her a lot. But I didn't know what I really wanted. We were only kids. And at that age you're as likely to fall in love with your pet hamster or your goldfish.

The last day of school was the best. A few of us padlocked the main gate to stop the teachers getting their cars out. We had a big punch-up with the prefects. It was great!

I had no qualifications but I started my first job a week later. Before I go into that, I have to say that I don't think my childhood was in any way different from thousands of others. I can't blame my upbringing for what I have become. Maybe I was a bit more headstrong than some other lads, maybe a little more quick-tempered and rebellious. But don't all boys fight, steal and take chances?

I took the first job offered to me, in Tesco's supermarket. I had to keep the fridge section stocked up and stamp the prices on the goods. From day one I knew it wasn't for me. It wasn't a man's job. I felt like a fairy.

There I was with my red top on, stamping the eggs, butter and cheese. But there were a lot of girls working there – and I met Sue.

I really fell for her. She was a couple of years older, but it boosted me that she liked me. I had a tattoo done with her name on. But that relationship didn't last – like the job.

Two weeks after I'd started at Tesco's, I ended up cracking the manager over the head with the stamping machine.

It was a chaotic Friday evening and he'd shouted at me in front of the customers because there weren't enough eggs on display. He'd made me look an idiot. He had another go in the back of the store, so I just lashed out. One of the store detectives escorted me off the premises and told me my cards and wages would be in the post. Luckily, the manager never called in the police.

Soon after, I left home again, this time with a good pal of mine called Alan. We packed some gear and off we went! We hitched lifts all over, and after a while I decided to go to see my mum's family who had moved to a small town called Ellesmere Port. It was near the seaside, a few miles from Chester and close to Manchester and Liverpool, but there wasn't a lot there. We didn't stay long. We ended up catching a ferry to Dublin, and from there we hitch-hiked to Belfast. Then, everything started going wrong; we were picked up by the police and questioned about a few things and then made our way back to Luton, where I had a big bust-up with my old dad.

Dad was working as a painter and decorator and got me a job with his mate Mick Collins, a local builder and a good footballer. I carried the hod for his bricklayers and he treated me well.

I was 15 and doing a man's job. My hands got cut and my shoulders blistered but it was good money. However, there was one worker I just could not get on with. I remember stacking up hundreds of bricks and he argued that they were the wrong ones. I'd just been doing as I was told, but he took delight in kicking the whole stack off the scaffolding. I knew I would hurt this guy, so half the time I didn't turn up for work.

I went from job to job – the hat factory, the dye factory – and got in a fair few scrapes. One guy in a group of lads much older than me just ran at me one night in the town centre, nutted me, and broke my nose. I had my hands in my pockets and was helpless as he went for me and kicked me in the groin. There was no reason for it. He was too fast to be drunk, but he was either out of his head on drugs or just plain nuts.

I was going to pubs at the time; I could easily pass for 18 even though I was three years off it. I started going out with different girls and dabbling in pills like Purple Hearts. They cost half a crown a pill. I never did anything other than speed, but I knew guys who were dropping a lot of acid. There was a lot of it about in the late 1960s, but not as much as there is now. It really wasn't my scene and I soon came to despise drugs.

A few of my mates had been sent to Borstal and I sure didn't want that, so I decided to start afresh and move up to stay with my grandparents in Ellesmere

Port – Mum's parents Martha and Gordon Parry. I got a job as a labourer with a plastering firm and then something great happened – Mum, Dad and Mark moved up, and I moved back in with them.

Me, Dad and Grandad would spend hours playing cards in the kitchen every Friday night. We'd be joined by three or four of the local painter and decorator lads. Mum would go down the market for us and we'd have a big cheese board with Stilton and a few beers on the table. Sometimes we went on until five in the morning. I became quite good at chess, too. Grandad and I used to play whenever we could. I was so keen, I even had a little pocket set I used to carry around.

My friends were older, and I didn't realise it then but they were false. If I didn't have money for a round they couldn't be seen for dust. And here I was, just 16 and knocking back a lot of drink in the pubs and clubs. I wasn't an alcoholic – I was doing it to impress. But I was drinking a hell of a lot. I'd wake up on my doorstep or someone else's settee. I was throwing away good money on drink; I even sold my watch to go out. I was being a first-class fool and I kept on swapping jobs ... window cleaning, building sites, factories. I also had a few run-ins with the police. Nothing major – until one Christmas time when I had a row with a girlfriend's dad.

Myra was a very pretty girl, in fact she was beautiful, and I'd fallen out with her father. She meant the world to me. I released my frustration by smashing up a load of parked cars. Then like a fool I hung around until the owners appeared. They beat me senseless, which I admit I deserved.

I was glad when the police car pulled up to take me away!

I was charged with criminal damage and had my first taste of Risley Remand Centre. They kept me in

the hospital wing for a week for a psychiatric report
and then moved me to the main part of the centre. I
was 16, but some of the lads looked 15. They were
terrified. The first guy I was doubled up with was a
half-caste called Snowy. He was a hard sort, up for
robbery. We became good mates and he taught me
how to survive in prison. We looked after our own and
we hated sex cases. During those couple of months, I
learnt more about crime than I could have done in a
million years on the outside. I was also put on to some
good people who could help if I ever needed anything
when I was out.

But I'd never felt so trapped. I hated being watched
all the time and having a number for a name. The
food was crap and the place stank of stale piss. I
couldn't understand why Snowy seemed so relaxed.
Mum and Dad saw me several times; the visits were
behind glass. I couldn't talk to them properly like
that. All I could do was smile, ask them how they
were, and assure them everything was fine with me.
Their voices were choked. I'd upset them again. But
my court case was coming up, and the lads had said I
was likely to get a fine and probation. They were
right. I was well pleased.

I soon got another job, this time as a furniture
remover. I was getting on well, but most of my wages
were going on fines. I was working all week and
seeing nothing for it. And I had to go to an office once
a week to talk to a probation officer.

I started knocking about with lads of my own age
and getting into petty crime again. I was always well
dressed and seldom short of money – after the fines
were paid off. But I was getting barred from pubs and
clubs. There was always someone who'd upset me – by
spilling beer on me, or insulting my friends or
girlfriends – and I'd fight them. There was always a
reason that sparked off a scrap.

Then I cocked-up big time. I ended up stealing a lorryload of brand-new three-piece suites with two so-called mates. It was late at night. We got to Cannock in Staffordshire no problem and were planning to drop the gear off when a set of headlights came from nowhere.

A car was bombing towards me and there was no time to stop. It went right under the cab, and my right leg smashed into the wheel. I was stunned for a few seconds, then I jumped out of the cab and hit the deck. My leg had given way, but I shouted to the others, 'Run!' I hopped and limped up the road. A bunch of truckers in an all-night transport café that we had just stopped at were yelling, 'He's getting away!'

I dived over a big hedge and lay there for what seemed like hours.

My leg was swollen badly, and I was praying like I had never prayed before – not for me, but for the driver of the car. Police searchlights scanned the fields, and then it all seemed to go quiet. I stumbled across fields, climbed over hedges and fell into ditches. It was a long time before I got home – over 90 miles away. I was cold, wet and in pain. But I'd made it.

The police were waiting. I was charged over the smash and was sent back to Risley. My 'mates' got bail. The driver was hurt badly and the police were waiting to see whether he died.

I saw a lot of familiar faces in Risley, lads who'd got off like me last time, but who were now back inside for something else. I learnt a lot about these guys. Some were born to hate. They had drunken fathers, no love at home. Some were dangerous boys; you could see the fire in their eyes. Others were just too young to be there. They had tears welling when the screws shouted at them. Society was surely to blame for the way they were. I could understand them being that way.

But me? I had no excuse. I hadn't had the hell kicked out of me as a kid. I'd had good parents. I had no reason to fight my way through life.

It was strange how, after a few months, my cell became like a home ... photos on the wall, a few bits and pieces, and a radio. I began looking forward to simple things like a pint mug of tea, a bowl of porridge, and an hour's walk a day in the exercise yard.

The good news was that the driver pulled through. And I got away without going to Borstal. I got more fines, more probation. I was banned from driving for life and was ordered to pay ten shillings a week for the rest of my life for the damage and injuries to the driver and his car. Naturally, it was my fault, and I was deeply sorry it had happened.

I was soon back on the buildings, carrying the hod. Then I bumped into my two 'mates' in a late-night restaurant. They had got probation.

I grabbed one outside and steamed into him. A guy called Johnny, who I'd only met that night, did the other one. Johnny and I were best mates after that – like brothers. We hung out at Rhyl, Chester, sometimes Liverpool and Manchester. They were good times, but nothing ever lasts.

We got nicked in Chester at a police road-block. Our motor was stacked with clothes, leathers, sheepskins, all sorts. They had us sewn up. It was back to Risley, but this time it was worse for me because I had a nice girl on the outside – Irene, who I would later marry – and this time I knew I was going away.

I kept thinking about Irene. Would she finish with me? Had she met somebody else? When would I next see her? My head was spinning. I'd never had pressure like that. I kept thinking about escape. I needed a break. I tried to pick a lock, I tried to pick a set of handcuffs. Nothing worked. Then our day in court finally came. We both got three months' detention – a 'short, sharp' sentence. We couldn't complain.

It was great to get home, and even better to see Irene again. She seemed prettier than ever. I'd met her at the Bull's Head, Ellesmere Port, and she seemed the most perfect girl on the planet. I used to love her near me, to smell her near me ... to touch her hair.

I applied for a provisional driving licence, just for a laugh and, to my amazement, I got one. Someone slipped up there!

I ended up getting a car. I always drove carefully when I was with Irene, but I had some close escapes at other times and I never learnt by them. My luck with cars was terrible – I was always smashing them up or blowing the engine. I was never insured, and hardly ever taxed or MOT'd.

I started to earn good money – self-employed, with two plasterers – but I was still at the stealing. Irene never knew what I was up to. She was a trained typist and had a steady job at Littlewoods Pools in Birkenhead. I loved her, but I couldn't seem to go straight, even though I tried. We moved into a flat, and Johnny and his girlfriend moved in. It was cramped, but it was a reasonable set-up. Even so, I was out more nights than I care to remember, either nicking, or going with other girls. Then Irene fell pregnant. I felt knocked sideways. We were so young. My mum said we should only marry if we loved each other, and should only have kids if we wanted them.

We married in 1970, but her parents didn't come – what an insult. Her dad didn't like me.

We lived with my parents for a while and I got a job with my dad's firm, painting bridges, steel works and petrol tanks. There was nothing I wouldn't climb to paint. It was exciting work – lots of heights. And I was excited to get home to see my Irene, too. Soon we would have our own home; we were already on the council list.

She was about six months gone when we got an invitation to a party. I didn't know anyone there, and I'm glad I didn't. The guys seemed posh, giggling and chuckling like schoolgirls. I wanted to leave but Irene didn't.

There was plenty of going up and down stairs, so I had a look in some of the bedrooms. They were just freaked out; some were naked. It was like some scene from a hippie film.

Someone passed me a joint and before long I had dropped a few pills and sunk some beers. My head was gone. Their faces seemed all twisted and everything was floating around me. Then it went black. I was flat on my back, with people crowding around me, looking down. What a state! I was helped home in a van to my parents' place and dumped on the doorstep. Irene never forgave me for that. Mum wasn't too pleased either. I'd let her down again.

I was only 19 when our son Michael was born, but it was a great feeling. I'd had a row at work and got the sack, but I was good at the painting lark and soon got another job. I felt I was beginning to settle. Wife, son, and now a council house as well as a car. It wasn't on a very good estate, but we were doing well for a couple of teenagers. I felt proud pushing the pram down the street. The problem was that Irene and I were drifting slowly apart. We loved each other but we seemed to have so little in common. And here we were facing the next 50 years together. We started rowing; I started going out and working away. And all too soon I was back to Risley, back in a stinking cell. I pleaded guilty at Chester Crown Court to a smash-and-grab – and the judge gave me the biggest chance of my life. I listened to every word he said. I was free, it was time to sort myself out. I had a suspended sentence over my head when I could easily have been sent down.

Irene was crying on the way back home and that night I lay awake beside her, thinking. I still felt trapped; I imagined bars on the windows and the door locked and bolted.

Grandad – my mum's dad – died soon after. He was liked and loved by so many. We were all so upset. I'd just been given my big break by a judge and now I was about to blow it. Don't ask me why, but I went out and got a shotgun and sawed the barrel off. Then I got a replica pistol.

Here I was, good at my self-employed painting work, and with a reasonable amount of money coming in, and I was about to throw it all away. I felt unsettled, unhappy at home. I was going out clubbing, meeting villains. But there was no real excuse. I was 21 now. It should have been time to put childish ways behind me.

Instead, I went on the week-long mission of madness that earned me seven years at Chester Crown Court in 1974.

I didn't know it then, but my time inside would almost double before I finally – and all too briefly – tasted freedom.

The gates of my personal hell were opening.

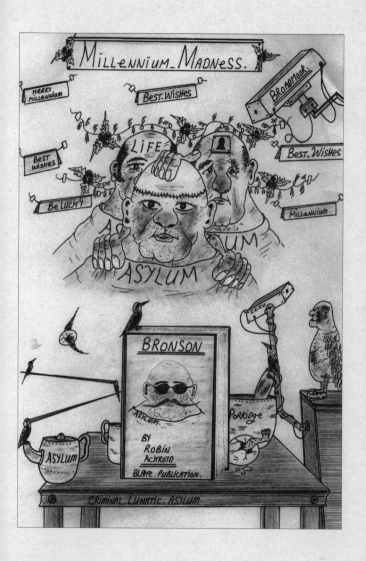

CHAPTER TWO

The first thing that hits you when you're banged up with long-term prisoners is the dead eyes. The dreams that have turned into nightmares, fantasy to reality, love to emptiness. Behind every door at Walton Jail there was misery. Blokes like me, newly sentenced, with the prospect of years inside. Wives and girlfriends isolated as much as us – at least at first. That gnawing, draining, feeling of hopelessness. The knowledge that your loved ones are left to fend for themselves. The numbed fear that you may never see them again.

Some convicts, of course, never do. Some are destined to live and die behind bars. It's never nice to see the old boys hobbling around the exercise yard, with their distant, watery eyes. Some of these old lags have been locked up for maybe 40 years. They know little else but prison life. Many actually don't wish to be freed; most simply die in their sleep. No family, no home, no contact. Their whole world is prison, and prison is all they have for family. Institutionalised ... beyond help. You might call it a living hell; dead men walking. Above all, it's just very, very sad.

H Wing at Walton was the long-term allocation wing. Below us was the punishment block. I was told I would be on the wing for six to nine months. I never liked this jail from the second I entered it. It was one of the old Victorian jails, in a suburb of Liverpool. Five storeys high, dirty, cockroach-infested, rat-infested, overcrowded, swill for food, rags for clothes. Everything was meant to bring a man down, degrade and humiliate him.

With hindsight, I suppose we were lucky in one sense. On H Wing, it was all single cells. We were long-termers – five years and over. My seven years was a short stretch compared with most. It was depressing to read the cards showing the names and sentences of the other inmates outside their cell doors. It was even more depressing to see a man walk out of his cell with vacant eyes. We were all losers, failures. It's bloody hard for a man to accept he's a loser. It's even tougher when you're behind a locked door.

Christmas was soon on us. In 1974, the Christmas Number 1 hit was 'It Will Be Lonely This Christmas' by Mud. I had a visit from Irene and my boy, but it never helped her at all. She was tearful and upset throughout it. An hour in six fucking months was all I spent with them! It was getting to me, and it was becoming harder to control my urges of violence. As lovely as Irene was and as sweet as she looked, I felt lost when I saw her. We were lost to each other. It was too much for her; she was slipping away from me. I could sense it.

I can remember that day so clearly. I was seriously wound up; six months inside, and sixty minutes with my family!

After the visit, I broke a con's nose and smashed up his ribs. I left him on the floor of his cell. He was a lifer (he'd strangled his girlfriend and assaulted his kid). I took my frustration out on him. Right or wrong, I emptied myself of tension. I felt better. Fuck him! This toe-rag had snuffed his girl and smashed his kid – and I was being torn away from mine.

A few days later, I smashed up a filthy grass in the recess. He was lucky, as I felt like cutting him up. That's not my game, but I felt hate bubbling up inside me like never before. It was as if I was on a suicide mission. I hit him with hooks, crosses. Insanely, I even tried to gouge his eye out. I was so far gone I was actually enjoying it.

Violence is an escape from reality. It can relieve tension. In prison, it's like being in a pride of lions, or being a lone wolf; the law of the jungle prevails. The victor will be respected. It's truly mad but it's prison life. I left the filthy grass on the toilet floor in his own blood and dirt. I walked out to be escorted to the punishment block.

This dungeon was a shit-tip, filthy, gloomy, no heating, damp – and the screws ran it with a fist of iron. There were a lot of unnecessary kickings going on down there. I was pushed into a cell, smashed up against a wall, and told what would happen if I stepped out of line. As they left, they slammed the steel door,

I felt a strange feeling of blackness come over me, a

sort of indescribable depression. With blood still on
my fists and over my shirt, I covered myself with a
blanket, lay on the wooden boards and drifted into
a nightmare.

This cell was freezing. It stank of stale piss; it
was dirty with bits of food stuck to the walls and
ceiling. There were stains where the cons had slung
their cups of tea. On the concrete floor were specks
of dried blood. It was enough to drive a sane man
mad. The cell was 12ft long, 8ft wide and 12ft high.
There was no window, no furniture, just boards for a
bed and a plastic piss-pot. The 'Judas hole' in the
door was the real wind-up for me. Every half-an-
hour it opened; that fucking eye staring at me,
watching me. It was invading my privacy. I was
becoming something I never believed existed – a lost
soul. My insight was fading, I was losing my head. I
screamed blue murder, I even tried to break out the
thick glass so I could poke them in the eye, but
they've got an answer for everything – they moved
me to another cell.

It's a battle of wits, but they will overcome
anything you come up with. Obviously you can make
it difficult for a spell, but you can't ever win.

Eventually they steamed in and kicked the granny
out of me.

They were doing it to the wrong person! I'd never
let it be. As they walked away I shouted to them: 'One
up on you bastards!' They must have taken it
seriously as I was let up on the wing the very next
day. I had one thought running through the back of
my mind … My turn will come.

Days later, I was involved in a 'sit-in' inside a
workshop over the way a con had been treated. He
was dragged out of the shop a bit heavy by a bunch of
screws. We didn't like the way he was handled.

I grabbed a pair of scissors and stuck them down

my overalls, ready to stab a screw if any violence broke out. I was ready and willing to go all the way!

Security screws came in to see what was up and some cons told them we were not happy. There were a good thirty screws. They brought in a con called Delroy Showers, a black guy from Liverpool, well respected and regarded as one of the top men in the jail. It was my first meet with Delroy. He told us that the con who'd been dragged out was OK and not injured. All the Scouse lads said Delroy was 100 per cent. We took his word and called it off. I was moved the next day.

As the cuffs went on my wrists and the van drove out of Walton Jail, I knew in my heart I'd be back one day to avenge that beating! No fucker beats me and lives to say I never come back. I'll always come back for more – until I win or until I die. It was to take ten whole years but, hell, did I get my revenge in style! As the van sped off, I wondered where I was going. It was even further north – and right on the other side of the country.

As the van drove up to Hull Prison, the first things that struck me were the electronic cameras all set on the walls and outside the prison gates. It may be common now, but this was 1975 – over a quarter of a century ago. Once inside the gates, I noticed even more cameras plus a 20ft barbed-wire fence within the walls. This jail was maximum secure. It housed some of Britain's most dangerous men: killers, terrorists, bank robbers. As my van drove in, Delroy Showers' brother Michael drove out. He was on his way to Albany Jail on the Isle of Wight. I was taking his cell! That's how jails work ... one leaves, one arrives. It's like a game of chess, but we are the pawns. Whether we walk to the van or are forcibly carried, we have no choice.

Once I was through reception, I was allocated to A

Wing. There, I met a few cons I knew: Tommy Tedstone, Harry Johnson, Wally Lee, Micky Ahmed and Jimmy Cassidy. Then I was introduced to many others who became life-long friends, guys who I respect – legends in the system and legends outside. Charlie Wilson was among them. He got 30 years for the Great Train Robbery in the '60s. He's a man I had so much respect for. He never cried about his sentence, he always helped other cons out – a truly lovely guy. Nothing was ever too much for Charlie. Some toe-rag shot and killed him some years later at his villa in Spain. A great loss to us all, but he will always be remembered.

Stan Thompson is another man I've always admired, a born fighter. He later made one of England's most dramatic escapes, in the '80s, from Brixton secure unit. Three top-secure cons dug through three walls and escaped! Stan's served years in top-secure jails, but he still fights his way through, keeps super fit and lives for victory.

Siddy Draper got life and 28 years for a robbery up in Scotland. From when I met him at Hull in 1975, it took him 'til 1987 to get out. He went out in a helicopter from Gartree, Leicestershire. It was the only helicopter escape this country has ever known. Sadly, he was recaptured some months later. Blackie Saxton was serving 24 years, a great guy who I love and respect. He's one of the old school, solid. His league is a dying breed.

Then there was big Les Hilton. A lot of guys didn't like Les. He was black and he was fearless. His 19 stone could, at times, be intimidating. I respected Les because he was a pure survivor. Eight Jocks once went into his cell to serve him up, but he fought them all and survived the stabbings! That's a survivor at his best. He was later stabbed to death outside. I liked Les; I love a born fighter. And there are plenty of other cons I met who became pals in the years that faced me: Kenny Wimbles, Ernie Page, Bertie Costa, Johnny Reed ... I can go on and on, but the guys I've left out know who they are.

The jail itself was miles ahead of Walton. It had a good gym (at the time the only prison gym in the country with a boxing ring). It had a football pitch, snooker tables, darts, table tennis and a kitchen to cook a meal. Everyone had a single cell – luxury compared to most jails. My cell window looked over the wall. I could see the Hull Dock cranes and the ships being unloaded. It was a smashing sight. I've sat for hours watching those cranes at work. The smell of the fish was strong in the air. The seagulls woke us up most mornings, screeching. Fascinating birds to watch, they rarely flap their wings. They just glide with the wind.

I used to throw bread out to them. Some would dive and catch the bread before it hit the deck. Incredible birds, so graceful. They represent freedom to me, total freedom! As I tell you my story, I'm in a cell with no window – just thick mesh and, through that, a grey view of concrete, closed-circuit TV cameras and razor wire. Sometimes, but only sometimes, I catch a brief glimpse of a little bird flying by.

From my cell all those years ago, I actually witnessed part of the Humber Bridge being built, a bridge I would drive across many years later. At least I had something of a window on the outside world.

The food was also good in Hull. There was variety, it was well prepared – and most of all there was plenty of it. I felt like I could get on with my sentence and settle down. But life never works out like we hope, does it?

After a week, they gave me a job in a workshop on a sewing machine. Me on a sewing machine! It just doesn't bear thinking about!

No possible way could I sit and work a soppy sewing machine. I told them 'No'. I started to sabotage the machine. They soon got the message. They knew it was senseless putting me on a job like that, so they moved me. I was put in a workshop with cons nicknamed The Dirty Dozen. Basically, it was a workshop for those who could not, or would not, work. That suited me! We sat playing Scrabble all day, drank tea, chatted, played poker. We were happy enough ... until one screw started his bollocks!

None of the cons liked him. He was a big man, ex-rugby player. He loved a row – what rugby player doesn't? People forget that a lot of screws are sportsmen; they love a rough and tumble. Some are ex-military, some are just boot merchants. Whatever, they are only human.

The uniform doesn't make them angels. Some are simply bully boys, some come straight out of the Forces where they never even had the wit to get past the most junior rank. In the Prison Service they get a bunch of keys and are called 'Officer'. Overnight, they've got the status they never managed in the Army. OK, it's not the best job in the world, locking up fellow human beings. And prison officers get more than their fair share of stick – and smackings. But the bully boys are a disgrace to the decent officers.

I don't know much about his background – I don't know and don't give a damn whether he was in the Army or not – but as far as I was concerned at the time, he had a bad attitude. It was all, 'I'm right – and you're wrong.'

He upset me.

I smashed the shop to bits. The furniture, the windows, the lights, the office. I'd told the other cons to stay clear. I slung a broken table at the screws – one caught it full blast on his crust and was carried out by his mates. Alarm bells went, screws came running, dog handlers were on standby. But I now had the workshop at my disposal.

This particular screw strolled in as if it was a picnic – obviously with a dozen heavies behind him. I had a stick in my hand. He said, 'Put that stick down before I ram it up your arse.'

I did as I was told. I put it down … sixty miles an hour over his crust! I went to smash him again but they were on me like a ton of bricks and I was pinned down.

Soon I was being carried. I couldn't breathe, I was choking and some bastard was squeezing my balls! Fists were smashing into my body. Once they had me in the corridor they were shouting, 'You bastard. We'll teach you for hitting an officer with a stick!' I seemed to have upset them.

By the time they got me to the punishment block, I was well and truly fucked. Pain is not the word. My bollocks were in agony, my body ached, my eye was cut, even my toes were throbbing. They stripped me off, then strapped me up in a body-belt. This is a leather belt that locks at the back and has a metal cuff on each hip, which locks your wrists. They also strapped my ankles. If this was not enough, they injected me in my right buttock with a hypodermic needle.

I felt a wave of fear; I began to panic. My head span, I felt sick and groggy. I'll never forget the burning sensation as they injected me. I awoke in a pool of blood and vomit.

For me, this was all torture. They had already beaten me, so why do more? They did it to me because I obliged one of theirs. These injections were used a lot in the '60s and '70s.

It was known as the 'Liquid Cosh'.

The doctors were using strong sedatives to control

unmanageable prisoners. This was my first shot of the Liquid Cosh, but sadly not my last. The drug – I believe it was a large dose of Largactil – knocked me out, but the side-effects were even worse: stiffness, muscular spasms, dryness of the mouth, blurry vision. It lingered for days. The practice is now banned in prisons.

I woke up in the 'strong box', a double-doored cell, sound-proofed and totally isolated. It's like a cell within a cell with no windows and no furniture. It's silent. And it's where all the kickings are given out. I spent weeks there.

I gained an extra six months over that incident, as well as punishment and fines. Soon after, Irene and Michael visited. But unknown to me at the time, it was the last I would ever see of my wife. And I wouldn't see my son for 23 years.

Irene said something to me on that last visit that has stuck in my head ever since. I can still hear her saying, 'You'll end up in a nut-house the way you're going.' How prophetic that was.

Life became more and more a battle to survive. My violent outbursts were becoming uncontrollable. Even locked in the punishment block 23 hours every day, I still got myself into serious trouble, smashing up cells, attacking screws. On one occasion I tried my luck at escaping!

I was out in the exercise cage, a small yard surrounded by a 20ft fence topped with razor wire and cameras positioned to monitor us walking around. This particular day, I spotted something worth a go. I can't say how I did it for obvious reasons, but I got out of the cage. I ran to a building that was being demolished. My plan was to pick up a large wooden joist, take it over to the perimeter fence, lean it up, climb up it, pull it back up, put it over the wall and slide down it. It all sounds so crazy now, but it seemed worth a go. Off I shot, but before I even got to the building, the alarm bells went off, the cameras were on me, dogs were barking and screws running. I was in trouble!

I ran as fast as I could back to the cage. I saw an alsatian dog 30 yards away coming at me with incredible speed and I could hear the pounding of boots getting nearer and nearer. I leapt on to a 20ft camera pole and shinned up it as fast as I could! From there, I leant over on to the fence and jumped – a long fucking drop! I left half my jeans and shirt up on the razor wire; blood was oozing out of a gash in my arm and out of a leg wound. My right ankle was smashed. Seconds after I hit the concrete floor inside the cage, there were dozens of screws surrounding the fence looking at me. Obviously the camera doesn't lie, but I still denied everything. I got another six months for that.

For five months I was on punishment, but I assaulted more screws and just went from bad to worse. My mind was beginning to wander. Then I had a fall-out with a con who would later come back to haunt me, John Henry Gallagher. He was directly above my cell in the punishment block. Nobody liked him. He was a Jock serving six years, always in debt, always in trouble with other cons.

One night he was banging my ceiling. It went on and on and on until I shouted up, 'Jock, give it a rest, mate. I can't think.' He shouted back, 'Fuck off, you English pig!'

To say I was upset is an understatement. For days afterwards, I prayed that my door would be open the same time as his, but with being in the punishment block we all slopped out alone. It was useless, I couldn't get to him.

I was getting badly worked up about him. Then after six months, I was moved back up on to the wing where I was allowed to mix with other cons. I was starting to get worried about Irene – I hadn't heard from her for months – but I was sorting out a big soft toy to be made in one of the workshops for my son. Two days went by and, to my shock, Gallagher walked on to my wing, bold as brass and twice as nasty! The screws knew that we didn't get on, so I wonder whether it was a deliberate case of encouraging us to fight.

I could take no chances, as he was a violent man himself. It was a case of attack or be attacked. I tore into his cell with a jug and smashed it into his face. I hit him again with the jagged handle. He screamed so I hit him again and again. Each punch was with the jug handle and it cut him every time – legs, body, arms, face, neck. I just kept cutting the bastard, and he kept on screaming. I was actually laughing as I was doing it – insanely.

My head was really going, the danger signs were there. For the first time in my life, I felt nothing but hate. Prison had created what I now was – a madman! I was taken back to the block covered in blood. Some of my clothes were put in a plastic bag for police forensic tests and I was charged with GBH. They took me to Hull Magistrates, then the escort drove away from Hull. I was being taken to another jail, and I really didn't give a fuck.

Gallagher would pop up again, I was sure. And pop up again he did.

A couple of hours after leaving Hull, the van pulled up to what appeared to be an old castle. This place looked evil; I felt a warning sign pass through my veins like a shot of adrenalin. The van drove slowly through the open gates. I spotted the reception area where a dozen or more screws with big shiny boots were waiting. As I got out of the van, followed by the six screws who were with me, the

other screws came marching over. One of them said,
'This is the fucker.' It was pure intimidation; they
were set for trouble.

I was taken through the tunnel that led to the
punishment block. There were a dozen cells with beds
outside the doors and I was led into a cell where they
began taking off my handcuffs. It was all eye-to-eye
contact. You could cut the atmosphere with a knife.

'Right, sonny boy, strip off.'

I told them, 'Bollocks.'

They never asked again.

They were on me like a ton of bricks, kicking,
punching, tearing at my clothes until they left me
naked, locked up in a freezing, dirty, stinking cell,
with no furniture, no bed. There was just a Bible, a
piss-pot, a jug of water and a lot of aches, pains and
bruises. I'd arrived at Armley Jail, Leeds.

The next two years, from 1975 to 1977, were like a
bloody merry-go-round: from Armley to Wakefield; to
Wandsworth then Parkhurst; Wandsworth again, up
to Walton, back to Wandsworth, and on again to
Parkhurst.

Counting bricks in a cell will drive any man mad,
so it was at Armley where I started my fitness régime,
a discipline which kept me occupied and in good
fighting shape for years to come.

My days at Armley were long, boring and totally
soul-destroying. The Governor came down soon after I
arrived to ask if I would behave myself. I told him,
'I've done nothing – but just look at the state of me.'

He said I was to remain in the block on 'good order
and discipline' for as long as I stayed in Armley. When
I asked him why, he replied simply, 'Because you're
too dangerous to mix.'

So here I was, locked up in the block, still no
letters from Irene, and living the life of a hermit. I
would go out on the exercise yard for my one-hour-a-

day walk, then be locked up for 23 hours. Those days, even a radio wasn't allowed. I had to plan a routine to survive.

I worked out in my cell every day but Sunday – press-ups, sit-ups, squats, step-ups, shadow boxing. During my hour on the yard, I jogged.

At first, they said I wasn't allowed to jog. I told them, 'Bollocks. What the fuck are you going to do, break my legs? Go and fuck off!' They left me alone to jog after that.

I only got one shower a week, so I used to strip-wash two or three times a day in my cell.

I still do that to this day. I get up at 7.00am, run the cold tap, and bung my head under for as long as I can before washing.

Night-times at Armley, I would have my light turned off by 7.00pm and I'd just switch off completely. I used to plug my ears, cover my eyes and go into myself. Deep thoughts; some good, some bad, some evil. I went through a period of searching myself.

I never found out a lot! I was just a mixed-up, confused young man with so much energy. I hoped my training routine would at least take the edge away and relax me enough to stop me becoming violent. I could never build up too much muscle, not with the diet I was on. It was swill. It seemed an eternity since I'd chewed a decent piece of meat or had a cool drink of milk. Prison food is mostly stodgy, uncooked plates of filth. Even the porridge is pig feed, but you become accustomed to it. Two pieces of fruit a week, when I used to eat eight pieces a day outside.

At times I felt fatigued and faint when I worked out, but I pushed myself to the limit. I persevered – I had to, as I had so much tension inside. I was given one letter a week to write out. I had stopped writing to Irene, so I mostly wrote to my parents.

It was pretty quiet in this block, but the block

cleaner was a complete toe-rag, a filthy grass. I actually heard him grass up a con who smuggled in some tobacco. I waited for the right moment, then I pounced. I hit him five or six times in a blind spot by the showers then just left him on the floor and went back to my cell and banged up. Five minutes later, the screws came in for me.

I denied hitting anyone.

The cleaner vanished and a new one took his place. Then Dougie Wakefield arrived. He got life for killing his uncle with a pitchfork. He was moved from another prison for the attempted murder of a screw. It was our first encounter, but it was the beginning of a long friendship. Dougie was facing years of hell and he knew it. I was facing years of hell but I never knew it.

Dave Anslow was the next to arrive. Dave had been in the control unit at Wakefield for six months. He was from Dudley in the West Midlands – fit, strong and fearless. They decided to let us out on the yard together. He was the first con I'd really mixed with for months. It was a treat. I respected Dave so much; he and his brothers, Eric and John, all became loyal friends of mine. I called them the Dudley Firm.

Dave and myself were getting pissed off with all the solitary so we decided to put something together. We plotted up and went to work. Our cells were next to each other. When we heard the eleven o'clock chime in the night, that was when we were going to execute our plan. On the last chime, I picked up my iron bed and began ramming it into the door. After a good 30 or 40 smashes the spy-hole casing was gone, the hinges were loose, the whole thing was breaking up. The plan was crazy, but that's how we were … smash the doors off, grab some screws and go home!

Nothing's that simple!

I could hear Dave's door, every thud rocking the walls. The whole fucking jail must have woken up.

Soon the screws turned up, some in uniform, some in civvies. There was the Governor, too, and there were dogs. We weren't going anywhere!

They went to Dave's door first. They shouted at him, 'Right, Anslow, stand back. We're coming in.' Next thing I heard a scuffle, shouts and Dave being carried away. It was a good 20 minutes before it was my turn. There was no warning; it was just bang, smash and they were in.

I ended up in a strong box at the other end of the jail, a box that had been out of use for years. When they slung me in and slammed the door it was total blackness. I could smell dampness and dust. I could feel lumpy things under my feet – dead cockroaches. The place had the smell of decay. I was itching, I felt dirty. I had a good seven hours in pitch darkness before they unlocked me.

It felt like the longest seven hours of my life. Dave had been put in the block box, but this box was the fucking pits!

When the door opened in the morning, I attempted to rush out. I was shouting, 'I can't fucking breathe!'

I battled with them, my head was gone completely. They grabbed me, bent me up and slung me back in! For two days I endured this hell-hole, and I can honestly say it was the worst pit I've ever had to climb out of.

Soon after, I was moved again – another mystery tour in the back of a van. I went to Wakefield and Dave and Dougie were moved to Parkhurst on the Isle of Wight. I got my charge dropped from GBH on Gallagher, pleading guilty to unlawful wounding. I received another nine months. As I left Hull Crown Court, I didn't even bother to ask where the van was going. I just sat there thinking. The strange thing was, nobody knew then that three years later Gallagher would be released and would kill four people. He was later sent to Broadmoor for the rest of his natural days. If I had killed the scumbag, four people would be alive today. But who can see into the future?

From the second I entered Wakefield top-security unit, I knew I would not last. The reception screws told me I was going straight into the block. When I asked them why, they just smiled and said, 'The Governor will tell you tomorrow.'

I went mad. 'Bollocks,' I said. 'I want to know now, not tomorrow!'

They surrounded me, led me to the block and locked me up. I wasn't too happy!

The Governor came into my cell with half-a-dozen screws to tell me that I was staying in the block on good order and discipline and would remain so all of the time I was there. When I asked why, he told me the Home Office wanted me isolated as they felt I was a danger. This was a fucking joke to me. Wakefield Jail housed over 500 cons, 450 of them lifers. I made it clear that I was not happy with this decision, but the Governor just smiled and walked out. I was now trapped, my reputation had preceded me. I felt hostility towards me – the screws were tense, ready to jump me at any time. Within hours of being there I blew. I went out to collect my tea. A good dozen screws were staring at me. One said, 'You! Back to your cell and put a shirt on.'

'Why?' I asked.

'Because that's the rules; you wear a shirt.'

'Fuck the rules.' With this I spat in his face and walked back to my cell. I just felt my head pounding and I blew up. I began tearing my cell apart.

They were in like a shot and dragged me out. I was put in the box, and all the psychological games began. They banged my doors, gave me cold food, half a cup of tea, no slop-outs, no toilet roll, no soap. They were spying on me every 15 minutes, waking me up with the bolts. All mental games – but what they fail to realise is, it just makes a man worse. It breeds contempt and distrust. It also breeds violence. If not right now, then later. It scars a man, it turns him nasty. If you keep poking a dog with a stick, eventually the dog will bite. They were loving every minute of it.

I was eventually allowed to exercise on my own. I had to walk around a little yard by some workshops. I could see the other cons looking at me. It was a cold, wet day. My feet were bad owing to the tightness of the shoes that they had given me. I took them off, and my socks, and slung them over the fence. The screws pretended they never saw it, but what I saw upset me. A con was at the workshop window talking to the screws and passing them cups of tea. He totally blanked me. I shouted at the rat, 'Where's mine then?' He still blanked me and went back to work. This really upset me a lot. I just couldn't work it out, couldn't understand it. I never locked his door at night, yet he gives the screws a cup of tea and ignores me. It just didn't make sense to me.

My next week was a tough one, very tense. They never gave up – but neither did I.

I was so close to hurting someone. Every time I came out of the box, I searched for a tool, a needle, a nail, a piece of glass … anything to hurt someone with. Punching them on the jaw isn't enough in situations like this. You've got to hurt them badly to show them you won't be messed about. I felt I was at war. My back was up against the wall.

I'd lost all track of time. I didn't realise I'd been in the box for ten whole days – it seemed like 100. On the tenth day of arriving in this piss-hole, they all piled in. Something was up.

'You're on the move now.'

I asked them where and they said I'd find out soon enough.

A row broke out, there was a bit of a scuffle, and the next thing I knew I was secured in a body-belt with my ankles strapped. They carried me out to the waiting van but there was actually a smile on my face! I was glad to be leaving.

The journey was a long one, trussed up and lying on the floor of the van. I wouldn't recommend it to anyone! Yorkshire to London is a fucking long way. I didn't know where the hell I was when I arrived.

The van stopped outside the punishment block. Then I was told where I was – Wandsworth, a tough jail with 1,000 cons. The only jail left in the country with working, if unused, gallows. Still, it felt better than Wakefield. In this place, everyone knew where they stood. Step out of line here and they knock you back (or try to). There are no psychological games. It's pure prison; it smells and tastes of prison. I was to spend my next ten months here.

The block was tough. But from the word go, the screws and the Governor told me what the rules were. There was no bollocks, no lies, just straight talk to my face. I respect that. Obviously, I did not like the prospect of staying too long there, but the decision had been made long before my arrival.

Unfortunately, after a couple of days, I blew. I chinned a hospital screw and a block screw – and, as I was being manhandled, I bit another screw on the hand. He was a senior officer called Mr Hastings, who was, in fact, a decent guy. I spent a week or more in the strong box. Bad, lonely, empty times – but the biggest shock of all was to come for me in this box.

Only days after I had survived a good kicking, a screw slung in a big brown envelope and said, 'Even your missus don't want you.'

Inside the envelope were divorce papers.

It was the smack in the face that I never recovered

from. I cried my fucking eyes out that night, in my own emptiness, under a stinking blanket.

I had thrown my whole life away, the woman I loved and the son I worshipped. I knew from that night that my life would never be normal. I'd lost everything, including my sanity. I could hear Irene's voice in my head: 'You'll end up in a nut-house ...'

I was beginning to believe her.

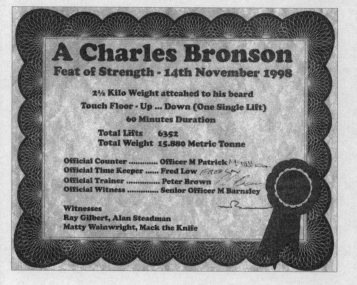

A Charles Bronson
Feat of Strength - 14th November 1998

2½ Kilo Weight atteahed to his beard

Touch Floor - Up ... Down (One Single Lift)

60 Minutes Duration

Total Lifts   6352
Total Weight 15.880 Metric Tonne

Official Counter .... Officer M Patrick
Official Time Keeper ...... Fred Low
Official Trainer .... Peter Brown
Official Witness .... Senior Officer M Barnsley

Witnesses
Ray Gilbert, Alan Steadman
Matty Wainwright, Mack the Knife

CHAPTER THREE

It was only a matter of time before Irene's prediction came true.

I managed a month or two without any incidents, then a big fucker arrived from Chelmsford Jail. His name was 'Sie-Sie'. He was black as coal and he was a bully. I hate a bully.

They put him in the cell next to me and we had words through the window. He was going to tear my head off, I was going to stab him in the eye. We were both going to kill each other.

The problem was – how? In this block we had to

slop out alone, we didn't mix. It was frustrating for us both. The tension was building and we couldn't get at each other.

But I had a plan. I was going to poison the ugly fucker! I'd never poisoned anyone before, but I felt happy to poison this slag. The only problem was, I had no poison. So I used glass. I got a piece of glass and crushed it up into dust and added it to some sugar.

I banged on his wall, 'Oi,' I said. 'Do you want some sugar?'

'Yeah, I'll have some,' he said.

So I arranged a hiding place for when he slopped out. After he got it, he banged my wall, 'Cheers, brother!'

Three or four days passed, then it happened. He began pissing blood. The security were brought in, the bag of sugar was analysed, I was questioned. He made a statement to the effect that I gave him the sugar. He also said, again, that he was going to tear my head off. I've never seen him since.

★ ★ ★

It's weird how the mind works in jail. You have to be mad to survive it. There's a lot of violence – it's facing us every day. Even talk of violence goes on all the time. I've lain on my bed listening to them until I've fallen asleep ... how the guy will kill the lover-boy when he gets out, or shoot the copper. Most, of course, is just talk. Pure hot air.

I saw a lot of cons come and go over the ten months I was at Wandsworth. Dave Anslow popped in, along with Stevie Lannigan, 'Mad' Frankie Fraser, Micky McConnell, Billy Armstrong, Cyril Berkett, Tommy Tedstone and Albert Baker. Not forgetting poor Dave Martin, who hanged himself in Parkhurst Prison some years after – a very sad ending.

I kept my training up every day and the ten months just flew by. I was getting my head together. It was now 1976.

However, my world was solitary confinement and it was obvious I was achieving nothing. I began to feel restless, aggressive. It was clear to everyone, including the Governor, that I needed a break. Soon I was on my way to the Island!

It was a weird feeling going over on the ferry. I was double-cuffed and had to remain in the back of the van with five screws. The Isle of Wight has three jails on it: Albany, Camp Hill, and the most notorious of all, Parkhurst.

Parkhurst is probably the most infamous jail in Britain. It's known around the world. It's seen it all: riots, murders, stabbings, hostages, fires, suicides, sieges, attempted escapes, the lot. The hardest villains in the country have spent time there. Legends, myths, have all been created. Stories have lived on for decades.

From the second I entered Parkhust, I could taste the atmosphere. It's the only jail that can throw off an aura. It reeks of history.

Every cell tells a story – mine certainly did. The first night I was there, some idiot upset me and I smashed up my cell. In the early hours, they came for me; I was on my way to the block. I spent the first night in the box, the next day I was moved to C Unit, where I was to meet the best two guys I've ever met in my life – Ronnie and Reggie Kray.

Obviously, I had heard of the Kray Twins, but meeting them was something else. As I tell my story 26 years later, I remember Reg as the loyal friend I met in 1976. Ron, too, I remember as a gentleman. Both passed away while serving their sentences. God bless them both.

The Twins were unique, a special breed of men.

Later, I was honoured to meet their lovely mother (who sadly is no longer with us) and also their brother, Charlie.

'C Unit' was known as 'Cooper's Troopers' – after the doc in charge – or, sometimes, the 'Psycho Wing'. There were 12 to 14 of us, most with bad problems. A lot of us had spent months, if not years, in punishment blocks. We had our own gymnasium, library, exercise yard. It was a self-contained unit, segregated from the other wings. Some of the guys I met down there included Dougie Wakefield, Eddie Wilkinson, Wally Lee, Chilly (from my home town in Luton), Colin Robinson, Joey Cannon, Johnny Bond, Johnny Brookes, Mad Jacko, George Wilkinson, and Nobby Clark.

I thought I might settle there, but it was strange for me to mix with people. Solitary can affect people in different ways. It turned me inside myself.

I was withdrawn and very bitter towards the screws – and the Parkhurst screws were really very relaxed compared to those in a lot of prisons. They just wanted a peaceful time – they couldn't afford trouble, not with the kind of cons they had in there. Thirty years is no fucking joke and some of the cons in Parkhurst had absolutely nothing to lose by sticking a knife in one of them. The screws accepted this. The policy was to keep us happy. But there was always a minority who upset us.

I had been doing well, thanks to a lot of the lads. I worked out in the gym with Ron, Reg and Robbo. I ate well, slept well, and felt a lot better in myself ... until this fat screw upset me.

I pushed the bastard up against a wall and spat in both his eyes. I told him I'd kill him if he upset me again. I meant it and he knew I meant it. I was moved the next day over to the hospital wing – F2. This wing was notorious, the wing that certifies people insane and sends you packing off to the asylums. F2 was a dangerous, bad, bad place to be locked up.

I fucking hated it, I had to get out. I was now plotting to smash a sex-case's head in with a brick. Me and another con were going to do it ... but for some reason I got moved out! After only a month in Parkhurst, I was put in the van and whisked away. I don't know if I was pleased or sad. Strangely though, I felt I would be back. They say that Parkhurst is a magnet which will always pull you back. How true that is.

The van drove off the ferry at Portsmouth and we headed for London. A couple of hours later, we pulled up outside the punishment block at Wandsworth. I was fucking sick! I knew one thing though – there was no way I was going to stay in this block for another ten stinking months ... no way. They put me in the same old cell and the Governor came to see me. He said if I behaved myself for a month I could go up on D Wing, the long-term wing. I thought it over. It had to be better than staying in this cell, as this cell was becoming a tomb.

There were around 250 cons on D Wing, all doing five years and over. A lot of faces, London mobsters, armed blaggers, murderers, terrorists. I never liked it; eyes seemed to be everywhere. I'd spent too long in solitary.

I sat in the mailbag shop, watching villains sewing bags for £1 a week. I couldn't understand it. I don't know if they were doing it for the money or for good reports. Whatever, I wasn't sewing fucking bags – not for £100 a week. I was sick to my back teeth of it all. It was time to put something together. Escape!

I got some gear to dig through my wall, I made a rope and I got a steel chair to make a grappling hook.

I began digging. Wandsworth is an old jail, the brickwork crumbles. I worked bloody hard on that first brick until it finally came out. I was buzzing, I actually felt convinced I was on to a winner. Once out of the cell, I reckoned it would be easy. Once over the wall, it's just fate. I would flag a car down and take the driver hostage ... my own taxi! Life's a gamble – win or lose, you have to take a chance. This time, though, unknown to me, the odds were stacked against me.

Through the Judas hole in my door I could normally see the light shining through a small gap. I was chipping away at the cell wall when I just happened to turn. There was no light! I rushed to the door to see why. Through the hole I saw a con walk away – a south Londoner, a flash bastard. Every time he looks in a mirror, until the very day he dies, he'll remember what he did.

Five minutes later, screws came down the landing – heading straight for my cell. Obviously, someone had grassed me up. Within minutes, I'd been hauled down the punishment block, put in 'patches', or escape clothes, and had lost 120 days. I wasn't happy.

This rat who'd grassed me up didn't only steal four months of my life, he stole a big dream of mine.

Escape is every con's dream. Even the trustees – the Governor's pets – dream of escape. Sure, we may only dream, but it's those dreams that keep us alive.

The dream had been snatched from me. And the man responsible became my dream.

I ended up back on D Wing and I stayed on the escape list for almost a year-and-a-half. But the shock was, I went to collect my lunch one day and the filthy grass was serving the chips. I couldn't believe my eyes! It was obvious that he didn't know I'd seen him on that fateful day. But he soon realised that I did know. It was all over his face. When I kept my plate in front of him for more chips he couldn't even look me in the face. He just kept piling on the chips. I said, 'Cheers, pal,' and smiled right at him. He managed to say, 'Nice to see you back up out of the block.'

I almost let him have the tray in his face, but I had something better lined up for him. I'll leave it there at this stage as I don't wish to incriminate anyone, but I'll just say that this con now has a scar from his right eye all the way down to his neck. They found him in a cell on D Wing, bleeding all over the floor and in a terrible, dazed shock. Probably self-inflicted ... it's terrible what some people will do for a bit of attention!

After he was found, the whole wing was banged up. The screws came to my cell and out of 250 cons I was the only one to be put down the block. The snitch had made a statement; his attacker wore a pillow-slip on his head and socks on his hands. No one was ever charged, but I was kept on good order and discipline for another year.

It was at this time my old grandad's house blew up and we sadly lost him. He was my dad's dad, Jack, and he'd had a good innings, but it's always gutting to lose people we love. I went through a silent period. I literally cut myself off from the world. I read a lot, slept a lot, and thought a lot. I now know I was making myself ill.

It was during this period that I really began to be badly affected by the isolation I was enduring.

Isolation twists the mind. It makes normal things, like daylight, or the sound of people's voices, appear magnified to almost blinding and deafening levels when the heavy door finally swings open. Normality becomes abnormal.

I have now had 24 isolated, lonely years out of a total of 28 inside. I don't expect you ever to fully grasp what it has been like. But imagine.

Imagine having to look out of the window of one

room for what seems like an eternity, at what is the only view you will ever see. Imagine never walking bare-foot on grass, never smelling a flower or stroking an animal, never waking up alongside the person you love; imagine never having choice – a choice about what you eat, where you go, who you see. Imagine never deciding what you will do today, tomorrow, next week, or next year. Imagine having all your reading material censored, and staring at a blank wall for 23 hours a day.

Right now, I don't even have the view out of the window. At Hull, I saw the docks in the distance; years later I was to be held in a cage, surrounded by steel, by concrete, by cameras and by bullet-proof screens. Although I don't like being compared to Hannibal Lecter, it is the closest that you will ever get to imagining how I was held. And he, of course, only ever asked for a cell with a view.

But, as I say, it was at Wandsworth in 1976 that I first began to be seriously affected by the isolation. I would hear noises and rush to the door to see who was talking. If I heard anything, I would be convinced that someone was talking about me.

I was definitely being affected in a bad way. I started getting urges to jump people for looking at me. Eventually, they got a doctor up to see me, but I lost control and went for him. Fortunately I was restrained. I felt myself disappearing under a very big, black cloud. Depression hit me. I always felt very close to erupting violently. It was obvious to everyone it was time I moved on ... but where to? Nobody wanted me.

Then the van pulled up, the cuffs went on, and away I went.

They put me straight into the punishment block at Walton Jail, Liverpool. I was told by the Governor that I would be staying there until I was moved to another prison, which would be as soon as possible.

Three days later I was piled into the van and heading back on the 200-mile journey to London. When I got back to Wandsworth, I was put in the same cell I'd left three days earlier.

It was now becoming insane. The system was fucking up my head!

The Governor was at my door right away; he couldn't understand why I had been sent back. He agreed it was completely wrong and said he would personally arrange another move somewhere else. Weeks went by and I was beginning to get fed up again. Then the Governor came back to see me. He told me no prison would accept me – except Parkhurst's notorious C Unit.

I had little choice. I said, 'OK. I'll go back.'

It only took a day before I was in the van and on my way back to the Island. But something told me a big fall was imminent. I was a more dangerous man than I had ever been in my life. I was now desperate.

This trip is like no other prison trip, as it's across the sea. It feels like you're being sent so far away, and that you may never come back. One day I'd like to make the trip 'unchained' and free.

Parkhurst's gates opened and in we went. I was back on C Unit in no time – but it was all different. New faces ... a lot of cons had moved on. It would never be the same for me because, on top of it all, the Twins had moved. Ron and Reg had taken the atmosphere away with them. It was now so dull. That's why they were special – they actually threw off a personality that would hit a place as soon as they walked in.

The Twins were now on the hospital wing, for some peace and quiet. This C Unit was the most violent in the country. Big George Wilkinson grabbed a hostage, so did Mad Jacko and Wally Lee. There were cons killing cons, cons cutting up cons. The Psycho Wing; the Nutters' Wing. The reputation was deserved – and it stuck. Obviously, Ron and Reg had seen enough and had had enough of it.

Years of C Unit could drive any man insane. Colin Robinson was on here, my best pal. We trained together and both got super fit. Life passed by fast. Obviously, there were days which went wrong. Like the day when I came out of a recess and dived on a screw. A mob of screws dived on me and the cons began a row. A riot was on the cards, but a senior screw had the sense to defuse it.

They let me go and walked me over to the block, only to be jumped again and slung into a cell. The next morning I slung my piss-pot all over a screw, only to be jumped on again. Life was becoming a battle! There was contempt in the air. Hate had set in and bitterness was eating me away.

Doctors came to see me. So did Governors, the Board of Prison Visitors, chaplains, Home Office officials. I told them all to 'Fuck off'.

They were all the 'system'. Let me tell you now, bitterness is an illness. It affects everything: diet, sleep, bowels, anxiety. It causes stress. I always felt a heaviness in my heart, a dull ache in my head. I hated myself for being so hateful. It's just not nice. I started to suffer terrible tension. I would get so highly excitable and at times lose control.

The ultimate had to happen – and it did. I seized up and had a breakdown.

A neurologist was brought in to see me. It was thought that I had brain damage. Tests were done. Epilepsy was diagnosed. Hysteria was also believed to be part of the problem. A Dr Faulk, a consultant forensic psychiatrist, did a report on me at the time. He said I was psychopathic, with very sensitive ways that caused paranoia.

I was let back up on C Unit. I had visits – Mum and Dad would come, so would my brothers. My cousin Loraine used to visit me as well. So did my Auntie Pam and Uncle Ian.

1978 rolled in. I should have been going out, but I had years left. I'd lost remission, plus I had time added on. But I consoled myself with the thought that I was still lucky, as all of the other cons on C Unit were lifers.

Poor old Nobby Clark was in his late fifties. He'd got life in the '60s and then he killed a con in Broadmoor. Now here he was with us. I liked Nobby a lot and I learned a lot from him. He was an intelligent and dangerous man. He said something to me once, which I will never forget. He said, 'If you're not prepared to die fighting the system, then don't fight.' Words of wisdom and truth, sadly.

Nobby passed away in Parkhurst Prison, but I still think of those words. God bless you, Nobby.

Colin Robinson was by this time causing me more fucking headaches than any other human being. I love Colin like a brother, but he sometimes became disturbed and dangerous. You have to bear in mind that he was only four years into a life sentence, plus he had another one added. Some days he stayed banged up in his cell, others he would march up and down the landing like a storm trooper. I would like to think that I helped him over this period. I always went into his cell to see if he was OK. Others, including screws, never dared. I used to sit with Colin for hours, trying to convince him that there would be a tomorrow.

Colin was famous for swallowing objects ... bed springs, tobacco tins, razor blades, nails. He's been rushed to hospital for more stomach operations than any man I know. In a black mood, he just used to do these silly things. I understand why he does it – it's a way to fuck up not just himself but the system. He almost died on some of those swallowing bouts, but I'm glad to say he's still alive. Alive, but caged up.

Johnny O'Rooke came on the unit soon after that stabbing. O'Rooke's a rat! He was a big, strapping six-footer with a shaven head. He not only upset me, he upset all of us. He wanted it all his own way – but he wasn't going to get it! This was a unit where you had to give and take. After all, we were all in the same boat.

This rat had either to stop his nonsense or he would be obliged.

One day, he borrowed my broom and mop and never returned it. I went to his cell and pulled him. This might sound silly to anyone on the outside, but little things like that get to you in prison. Anyone can borrow something, but they have to return it. This arsehole didn't – but he apologised so I left it.

This didn't stop him doing it again and again. Eventually, he'd finally done it once too often. It was time to put an end to it. I told Colin I was going to do him. He told me not to, but my mind was set. I steamed into O'Rooke's cell with a jam jar and smashed it into his ugly face. He fell to the floor and crawled under the bed.

Then I really lost my senses. He was already cut badly facially and I should have left it at that – but I went crazy. I kept lashing out at his arms and legs. He was now screaming, like all rats do. I just wanted to shut him up.

I don't know how many screws turned up. The whole unit was swarming with them. They took me to the block, stripped me off and left me.

That night a big, black hole sucked me in. It was the depression of all depressions. I'd lost everything now.

I didn't actually care. I felt empty; I was nothing.

My life had spun out of control and I now felt completely hollow. A young man, a fit man. But I was in absolute turmoil. Four years had turned me, mentally, into an old man. I was utterly lost; nothing to gain from life, nothing to lose. Tomorrow simply didn't matter.

During those four years, I'd had the lot: punishment blocks, beatings, units and violence like I would never have believed was in me.

There was no love in my heart as I sliced the razor through my own wrists and arms. I truly didn't care.

For once, the Judas hole saved me. A screw looked in and saw blood everywhere. I was moved to F2 and treated. My head was now in bits. I was charged with GBH and kept on F2.

Weeks later, I *really* fucked up.

It was a day I'll always remember, a day the system will never let me forget – the day I lost my sanity and gave up the thought of ever getting out.

It was a Sunday. I had a visit booked for that very day. Loraine, Ian and Pam were coming to see me. All week I was looking forward to it. I woke up early and stuck my head in a bowl of cold water and just kept it there for as long as I could. I felt fresh, alive, and I was ready for a new day.

A hospital screw called Taffy Jones opened up the hatch in my cell door. I told him to 'fuck off' and with that he slammed my hatch. This set me off.

I was so upset my head started throbbing. I thought about Loraine coming to see me that very afternoon. I thought about how it would hurt them if I was in more trouble. But Taffy Jones was in my head.

Someone unlocked my cell door and brought my breakfast in. I leapt out and cut him. All hell broke loose. Bells were ringing, I could hear running, and there was shouting. It was like a film – but this was for real. A fight broke out.

Taffy jumped in. His blood was dripping all over my face and I was screaming blue murder. They dragged me off to the strong box. I thought it was all over. They left me naked, beaten, aching and totally demoralised. I covered myself with a dirty, bloody blanket and lay motionless on the wooden boards. I cried. It was the worst time of my life.

My life was a senseless existence, violent and loveless. Never mind all the talk about tough men, hard men. I cried like never before.

I was crying for all the pain I had caused my family. Loraine, Ian and Pam would travel down today, only to be turned away. They were told by Dr Cooper that I was too ill for a visit. He told them what had happened and they left broken-hearted.

All my life I've hurt the ones I love. If I'd had a gun, a knife or poison, I'd have ended my life that day.

I stayed in the box for some time.

My life was four walls. I went deeper and deeper into a hole. Every thought I had was violent. A Dr Tidmarsh came to see me from Broadmoor asylum and Dr Cooper gave me drugs.

I went to court in a haze of gloom. I can't remember much about it.

The courtroom appeared like a dream ... faces were blurred, speech sounded slurred. The doctors read out their reports while I sat there half-asleep.

It was over so quickly. I had been certified insane – unfit to plead! The judge sectioned me under the Mental Health Act. He said I would be sent to Rampton Secure Hospital, Nottinghamshire, for an indefinite period.

In other words, I had effectively been sentenced to life with no date of release. I would remain in a top-secure hospital until the doctors agreed I was safe to be freed.

I was to be taken back to Parkhurst Hospital Wing until there was a bed available for me at Rampton.

I mumbled to the judge that I wasn't mad, but I was taken away. I hobbled off like a man twice my age, drugged and destroyed. Fortunately, none of my family were in court to see it.

I went back to Parkhurst a broken man. Dr Cooper told me that I would be going to Rampton in a few days. He allowed me to see Ron and Reg, Colin Robinson and a few of the other guys.

I was going to smash a con over the skull with a lump of concrete so I could stay in jail, but a mate stopped me. I just didn't want to go to a nut-house.

I wasn't mad – or was I? Was I really insane?

It's a frightening thing when you don't know your own mind. Obviously, I had my problems, and I was violent … but was I mad?

Looking back on it now, I must admit, I was.

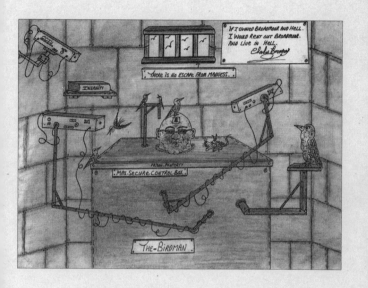

CHAPTER FOUR

On 8 December 1978 I left Parkhurst for the asylum.
The Boomtown Rats had a hit with 'Rat Trap'. I was
like a rat ... caught in a trap. I was now officially a
madman, a label that never goes away.

Both Ron and Reg saw me go. So did my pals Colin
Robinson and Johnny Heibner. Johnny was a great
boxer in his day – he had it all, hooks, crosses, speed,
footwork, and one hell of a punch. But he'd got life and
25 years over a contract killing. I've always respected
Johnny. I knew in my heart that it's never goodbye. I'd
see them again. I wished them good luck.

Before I take you on my journey through the asylums, I'd like to mention a few of the other lads who remain in my thoughts, who saw me through those four-and-a-half years in prison. There was Rooky Lee, Billy Armstrong, Roy Walsh, Bertie Costa, Paddy Hill and Johnny Bond, who I've deliberately left until last. Johnny got life for killing his girlfriend in the 1970s and was on C Unit with me. A super-fit man, but he suffered terrible depression over what he'd done. We all tried to help him. Everyone liked him and you could tell that he still loved his girl. But it was too late to help him come to terms with what he did.

He hanged himself. He could never forgive himself so he ended it all. Years later, he still flashes through my mind. It's a sad, sad, life.

C Unit remained what it always was – a very unpredictable place. Dougie Wakefield strangled Brian Peak. Brian was our hairdresser. Dougie got another life sentence.

The day I left, seven screws went with me. It was a journey into the unknown, a journey I did not want. All the way to that madhouse in Nottinghamshire I prayed we would not get there, but my prayers were not answered.

As we trundled up the driveway, there was a big Christmas tree, all lit up. It looked lovely. Once in admission, I noticed another tree, also lit up. This one was tiny but it still looked lovely.

The six guys in white coats looked the exact opposite. Big, ugly bruisers, all of them with boots on.

These were psychiatric nurses and they would have done any rugby team proud. One of them came up to my face, just inches away. This was bound to be the start of something. A scuffle broke out within seconds. I was carried to one of the wards where I had my clothes cut off with scissors, and was put in a bath of cold water.

Then they used wet towels on me, dragged me out of the bath and put me, naked, in a cell. This was my entry to the mad house.

They soon came back and told me the 'rules'. I was to do as I was told, when I was told.

One of the nurses held out his hand with loads of pills in it and told me to swallow them. I looked at him and said I wasn't taking any fucking pills. Why should I? Doctors prescribe pills, and I'd seen no doctor. He asked me if I was refusing to take them and I answered, 'Yes'. He just smiled at me and left. The next minute the door swung open. In seconds they had me down. I felt the hypodermic syringe pierce my right buttock. A burning sensation coursed through me. I screamed, 'You dirty bastards.' I couldn't believe this was happening to me. I was dazed, drifting into a deep sleep.

Why was this happening to me? I'd done nothing in the hour I'd been there to deserve this treatment. What would they have done if I'd actually done something wrong?

As I drifted off, I could hear Irene's words in my head ... 'You'll end up in a nut-house the way you're going.'

Sadly, most mental patients are helpless. They've got no family, no support, and unfortunately have no way of expressing themselves or defending themselves against these brutal people. Some can't read or write. Some can't even blow their own noses, let alone control their speech or their bowels. They are really sad, pathetic cases, largely forgotten by society – perhaps because of the terrible stigma still attached to mental illness. I say all of this out of compassion, not contempt. And I have to say that around the time I was in Rampton it was the worst place.

My doctor was always immaculately dressed, a man of good taste. But I hated drugs. I despise drugs.

There was no need to force them on me. They are used for mental illness, either to control or sedate. Long-term drug therapy is basically for illnesses like schizophrenia. It doesn't cure it, but it helps the schizophrenic accept reality better.

I didn't want any of it. But at this time, I didn't have any choice. I had to take drugs either orally or by injections. One way or the other, we all took them.

So my world was now an asylum, and I saw it through a permanent haze. I was a zombie. I slept a lot, my hands trembled like a drunk, I dribbled like a baby. My memory was affected. I was a 26-year-old wreck.

I'll always remember the first clothes they gave me. My trousers were three inches past my ankles. The jacket sleeves were so short that when I bent my arm they almost touched my elbows. It was a fucking joke. Most of us had badly fitting clothes. It was obvious to me that it was done deliberately to make us look stupid.

I tore mine up in front of them. I said, 'Get me clothes that fit or I'll wear nothing. I'm not walking around like a fucking lunatic!'

On this ward there were 30 loonies, all fresh from the courts. We were being observed and monitored to see where we should be allocated within the hospital. In the system's eyes, we were all potential madmen, not to be trusted, so we were treated like naughty kids.

I soon found out that a good three-quarters of these loons were monsters, sex killers, rapists and child slayers. I started to despise being in the same room as them. Eating with them made me puke!

One in particular, John White, was a slimy rat. He had killed a little girl after he had had his evil way with her. This monster had evil all over his face.

I had to sit in the dayroom with these animals for a

week. I listened to their madness, I smelt their madness. I knew that either I had to go or I'd end up completely mad myself. Out of the patients on my ward, I could only relate to a couple. The rest were either sex-cases or nutters who thought they were somebody famous. The Pope, Adolf Hitler, Jesus – they were all there.

I met one who actually thought that he was the Elephant Man. I gave him my supper buns, as elephants love a bun!

These people were not just crazy, they were dangerous fuckers. If you told them that you didn't believe who they said they were, they would get upset and violent. So you had to pacify them.

The one who thought he was the Pope kept blessing us all. In the end, I grabbed his throat and head-butted him in the face. Not a nice thing to do to the Pope – but there you have it, I nutted the Pope.

The time had come. A week was my lot. I decided to kill White.

My plan was simple. I thought it all over very carefully. If I murdered the monster, I'd go back to court and be sent back to prison for life. I believed I would never be freed so I might as well kill someone to justify my wasted life.

I thought that I would be doing society a big favour by topping him. I thought about the parents of the little girl that he had killed. I thought they would be pleased. She had died, so he was going to die. Simple. And as for myself – well, I was locking myself up for the rest of my days.

For a couple of days, I plotted the monster's departure ... how would I do it? Strangulation was the only way. But it was difficult for me as I was being watched more than anyone else. I almost always had two white coats with me. There was only one real chance – to grab him in the dayroom.

I sat right behind him while we were watching TV. Some were just looking into space, some were reading, others playing cards. The white coats were reading and were watching us. I waited for the right time ... it was now or never. I whipped off my tie and wrapped it round the pervert's neck. I pulled it as tight as I could. Strangely, there was no sound. Obviously, there were other loons watching. Some were laughing, some staring, but none of them said a word. It really was insanity at its best! I was killing a man before their very eyes and getting away with it.

I bent over to see the monster's face. It had turned blue, his eyes were bulging and his tongue hung down on his chin. His whole body was shaking like he was having a fit. I heard the death rattle. This monster was on his way out, and I felt so happy. He was getting off lightly after what he done to that little girl.

Then it happened so fast. A white coat shouted and they were on my back, punching and trying to prise my hands free of the tie. I was shouting, screaming and laughing. I was now completely mad! I was biting and kicking as I was being dragged away. I heard shouts for oxygen, and people running, but most of all I could hear my own laughter as they dragged me away.

They slung me in the cell and cut off my clothes with scissors. Then they injected me. I was still laughing and shouting.

'I've killed the monster. I've killed him!'

I was now starting to feel a bit groggy. They grabbed me and led me down the landing towards Drake intensive care unit.

White coats were waiting. It was like a dream turning into a nightmare. I was left in a cell with a mattress on the floor and a blanket. It was cold. I drifted off into a sea of misery.

For the next three weeks I was kept in total

seclusion. My letters were read to me through the hatch in the door. I wasn't allowed to read papers, books – nothing. I had to wear a canvas suit, a bit like a boiler-suit, and every morning I was shaved outside my door while I sat on a chair. If I wanted water, a cardboard cup would be passed through the hatch. If I needed to go to the toilet, I had to ask for a chamber pot.

Drake housed 15 loons. We were all down as highly dangerous, disturbed and unpredictable. This for me was the pits – and this unit was to be my life for the next 11 months.

White survived my attack. They started his heart with an electric current and gave him oxygen. So if he ever gets out and kills another child, you know who to blame. I asked for the police to be brought in to charge me with attempted murder, but my doctor said that I was too disturbed to stand trial. I was Rampton's Public Enemy Number 1. They now knew I was prepared to kill. I wasn't allowed to go out on exercise; I was denied fresh air for 11 months. My life was total humiliation.

I'll always remember one night when I couldn't sleep because I was so restless. I got out of bed and stuck my mattress up against the wall so I could use it as a punch bag. I hadn't had a work-out for ages, mainly because I was too tied on drugs, but this night I just fancied a session. My door was suddenly flung open and in they piled.

The routine on Drake Ward was crazy, and so demoralising. We got up at 7.30am and went to bed at 7.00pm. That's if we were good boys – otherwise we stayed in seclusion. We all had to stand in a line for our tablets. They put them in our mouths on a spoon and we then had to show them our tongues to prove we'd swallowed them. We then had to march to the dining room in a line. It was to belittle us. If official visitors were due, we were warned not to speak. The place was run on fear. A prison could not be run in this way or there would be a riot. Most of the inmates in Rampton were looking at 20 years, and some would eventually die there. Lunatics are basically forgotten faces.

Right now, my life was not good. I hated it and I had to escape it before I ended up a forgotten face, too. This was my one fear, becoming a madman true and proper.

Out of the 15 of these lunatics, I guess I spoke to about three. The others messed up my head so badly I couldn't think straight.

One of them, 'Hutchy', really took the biscuit. In a strange sense, I felt a lot of compassion for him. His neck was all twisted – it hung down on to his right shoulder and he was forever staring at the ceiling. It was weird to watch him.

Hutchy had his violent bouts so he was kept on Drake for years. I saw him lose his marbles many times. It was so sad to witness him being dragged away to be injected. The saddest day was when Hutchy's mother was coming to see him. She only came once a year so this particular day he was so excited. He went funny and smashed both his arms through a window and tore them open. His mother had to see him in the infirmary. This, to me, was so bloody tragic.

Jip Carter was the legend on Drake. His life was the most tragic case I had known up to that point. He was an old man and had been in Rampton since the Second World War. The poor old sod had been on Drake Ward for 20 years. He had actually refused to move. Mostly they left him alone because of his age, but Jip told me stories that made me cringe. He knew Frank Mitchell and he told me how Frank had escaped from there in the 1950s. They were all great stories from an old man who had survived so much. I'll always remember Jip's little brown case, one that he kept locked. This case was Jip's whole life and every once in a while he would sit alone and open the case up and look through it.

I often wondered what was in it that made him go so quiet. Then, one day, he called me over to show me. I was one of very few people to have had this privilege. He showed me some old faded black-and-white photographs of his family who had long since died. There were photos of himself in the '40s and '50s in Rampton. There were also some old letters. I really liked old Jip. I often wonder what has happened to that old brown case. Jip sadly died in Rampton, a lonely, sad old man.

Then there was 'John Boy'. John's case was unique. He really was the only one of his kind in Rampton. This is an incredible story and to me it is tragic. John's IQ must have been an all-time low. He was subnormal and mentally ill. He couldn't talk or do anything for himself. His life consisted of sitting in a specially-designed chair, into which he was strapped. When I first saw him strapped in, I thought, what the fuck is going on here? I soon found out why he was restrained – he was lethal!

Every morning, John used to run out of his cell, covered in his own mess. He would run to the bath and jump in. One of us had to scrub him and dress him, then walk him back to the day-room to be strapped into his chair. At times he was so violent he had to be put to sleep.

He had no teeth and wasn't allowed to eat with us. He ate alone for years and years.

John had been sent to Rampton in the '60s – tied between two mattresses – from a county mental hospital where he couldn't be controlled.

All I can comment on is what I actually saw

myself – and it wasn't very nice! He'd sit in his chair making animal sounds. I'd pat him on the head to calm him down. I'd never felt more sorry for a human being in my life. Sometimes they let him outside the ward on to a patch of grass with a little fence around it. God knows what was going through his mind as he sat there. I spent my days looking after John and scrubbing the floors on the ward. I wasn't allowed outside for fresh air or a walk, unlike all the other inmates.

John Boy later died in Rampton. He attacked me several times but I never once retaliated. I felt so sad for him. I used to buy a bag of chocolates every week, just to give him the soft ones. He was crazy, but he didn't deserve to die in a stinking hole like that.

I didn't feel so charitable towards Mad Taffy. This fucker was bang on target for a right hook. He was completely off his rocker! He kept telling me about his Rolls-Royces, jet planes and boats – so for a joke I asked him to lend me half a million. The bastard went and told the white coats that I was demanding money off him!

Later, I pulled him to see what his game was, but he went to the white coats again and told them I was now going to kill him if he didn't pay up. I busted his jaw.

Some nights I couldn't wait for 7.00pm so I could escape the madness. It was a life of emptiness for me. I was losing my mind.

My family visited me there and none of them liked what they saw. My visits were not allowed in the central hall. I had mine in a cell on Drake with white coats standing by the door. Out of the 11 months I spent on Drake, half of it was in seclusion. I was even denied a pen to write a letter. It was all set to destroy me – so it was time I destroyed them!

I got out of seclusion to set my plan in action. I was

going to smash a nurse's head in with a lump of concrete. This twat had to have some of his own treatment. I knew that I would be doing every loony in Rampton justice if I did this rat in.

Outside the unit was a concrete shop that made paving stones and kerbs. I made a deal with a loony. I'd give him five packets of fags for a good piece of concrete. He agreed, we made a meet, I gave him the fags ... and the little bastard ran off! I couldn't believe the loony had ripped me off.

That wasn't the end of it, though. I was called to the office and asked why I wanted some concrete. Obviously I denied it. Then they produced the fags. I still denied it but they put me back in seclusion. They never did find out why I wanted the concrete, but all the windows were screwed down after this.

One of the best guys I met in Rampton was Stevie Booth. Steve came into Drake from another ward where he'd broken some loon's nose. Steve's an old pal, one of the old school, good solid principles. He had done the rounds, prison to prison, then finally the asylums. The system has had Stevie a long time, but I'm pleased to say they've never broken him and never will.

He helped me so much, even though one day we had a punch-up. It was more of a brotherly clash. We both got carried away and injected, but later we hugged each other. Steve is just Steve. He won't ever back down, but I love the guy. He kept me in order, kept me sane. Without him I was doomed.

I was called into the office one day to see the doc. He told me that Rampton could do no more for me. I was to be moved to Broadmoor very soon.

I went back to tell Stevie. His eyes filled up with tears. He was pleased for me but he would miss me. I knew that I would miss Steve and a few others, but it was a godsend to me. I gave him my suit – the one I'd got married in. He was made up with it. I also gave him some chocolates to give to John Boy every now and again.

The morning I left I took a last look through the hatch at John Boy. He was sitting up, shit all over him, poor sod. I thought to myself, Who's the lucky guy who is going to bath him today?

Before I left, I shouted to Steve, 'Don't forget to wash behind John Boy's ears!'

The time I spent in Rampton will remain in my head for ever. I'm told Rampton has changed, but I'll always remember it how it was.

On 20 November 1979, as I was passing through the Nottinghamshire countryside in the van, I reflected on this so-called hospital. My final opinion is that it was a hell-hole on earth, a god-forsaken pit of human misery. I still carry the scars.

Still, I was glad that I was finally getting out of the place. I left Rampton a very sick and disturbed inmate, thinking that Broadmoor couldn't be any worse.

Little did I know.

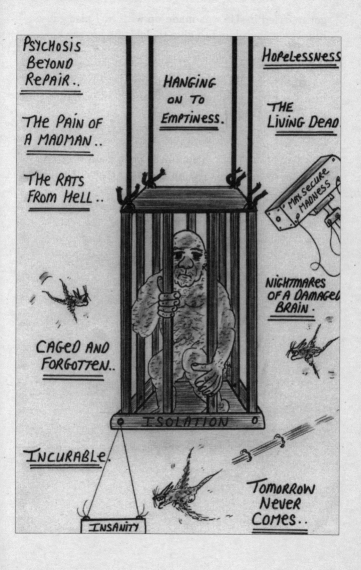

CHAPTER FIVE

Broadmoor is known as 'the end of the road'.

It is perhaps the most infamous mental institution in Great Britain. Broadmoor is legendary.

All the top-security mental hospitals – Rampton, Broadmoor and Ashworth – have been trying to shake off their terrible image in the last few years. They now call their inmates 'patients', 'clients' and 'service users'. But they still fuck up.

Reality stops at the gates of these institutions. Broadmoor, to me, is simply an institution for the criminally insane. Behind these Victorian walls lie stories that would turn your hair white overnight – stories of madness, pain, anguish, torture, murder, suicides, escapes, sieges, protests, drug abuse, force feedings, electric shock treatments, brutality, sex crimes.

The place is riddled with horror. It is a monster's paradise and a psychiatrist's dream. This was to be my home for the next five years.

Broadmoor is situated on top of a small hill in the Berkshire countryside, in a village called Crowthorne. It houses both male and female inmates. Some have been locked up since the Second World War. Thirty years is not an unusual stay in Broadmoor.

From the second the gates opened and let us in, I felt a strange sensation. I could smell the madness. The place was full of despair, full of souls that were lost. I could sense the broken hearts, the dreams that never were.

For the first time in my life I felt fear, a fear that I would never be free again. This was reality. I was now a Broadmoor patient.

I was taken to reception, which was the opposite of Rampton. The staff seemed decent; they didn't intimidate me. It all seemed relaxed. I was led to 'Somerset House' and given a plastic mug of tea and some sandwiches. They told me about the place and what they expected of me. They said I could do it any way I wanted – easy or hard. Either way, I would do it! Broadmoor could be heaven or hell, they said. If I behaved, I would have an easy ride – TV, snooker, social events. On the other hand, if I messed about I would have a bare cell for a very long time.

As they told me all this, I thought one thing: Fuck Broadmoor!

They started asking me questions ... name, date of birth and so on. No way was I going to accept all this shit – no way. I told them to read my file if they wanted to know anything. After all, it was as big as a tea chest!

After my bath and something to eat, they locked me in my cell. It was bare except for a bolted-down bed and a piss-pot, but at least it was warm. I lay in bed, nice and relaxed, thinking. I thought about how many lunatics had slept in this cell. I also thought about my past and my present. There was no future that I could see for myself.

All I felt was a big black hole. There was no light. Just a big, black, bottomless pit. A lot of inmates die in asylums. They will never be released so they are the ideal guinea pigs. Even if they complained, who would listen? Who would believe them? Who really gives a fuck? After all, they're mad, aren't they?

I counted the bricks and recounted them so many times, but it was never the same number. I tried to picture in my mind everything that I saw as I arrived: walls, gates, doors, drainpipes. I thought of a way to escape. I didn't like this place and I didn't like the stigma that went with it.

I was on Ward One of Somerset House. All the new inmates went on this ward to be put through psychological tests. An assessment lasts for anything from three to six months.

As I lay in my cell, I heard a tannoy announcement: 'Will Ronnie Kray please go to the office.'

I knew Ronnie had come to Broadmoor from Parkhurst only a short time before, but obviously I never knew he was going to be on my ward!

This put a smile on my face. Half-an-hour later, another message came over the tannoy: 'Will Colin Robinson please go to the office.'

Robbo was sent to Broadmoor for his 'unusual ways'. I couldn't wait to see them both again.

The staff came to my cell for a chat. They said that

Ronnie and Robbo were both settled and doing well and were soon to be allocated their new wards.

Strangely, I was excited on my first morning inside Britain's most notorious madhouse. Sure, I had to face facts. I was criminally insane. I was only 26 and I was desperate. I had been caged for almost five years and I had lost everything. I truly felt that I had nothing else to lose. Maybe I was mad and deserved to be in a cage but there was no way I would go along with their mental games.

I knew from day one that I would be a lion. They knew they would have to tame me. It was going to be a long battle and, admittedly, a battle I could never win.

That first night's sleep was a strange one. I woke several times. On one occasion, I could hear screams; some poor sod was having a nightmare. It was a restless night.

I was too excited to sleep. Tomorrow I was going to be allowed up to see Ron and Robbo!

In the morning they gave me a mug of tea, porridge and a bacon sandwich. They told me that I'd be slopping out later, after all the others, and then I had to collect my new clothes from the stores. I was excited; I told them not to keep me waiting! After breakfast, I walked up and down my cell. I soon got fed up so I lay down on the cold floor and started to bang the door with my feet. They arrived with my clothes.

They led me to the recess where I was allowed to empty my pot. I was given a clean towel, soap, toothbrush and, to my amazement, a safety razor. I shaved myself for the first time in a year. It felt great! And it felt really good to be trusted with a razor.

After my wash and shave, I got dressed in my new clothes. I felt human again. The time had arrived ... I was led to the day-room. There, facing me, were 24 pairs of eyes. It only took me a split-second to find the two pairs I wanted to see. Ronnie came straight over and gave me one of his firm handshakes and a friendly hug. Then Robbo did the same. At that moment I felt elated – on top of the world!

Ron had lost weight. He had been through a bad spell at Parkhurst. It is no secret that Ron was a paranoid schizophrenic. He could become violent, but Parkhurst had never helped him. I know about Ron's final few months in Parkhurst. After nine years there, they certified him mad. He suffered. He'd been in the same evil room as me – the silent box. The same evil room that drove me mad.

Robbo looked his usual self. He had recently recovered from his latest swallowing bout.

They both gave me tea bags, biscuits and chocolate. Ron's locker was jam packed with tins of salmon and tuna. He knew how to eat well, even inside. And when Ron ate, his pals ate! He looked after his own – a good-hearted man.

We all had a good chat; we had lots to talk over. I hardly noticed the other patients, I was too engrossed in our conversation. I was too excited. But it couldn't last – nothing ever did with me!

In that room there were 25 of us. All of us had our own problems, but I can honestly say that three-quarters of those guys were so mad it was impossible to relate to them. They were the craziest fuckers I'd ever met! There were all sorts in the room, all dangerously disturbed men and all on observation.

Dr Pat McGrath was in charge of Somerset. He'd also been the Superintendent of Broadmoor for over 30 years. I personally respected the man. We had several discussions and I found him very interesting. He'd seen it all.

I was put on an anti-psychotic drug called Modicate which was injected into my buttocks every two weeks.

Other drugs I had were taken orally – Stelazine, Chloral Hydrate and Largactil. I hated them. I despised having to take them, but I had no choice.

If I was asked what I believed my problem to be, I would say that I was suffering with anxiety and stress caused by five years' mental and physical abuse. Stress is a very touchy subject. Unless you've really suffered it, you'll have little or no idea. Some doctors don't even understand it – and many don't want to.

It is not about being under too much pressure, having too much grief. Anxiety is the same – it's not about panic attacks. Anxiety and stress can cut you to the core. Your body is not your own; you shake uncontrollably, you have to piss when you don't want to, you forget things, you cry, you shamble around like a man three times your age. It affects a lot of people and it's not nice!

I truly believed by then that I was a very messed up and dangerously disturbed man. Maybe I was a psychopath. Who knows? I honestly don't.

But I did know one thing – once Ron and Robbo moved on, I would flip my lid!

After a few weeks, Ron and Robbo left. Ron went to Somerset Ward Three and Robbo went to Cornwall House. And me? I went to fucking pieces! My mind began to wander. Then Gordon Robinson arrived.

Gordon Robinson was a black guy. From the start we didn't hit it off as he was just a big-mouth. We had a few words and I managed to slip into the toilets unseen. I hit him so hard with a right hook I thought I'd killed him. It was a perfect punch. I didn't need to follow it up, but I did. As I left the lunatic in a pile on the floor, I knew our paths would cross again.

Then young George Shipley arrived from Feltham Borstal in Middlesex. The second he strolled into the room I took to him. I called him over. I sorted him out, told him what's what.

He was a breath of fresh air for me. He lifted me out of a low period. George was a violent, aggressive lad but conducted himself well. He frightened a lot of the loons but I loved the guy. He represented 'prison'; prison was all over him – he was a 'time man'. I could relate to him. I could trust him and that, to me, was marvellous.

We played chess and Scrabble and I knew we would end up good pals for a long time. I was beginning to realise that in these asylums good friends are so few. They were riddled with grasses. The lunatics never even saw it as grassing. It used to make me and George sick to witness it.

'Please, sir – he's just taken two cakes'; 'Please, sir – he's just torn a page out of the *TV Times*'; 'Please, sir – he's smoking in the recess.' All silly bollocks like that.

George and I tried to switch off and play our games. We wanted no part. But, sadly, it was impossible being in the same room as them.

It caused us a lot of problems but there were ways of dealing with the persistent loons who kept upsetting us. Even though the wardens were in the same room as us, I stabbed one rat in the eye with a lighted fag. I got another one with a kick to his bollocks as he was going out of the room.

One fat bastard who had killed his wife and kids arrived on the ward. Within a week, he was the staff's tea-boy. It made me sick to watch the fat slob grovelling. I said to George I fancied taking him hostage. But the snivelling shit was lucky, as it was my turn to move on. I had to leave poor George on his own ... but I knew that we would get back together.

Another nice lad that I left on Somerset One was young Michael Martin. He was fearless, strong as a bull, and he'd fight anyone. Five years later he was to die in the hospital's Norfolk House – a sad, sad ending. I witnessed Michael arrive and I witnessed his deterioration. He was ten-and-a-half stone on arrival and fourteen-and-a-half stone at death. A tragic waste of life.

As soon as I entered Broadmoor's Gloucester House, the whole atmosphere hit me in the face like a pick-axe handle. It was the lunatic eyes staring at me … mad eyes, dead, zombie eyes. They were all lost souls. Some were old men who had been there 40 years.

My heart felt heavy for them. I felt a sense of doom. The sight of them convinced me I'd never accept being a lunatic.

They put me in a dormitory with seven others. Jesus, it was bad enough even to be in the same building as them, but now I had to sleep with them! It was here that I learned about real insanity. They would get upset over crazy things; it was paranoia at its worst. Some would laugh out loud, some would talk to themselves and some would accuse others of being spies. They heard voices in their heads.

I soon learnt the danger signs. It was a case of being alert at all times. A madman is a dangerous and unpredictable person, believe me.

Here I was, Prison Enemy Number 1, in a fucking dormitory. It just didn't make sense. The first night was crazy. A loony was keeping me awake with his persistent snoring. I'd had enough, so I walked over to his bed, picked it up, and started shaking it. He woke up and got very abusive, so I punched him in the mouth and went back to my own bed. He didn't snore again. I'd cured him!

The funny thing is, my friend Neil Adamson, who was sentenced to two life terms back in 1970, had been in Broadmoor a couple of years before I arrived and had slept in the same dormitory. He chinned the same bloke on his first night! If that isn't fate, what is? I often smile over this. Luckily, Neil has moved on, out of Broadmoor.

I survived on the ward less than a week – a week of sheer madness for me. I saw things that disgusted me and I was sick to the teeth. On the second night, I got out of bed to go to the toilet only to walk in on a lovers' session. They didn't even stop when I walked in. I went mad. I told them to 'Fuck off' and kicked one up the arse as they ran out. I don't give a toss what anyone gets up to but I do care when it's in front of me. They stayed clear of me after that. I lay in bed that night, brooding. I felt the danger signs.

The next day I pulled David Francis. He put himself about as one of the lads. Tattoos, ex-Dartmoor con … he gave the impression he was tough. He worked in the kitchen so I did a deal with him. My plan was taking shape.

Dave was going to get me a knife, snap the handle off, and bury the blade in a large potato. I didn't tell Dave why I wanted it. Only I knew.

The day after we got it together, and he agreed to get the blade for me, was the day six white coats came for me. I was put into a seclusion cell, stripped naked and then left. They never spoke a word. Soon after they returned with Dr Tidmarsh. He asked me why I wanted a knife. I just couldn't believe it! Obviously, I denied any knowledge.

I was given pyjamas, slippers and a dressing-gown and escorted out of Gloucester House. The six attendants walked me in silence over to Norfolk intensive care unit.

I had heard about this place. Most patients feared it – it was the dungeon of the asylums. The security door opened, the red light went on. As we walked through, the door locked, the red light went off, and the next door opened.

There, facing me, were a good dozen nurses in

brilliant white coats. I could smell the tension. They were ready, like a boxer waiting for the bell. I was led to a double-doored cell. No words were spoken. They locked me in, first one door, then the second. The bed was a plastic one, the walls were filth. This was a shit-hole.

They returned five minutes later and told me to take two tablets and a medicine tot full of syrupy liquid. I'd already had this bollocks in Rampton. I knew they meant what they said. I was being forced to take these drugs for one reason and one reason only – *control*.

I took them ... and my hell began. This liquid medicine was an anti-psychotic drug with bad side-effects. I felt as though my whole nervous system was breaking down. It caused muscular spasms so bad that I collapsed in a heap on the floor. My head span, my tongue seemed to double in size. I had no saliva, my body trembled and my eyes blurred. The pain in my neck, shoulders, spine and arms was agony. I couldn't stand, I couldn't even sit up. I was confused.

I lay on the floor of the cell a beaten man. This was beyond any pain I've ever known. It terrified me as I was twisted up like a cripple. What if I stayed this way? My next attack was on the exercise yard. The pain got so bad, I had to lie down on the concrete. I was crying. I couldn't fight it. It was a torture worse than any I had ever experienced.

I had been injected many times before, both in Rampton and in prisons, for my acts of violence. I'd been given Largactil, Valium, even Modicate, but I had never suffered side-effects like these. What were they doing to me? It was inhuman. The worst humiliation was to have to be carried back inside. This was the final kick in the arse.

It hurt me badly. I felt bitter and hateful. I knew in my heart that I would get my own back. Time would tell.

It's strange how a drug can become part of your life. Anyone who knows me knows how I feel about drugs. I won't even take an aspirin. Obviously, there are times when drugs are necessary. But who knows what some of the permanent side-effects might be?

My whole life turned upside down. My sleep altered, I woke in a confused state and suffered constipation. My weight just went up like a balloon. I had always been super-fit; now I was fit for nothing. I was usually around 12 stone. I was soon up to 17 stone – a fat, weak, breathless, soul-destroyed man.

One of the doctors even wanted to give me electric shock treatment, but I warned him my family would have a hell of a lot to say about that. Many doctors are against electric shock treatment. It can be barbaric, but it's still used. Guys have bitten their tongues and had fits while being given this treatment. Electrodes are attached to your head and, as the pulses of electricity go through your brain, your whole body experiences spasms and convulsions. You lose control of your bladder and bowels. It's fucking terrible.

Before the treatment, the patient is given a muscle relaxant and sedative, but you still feel it! I've witnessed the trolleys carrying the patients, being pushed into the room where it was done. I've seen them being pushed back out – blood on their pillows. And I've seen the confused state of the patients hours later.

Life in Norfolk was depressing. These loons were the cream of the madmen, violence was like a walk in the park to them. Their crimes were beyond belief.

One had killed his mother and decapitated her. He was caught on a bus with his mother's head in a shopping bag! Some of their crimes are so insane I couldn't even relate them. It's just repulsive.

But it was their behaviour that did my head in. I witnessed them running into walls, using their heads as rams. I've seen them fall unconscious doing this. They stabbed themselves with pens, needles, scissors. One even blinded himself in one eye and another tore out his own testicle. There was one who just kept trying to eat himself, biting his arms, legs and feet. This all scarred my brain.

I was being watched all the time, and one bad report could increase my dosage of medicine. It's a sad fact that most inmates in asylums are forgotten people. A lot have never had a normal life or stable relationship. I was different to most. I had my family behind me. Escape was constantly in my mind, but it would be near-impossible on this unit.

I made it up to Ward Two. There were 15 of us and we all had to sit in a room. We couldn't leave our seat unless we asked. Some of these guys were so dangerous it was unreal! One guy stabbed himself in the stomach with a biro, one cut his own throat and another stabbed an inmate in the eye with a plastic knife.

I fear nothing – but even I was on my toes with this lot! My survival instinct told me to be prepared.

Soon, I made my way up to Ward Three, where there were 12 of us. It didn't take long to get out of Norfolk. I was on the way to Kent Ward.

This ward was to be my last chance. Dr John Hamilton was in charge of Kent. It was spotlessly clean and there were plenty of reasonably sane guys I could relate to. Dr Hamilton was a Scotsman, a pretty fair guy. He practically took me off all the drugs. I began training again. It was hard work but I fought it.

There was only one problem: I was back in a dormitory and Gordon Robinson was in the very next bed. He was bugging me. I knew when I hit the idiot on Somerset Ward our paths would cross again, and here he was, as arrogant as ever, and in the next bed! But I swallowed it for the time being.

I had something much more important to occupy my thoughts. I had to escape. My whole time was spent plotting. It wasn't like planning an escape from jail, it was double the trouble as there were a lot of grasses around.

I had one or two ideas. One seemed half-decent, but it was a terrible gamble.

All the time I was being plagued by fucking lunatics. I was gradually losing my cool. One in particular completely messed my head up. I was sitting watching *Top of the Pops* and he was staring at me. It made me feel tense. I asked him what his problem was – and he asked me to hit him! He kept on and on, so in the end I hit him. He loved being hit, the harder the better. He used to buy me sweets and chocolates just to get me to hit him again. He said I was the best puncher he'd ever had! I couldn't understand it. I really felt I was going mad myself.

I ask whoever reads this book to go to the library and look at the *Guinness Book of Records*. Turn to the prison section and you'll see that Walter Giles served 72 years in Broadmoor. He arrived at the age of 12 and died there aged 84. It is terrifying that someone could be in a place against his will for 72 years! Just thinking about it did my head in.

Once a month there was a disco. Yes, I know it's hard to believe. Broadmoor has male and female inmates and every four weeks we were allowed to get together for a party. I only went to one disco the whole time I was in Broadmoor … it was enough for me! The girls strolled in and the loons began to buy chocolates for them. The staff were in force watching every move.

Bear in mind, some of these madmen were sex killers and women-haters. Some of the women were no angels either. I know of one who had put her baby in the oven and cooked it. Another bit a man's private parts off, and one strangled a man with her bare hands. There were also the hard cases that women's jails like Holloway could not control. These were pure psychopathic maniacs.

I watched it all from a table. It was madness at its best. One girl got over-excited on the dance floor and started to kick her legs up like a Tiller Girl. She was soon taken away by the staff! It was really amusing.

I even had a dance – a slow one. She was a big black girl. She grabbed me close and her arms were closing tighter round my neck! I could hardly get free. I soon pushed myself away. It was to be my first and last dance!

After only weeks of being on Kent Ward, all my hard work came to an end. All my dreams were wiped out, all my escape routes blocked.

I had fallen over the edge. If I wasn't insane before, I was now. Gordon Robinson pushed me too far. Now it was time to show every fucker who I was!

My mother and father had just been to visit me; I was happy. But after the visit I went back to the ward and found Robinson with his key in my locker. The toe-rag was trying to open my locker.

I pushed the scum-bag away. He started a load of verbal abuse – so I chinned him. But this wasn't enough for me. I wanted to kill the motherfucker! My sanity was gone; he was going to die. I was a very desperate man. I saw no future for myself, so what the hell.

I got a silk tie and locked myself in the toilet to test its strength. It held my weight. I was going to strangle him that very night.

I was excited. It was the same buzz you get from an armed robbery, waiting to attack. I can't fully describe my feelings. I was on an all-time high.

The time arrived. I walked into the dormitory in my pyjamas, the tie around my waist, out of sight. I climbed into bed and waited. Robinson's left eye was nearly shut where I had hit him earlier.

His right eye was alert, watching me. I smiled my best smile.

The dormitories were well watched throughout the night. The night patrol nurse looked in every half-an-hour, through the observation slit.

I only needed a couple of minutes. Fuck the night shift! I lay there, still, deep in thought, just waiting. I had all night. And this was *my* night.

Some will read this and think that I am a heartless animal. I know I was over the top, but that's how I am. I don't claim to be something I'm not.

I was buzzing. Twelve o'clock came, then one o'clock. I waited patiently, watching the night nurse. All of a sudden, Robinson moved. He sat up and bent over to put his slippers on. I leapt out of bed.

In a second, the tie was wrapped around his neck. I was strangling the bastard and it felt great! Surprisingly, there was little noise. I pulled tighter and leant over to watch. His eyes were bulging and his tongue was protruding. He was on his way out of planet earth.

Then it happened. The tie snapped. I was in shock – I had half the tie in one hand and half in the other. He began to make a lot of noise – grunting, moaning, and all the others woke up. I was in trouble!

I acted fast. I hit him, straddled over his bed and told him he was having a nightmare. I was now strangling him with my hands. Unknown to me, one of the loons rang the emergency bell. They came charging in.

Gordon Robinson survived but the welts around his neck tell the story.

I hit the Norfolk unit so fast my feet didn't touch the floor! My next four years were to be spent in this hell-hole.

When the double-doored cell cut me off from the madness, I covered myself with a blanket and cried in frustration at what I had just attempted. I went through a bout of sheer panic, and a loss of hope.

I tore up my photos and destroyed all my letters. My dreams were no more. I was empty. I wasn't the person I once was. Once a punch in the mouth was enough, now I had nearly taken a human life.

I wrote letters to tell everyone to forget me. Suicide passed through my mind more than once. We all go through bad spells, it's what life is all about. But this was my lowest point. I felt sure I would die a lonely old man in Broadmoor.

I don't know what really saved me, but Ronnie Kray played a big part in it. One day, I received a note from him. He had heard that I was feeling low and arranged for a friend of his on the outside to visit me. This friend was Terry Downs, former middleweight boxing champion of the world.

He was the lift I needed. He gave me a massive boost – the kick up the arse I needed. So thanks to Ronnie, I started to pull out of my depression. God bless you, Ron.

I got my act together. I fought back to fitness. I beat the evil drugs and the psychological games. The time was right; my plan was simple. It took me three months to work my way up to Ward Three. It was my turn to break loose and let fly. I'd come alive again!

CHAPTER SIX

My heart was pounding. I leapt on to a metal beam. It was slippery but I managed to pull myself up. Some bastard had grabbed hold of my right foot. I lashed out with my left and I caught him on the head. He let go – and I was up!

I was the first lunatic to ever break free and hit a roof from Norfolk Care Unit in over 100 years. Three months I had been planning this. I was going to fuck the whole system.

Broadmoor was medieval, a very old, crumbly institution. It was madness even to think of climbing the 30 feet to the roof, but I had everything to gain, nothing to lose.

I achieved it.

Twelve of us were being escorted to the canteen. This day was the highlight of our week. Time to buy chocolates, toiletries, writing paper and stamps. We all marched in a line. But this was going to be my day. I had prayed for this moment.

The rain was chucking it down, which made my task doubly hard. Doubt entered my mind.

Fuck it!

I was off like a rocket! I ran a good 20 yards, and I never looked back.

I heard a whistle blowing and shouting. I got on to the slippery beam, scrambled free of the screw trying to grab me, dived to a cell window and made it up a drainpipe.

Up I went! I was on top of the world! The rain was pouring down but it felt magic. My friend Jimmy Boyle wrote a book called *A Sense of Freedom* ... well, this was *my* freedom. I was the King Loony on top of the Loony Bin!

Dr McGrath came to a cell window on the top floor. He asked me to come down. I shouted to him to 'Fuck off'. I had begun my mission, a mission of destruction. Slates flew through cell and office windows in the opposite building. I aimed them at workshop windows and anybody within distance. I tore out electrical wires, TV aerials, copper pipes, timber. They had to evacuate Kent Ward Three, which was below me, and they turned off the water supply and electricity at the mains.

Hour after hour I emptied myself of years of pain; all the hatred oozed out of me.

My hands were bleeding and my head was cut. My body was soaked with the rain, sweat, blood, grime and dust. My eyes were full of dirt, my muscles ached and my back was sore – but I loved it!

Every slate I slung off that roof represented a day of my life caged up. It felt great! I started laughing, shouting, singing and screaming. Madness enveloped me. Here was I, making history! They wouldn't forget me.

Obviously, it had to come to an end, but it took 'til nightfall.

I'd found a place out of the way of the searchlights they had on the roof. I lay there cold, hungry and tired. I wrapped myself up in some polythene I'd found.

This was the first night I'd spent looking up at the stars for almost eight years. Eight fucked-up years. My son was now 11 years old. I had not seen him since he was three. Life had passed us by. I thought about my family. I remembered once looking down at my son sleeping in his cot. He was sucking his thumb; I touched his warm little face. Yeah, I'd thought, that's my boy.

I remembered going into the bedroom and settling down beside Irene.

'I wonder what Michael will be when he grows up.' Irene just looked at me. 'Sane, I hope.'

A lot of water had passed under the bridge since then, since I was a free man. Right now, this roof was my freedom. I was the Governor!

The Berkshire countryside was lovely to see. The lights shone for endless miles – I could see it all!

All the villagers were beyond the wall. They had been watching for most of the day. Kids were shouting, 'Jump, jump.' This upset me, but mostly it was peaceful, time to reflect on my life.

Broadmoor has always been a source of fear for the public and the media. John Straffen caused the biggest scare in the 1950s. Straffen was sent to Broadmoor for strangling two little kids in a park. He was found to be subnormally insane. After five years of incarceration in Broadmoor, he escaped and within

24 hours a little girl's body was found a mile from the hospital. She had been strangled. Straffen was eventually caught and was again 'lifed off'. Over 35 years later, he still went out into the prison exercise yard, a walking shadow of death. Straffen was a monster, but there are many other old lags who have been locked away for 30, maybe 40 years.

There was one film, *The Shawshank Redemption*, which I'm told got close to the mark. But unless you've witnessed it with your own eyes, you'll never fully understand the utter emptiness of these old boys, shambling around with their hearing aids and walking sticks.

It was Straffen's escape that really put the fear into the people living in Crowthorne. Every Monday morning a test siren blares away. It can be heard for miles around. The villagers must dread those Monday morning calls, especially those old enough to remember 'Straffen the Beast'.

As far as I was concerned, I was just another madman on the roof. But I knew I would not get much help from the media. I thought of my mum and dad, my brothers, the rest of my family and the closest person alive to me, my lovely cousin Loraine. But here I was alone. Lost in a world that had left me behind.

I actually felt a sadness come over me. I was going nowhere. To stay where I was would be to die; to jump would be to die; and to climb down would be to die. I had no life to look forward to. A double-doored cell. Solitary and emptiness. Drugs, boredom and no company. Just every day the same.

I thought about it all, about Ron Kray and Colin Robinson. They had settled in – why couldn't I? I knew then that I never would. Escape must be my only goal and to escape I had to stay strong, train and be prepared. I decided to climb down. I would take the treatment they were going to dish out – I had to.

I came down.

One whitecoat, one of many surrounding me, grabbed my arm. I told him to fuck right off, and a big charge nurse called Roger Russell told them all to leave me alone.

Roger's 6ft 7in tall and 16-and-a-half stone. A good footballer in his day, he respected me and I respected him. He was always decent with me. You see, I don't hate all screws and whitecoats – I just want to be treated fair; to be told the truth about where I'm to be moved. Fuck! They're the most basic of rights.

Sure, I've caused damage. A considerable amount. I've laughed, sung and cried while I've been on jail roofs and while I've held my hostages. But I've never killed a hostage – or even seriously harmed one. I've certainly never stabbed one.

They are just pawns in the game. But, unlike pawns, I don't sacrifice them. I don't mean them any serious harm.

I was covered in blood and dirt when I came down from Broadmoor's roof. I was a mess. I was led into Norfolk and allowed a bath. Roger took all the splinters out of my hands. He patched me up and cleaned my eyes.

A doctor gave me some medicine. They led me into the cell and I climbed on to the plastic bed. I can't remember any more. I felt like I was in heaven but in my subconscious I knew that the opposite awaited me when I woke up.

I slept all that day and most of the night. I woke stiff, aching and in a lot of pain. Every time I inhaled, I was in agony. A doctor came in to examine me – I had pleurisy. It felt like Marciano had worked out on my body for 15 rounds. Just breathing was an effort, and moving was even worse.

Let me tell you about another guy on Norfolk. I have to say I hated Jonathan Silver at first. But my anger turned to compassion.

Jonathan was a legend among us loonies. Every institution has one, whether a prison or an asylum or even an old people's home, anywhere where people are crammed together, someone special sticks out. This guy, all 6ft 10½in of him, was the most talked-about loony in Broadmoor. He was a giant; size 14 shoes, hands like shovels. Sadly, I never spoke to him the first two years in Norfolk, because I knew that back in 1969 Jonathan Silver had killed his three children and attempted to kill his wife and himself. It was a horror story.

I first heard about his case from Ron and Reg Kray back in the mid-'70s. He'd been in Brixton Jail on remand at the same time as them. Anyone who kills children is a hated prisoner – by cons and screws alike. It's unacceptable, it goes against humanity. He was found unfit to stand trial and they sent him to Broadmoor. Most of his time there had been spent in seclusion because he was forever attacking the staff. He was famous for his right hooks. He'd even hit Dr McGrath, the Superintendent.

We lived in neighbouring cells for almost two years and no words had ever been spoken between us. I heard him get beaten up and his screams when they pierced his skin with the hypodermic needle. At times, I had to stop myself from banging on his wall to see if he was OK.

I often wondered why he'd killed his kids ... what makes a man snap like that? But my code of conduct always stopped me getting close to him.

Then, one night, it happened. It was a quiet evening. I was lying there, staring at the ceiling and just thinking, when all of a sudden my wall knocked. After two years he shouted, 'Micky, come to your hatch.'

I got up and he shouted at me again. This time he

asked me for a plastic bag or a razor blade. I told him I hadn't got them.

It didn't take much working out that he wanted to commit suicide; this place had driven him to try to kill himself. I told him to slow down and take it easy. That evening was the beginning of a long friendship.

I found out later that Jonathan killed his kids because he thought the world was too evil for them. I saw photos of him pushing his children on the swings and them sitting on his shoulders. He had a lovely happy family but he wanted them all to go to a better place.

I am not justifying what he did, but I felt this man's agony. Some people asked why I was talking to him. My only answer to this is that I came to know the real guy. I felt the man's sorrow.

Then there was George Shipley. I knew from the moment I saw him that our paths were destined to cross over the years. He hit Norfolk Wing and ended up a long-term inmate. He had had a bad day, picked up some scissors, and stabbed another loony. The loony had multiple stab wounds.

When I next saw George he was heavily drugged. His eyes were heavy and his speech slurred. I felt sad for the guy, as basically he was a good lad although a little headstrong and quick tempered. He did the stabbing to brighten up the day; he was bored! But George was to pay for it with more years of his life locked away.

Dr McGrath retired a few weeks after I completed my demolition job on his precious roof. I was told the incident broke his heart. It was an embarrassment for him; he had a lot of questions to answer for it. He'd once said to me, 'We only take the best in Broadmoor – and you are the best, Micky.' I don't know to this day whether that was meant as a compliment or an insult! But for all it's worth, I did respect the old git!

I can put my hand up and say that I have

experienced my share of pain, but nothing could have prepared me for what was about to happen next.

I woke up in agony. I couldn't eat, couldn't talk. The right side of my face had all swollen up. This was like toothache and earache and a lot worse all rolled into one ball of agony. I was sick, but no one would believe me. I went berserk.

Again, I was injected, only to wake up in more pain. A couple of screws, Stuart Elliott and John Turner, saw how bad I was. They made sure that I had pain-killers but, apart from that, no one helped.

I'd got an abscess. It finally burst and treatment arrived immediately. The pain was so bad by now and I was actually banging my head and face so hard that I caused myself concussion! My pillow was covered in blood.

They took one look at me and called in an ear specialist. He examined me properly. It had been a giant abscess, deep inside my ear, which had burst open.

I hate the sight of prison doctors!

Little George Heath arrived. He was a breath of fresh air to me. Just nine stone and 5ft 2ins, he was fearless. He lasted only days on Somerset Ward and ended up on Norfolk with me. George got life for stabbing someone to death in London, then got another life sentence for a stabbing in prison. He always says that he's not big enough for a punch-up, so he stabs himself out of trouble.

George was just too much for them in Broadmoor. He wasn't mad, he was just living by his code – kill or be killed. He is still plodding on with his sentence all these years later. Last I heard, he was in Parkhurst. God bless him.

There were two escapes in 1981 – Alan Reeves and James Lang. Alan is a personal friend of mine, a smashing guy. He was sent to Broadmoor at the age of

16 after he'd killed a friend. While in Broadmoor he was found guilty of murdering another inmate. Twenty years later, he still had no hope of release. He escaped from Essex House.

Essex is a 'trusted' house. Most on there have served 20, 30, even 40 years. They have long accepted Broadmoor as their home.

Not Alan! His escape was a classic. He used a TV aerial to get over the wall and a car was waiting. He hit Dover, went over on the ferry, and was free. Three months later, in Holland, he was walking out of an off-licence when a copper shot him. Alan spun round and shot the copper dead. He got 15 years. As I tell this story, he has been freed.

James Lang's escape was similar but his was not to last, simply because he is a sex killer.

Lang had been sent to Broadmoor in the early '70s for the rape and murder of a 16-year-old girl. He made it over the wall, breaking his ankle. He limped to a field and gave himself up hours later. He realised that nobody would harbour a sex monster!

He was later sent to Ashworth Hospital on Merseyside and released in 1985 – only to rape and torture two women. Once a monster, always a monster.

Escape was still going through my mind.

I again worked my way up to Norfolk Three. It was bloody hard work but I managed to do it and stay in one piece. I got hold of an 'angel wire', which can cut through prison bars. I also got hold of a car key, money and a screwdriver. I was ready to go!

We were allowed nothing at all in our cells. No clothes, shoes, nothing. We had to strip off outside the cell. But I managed to smuggle in all my equipment and also clothes and shoes, which was a great achievement on its own.

First I had to work on the shutter against the window. This was going to be very difficult, because of the noise it would make. With my head, I held a blanket against the shutter to deaden the noise. As I worked at it, I could hear the chimes of the Gate Lodge clock. I made it by 5.00am – the shutter was only hanging by a silly piece of metal which I could snap with my bare hands. There was now only two-and-a-half hours left to cut through a bar. Impossible. So I decided to clean up and climb into bed and play sick when the staff arrived to open us up. I'd stay in bed all day and do it through the night. It was easy! I was buzzing!

At 7.30am my door was unlocked. They told me to get up; I told them I had flu. They wouldn't have it. They insisted that I go up for a shower. I didn't want a row to get them suspicious so I did what they said.

While I was showering, they went into my cell and found the loose shutter. My visits were stopped and I was put back in Ward One!

My belief was that I had been grassed. I have my own ideas about who it was, but I never got the chance to sort it out.

Depression set in. I had to put something together; but what?

I kept thinking about hanging myself. Fuck me, was I feeling low!

Luckily, it didn't last – what does? Within months, I was on top of the world again … shinning up an old drainpipe to be King of the Castle!

This time I didn't just take over one roof. I had the run of two roofs – and demolished them.

It all started on a glorious, hot summer's day, a day that was to be the greatest of my life. It was too lovely a day to be caged in a madhouse. I was having none of it!

It began at 10.00am in the exercise yard. Young George Shipley was with me. He wanted to come as well, but I had to say no. He was on a lot of medication at the time, too much to make a climb like this.

This was to be the greatest climb of my life. I couldn't chance it. And I didn't want George to fall and kill himself.

This was not like the last roof. We were in a different location and I was about to go up a 100-year-old building on pipes and guttering that were falling to bits. If I made it, then two roofs would be mine as Kent and Essex were joined together.

There were ten of us out on the yard. The staff were at their observation points. The time was now.

I ran past a warden so fast he couldn't believe it! In seconds, I was up on the top of the toilet ledge and I heard the bells go off. In a second, I pulled myself up on to a cell bar and swung over to another cell. The risk was now the drainpipe.

I looked down at the staff who had formed into a mob below. I saw the other loons being led back inside.

It was as I had thought – a difficult climb. My knees were cut, my hands were grazed. And then it happened. Just a few feet from the top, the pipe started coming away from the brickwork! My heart stopped. I truly believed this was my lot. I let go of the pipe and dived for the old metal guttering.

It worked! I was now on top of the castle. A beautiful sensation passed through me at this moment. It was electrifying, beyond explanation.

I shouted down to them all, 'This is the fucker! Anybody comes up here and I'll sling them off!'

I was the Governor of Broadmoor again. My last ten years had been a war. I felt exactly what I had become – a desperate, dangerous man who didn't give a shit about life.

I started my demolishing act. I began by smashing out all the windows in the workshops with the slates that I had ripped off. I threw slates at the parked cars down below, then I tore out the water pipes and the cables.

For three days, I destroyed Kent and Essex roofs. The TV cameras were out. I shouted down at them. They put me in the daily papers under headlines such as KILLER ON THE ROOF. They said I was 'Reggie Peterson', a convicted killer. You can never trust the press to get anything right!

My mother suffered terrible anxiety over this. People were coming up to her in the street asking if I killed someone.

On my second day up there, my dad arrived. They had phoned him up and begged him to try to get me down. I told him, 'Leave me, Dad, I can't come down. Tell Mum I love her.' I watched my old man go. He walked away with his head bowed, got in his car and drove off. I swear I saw him wipe his eyes.

I cried my heart out. I cried for the pain I had caused them.

All I ever did was hurt them. I was so strung up that I tore out 12ft joists from the roof. God knows what they weighed. This was pure hate coming out of my body – hatred for the system, hatred for the hurt I had caused those nearest and dearest to me. I would have killed any man who had come up there after me.

Late that night, I could see the female wards over at York House and Lancaster House. I could see the lights shining and the women's silhouettes in all shapes and sizes. They started to shout, 'Show us what you've got, Micky,' and 'Come down, you lunatic.'

I had to smile. They were as crazy as me!

I dropped my trousers for them – they loved it! I shouted back at them, 'Now show me yours!'

Bums were up at the windows everywhere. Bloody hells bells, what a laugh! Later that night, all went silent. Reality finally hit home.

I was starving. I ate some pigeons' eggs and some moss out of the gutter. In a proper jail, cons would have been throwing me up food and blankets, praising me. Here in this asylum, they were slagging me off.

Broadmoor has more than its fair share of bats, believe me! They were in the rafters, looking at me and whizzing past my head. I even saw an owl – it was a beauty. Those nights are treasured memories. The destruction was heaven, but the peace at night was paradise for me. A true feeling of being free. Being up on that roof was the answer to every part of my life.

I knew I was disturbed, but I had to live with it.

No fucking head shrink could cure me. I was the ultimate challenge to the system and right at this moment I was actually winning. So fuck them!

The next day, my third on the roof, my dad came back, this time with my brother Mark. He was in the Royal Navy. We've had our differences. Mark doesn't agree with the way I take on the world, but I love him. We shouted to each other. Our hearts were heavy, emotions flooded us, and even from up there on the roof I could see their eyes fill up with tears. Mum was the sole subject of conversation. They said I was making her ill.

I'd had enough. I decided to come down.

I was aching, cut, dirty. No way could I climb down. They opened up the attic shaft and I climbed down the ladder. My dad hugged me, so did my brother. They let me phone Mum.

Later, after treatment and a clean up, the double doors banged shut on me once more. I heard later that the damage came to almost £250,000.

I now felt that I had truly buried myself. My mind was tortured. There were only four walls to look at – and no future.

It took weeks to come to terms with my life after that. During this period, my poetry began. I wrote one verse called *Life*.

John Turner, a charge nurse and a good man, had it typed up for me and encouraged me to write more. I wrote 30 poems in all and compiled them into a book. To my amazement, it was published (a limited edition). A great achievement for me. I was soon known as the 'Psychopathic Poet'. I recommend writing to all prisoners in any type of institution. It's a great thing to do to pass away the time.

I've since won more prison awards than any other con for my poems, prose and cartoons. It's my only escape. I sit at my cardboard table late at night, my ears plugged with cotton wool to blank out the ceaseless sound of doors slamming and lost souls screaming out their nightmares, and I create. People ask why I only draw scenes from prison. The answer is simple – it is all I ever see. I'd love to sit in a field of long grass and paint the flowers, trees and animals, but I can't. I've hardly watched television in over 20 years. I don't have a proper window. I see little more than concrete and razor wire. My 'freedom' consists of one hour a day, exercising outside on my own, outside in a cage. Sometimes it rains, sometimes it snows, sometimes I feel the sun beaming down on my face, glinting on the steel of the exercise cage. I love the sensation. I love the wind and rain on my face.

That's the limit of my life. I challenge anyone in the Home Office to survive one day of it – *just one day*.

Survive it I have. Prison survival is a tough game. So many don't cope. It's never nice to see, or be in the next cell to, a suicide victim. The smell lingers for days. It's a smell of despair. I've seen it, smelt it. I've seen the loss of real friends. Some guys cut their own throats or wrists, some take an overdose, some choke themselves to death.

A cell death is such a tragic end, and there is so much pain left behind for the families and friends. I'd say to any con; if you get the urge, just fight it. Life really is too precious.

Prison is crowded, but it's a strangely empty place. People are in your face all the time, yet ultimately you're alone. I've learned to switch off. I have to – otherwise I'd be blowing up all the time.

Prisons and asylums are full of noise and aggressive people. Doors slam, cons play their radios at full blast, shout and scream. The answer is to cut it out – block up your ears, just like I do when I'm doing my art. Let the others get on with it. Ignore them.

But if they really get in your face, you've got no option. Prison bullies take liberties. They prey on the weak. You can never say 'yes' to these gutless characters. They all end up with a smack in the face one day. If necessary, I say punch them. You've got to stand up and be counted. Cut the bud before it grows. Thing is, you've still got a life ... of sorts!

One of the great highlights for me in Broadmoor's Norfolk House was when Acker Bilk came to play for us.

Jimmy Savile arranged it. He's long been a frequent visitor to Broadmoor and a staunch supporter of what good work there is. The concert was held on Ward Three in Norfolk. It was brilliant! For a good hour Acker played us all his old classics. My favourite was 'Stranger on the Shore'.

We all behaved ourselves. Even Acker said we were the best audience he could remember for a long time. He gave us some signed photos but, above all, he gave us all a nice memory. Cheers, Acker, you cheered us all up – even me!

Life soon became month after month of boredom. I was achieving absolutely nothing. It was as if time was standing still ... same routine, same faces, same food. I was getting sick of it. Only my family kept me from losing all hope.

My yearly tribunal was due. This is a mental health review to which all lunatics are entitled by law. We were given Legal Aid, so we could have a solicitor represent us and we were also allowed an independent psychiatrist's report to be read out.

My solicitor was Lucy Scott-Moncrieff. She got me Dr Bowden, a consultant psychiatrist from the Maudsley Hospital, Kent. We prepared my case carefully as I was told I had a good case for discharge – on the grounds that three psychiatrists' reports all suggested different diagnoses.

The tribunal day arrived and, to my utter surprise, the turn-out was amazing. Most of my family arrived and so did a few friends. They all spoke up for me and all did me proud.

I stood before a judge, a Home Office-appointed doctor and a 'layman'. Lucy and Dr Bowden did a great job.

We lost. It would be another year before I could even be considered again. Another 365 days to go.

I knew something that even my own family didn't know that day as we hugged and said our goodbyes. I knew in my heart that I would not stand another tribunal in Broadmoor. It was a farce.

There was only one real choice – to move me. I'd had enough. I had a word with Clive Mason, a charge nurse and a man I respected a lot. I explained how I felt and what I wanted. He told me to give him a few days, which I did. When he came back a few days later he told me that they couldn't move me, mainly because no one wanted me. There were only four special secure hospitals – Broadmoor, Rampton, Park Lane and Moss Side.

Rampton refused to have me back (which I was glad about). Moss Side was for subnormals and Park Lane was a brand-new secure hospital that wasn't prepared to accept me until I was more stable in my behaviour. (Moss Side and Park Lane later merged to become Ashworth Hospital.)

So I was fucked! There was no where else to go. I

was now an undesirable and untreatable inmate. For the first time, I feared I would become one of the old men of Broadmoor, the men with the lost eyes.

My sleep was becoming affected. I was getting stressed out. It was only time before I exploded!

Three times lucky, they say.

Yes, I made it back on top of the world. It's no wonder I joke I've been on more roofs than Santa Claus!

This was even too much for me to believe. The sun was beaming down on me. The scaffolding was still there from fixing the last roof – so I used it to get up!

This was the ultimate kick in Broadmoor's bollocks. And I knew that this time I had the power to demand what I wanted. I demanded to see Dr John Hamilton, the medical director. He was there in minutes. He came to a top window and we talked for over an hour. I told him my grievances and he wrote them all down. He passed me some sandwiches and tea. To be honest, he was terrified of losing another roof.

I sat there quite cool and listened to all he said. The sun was lovely, so were the sandwiches. I was dying to demolish the place but something stopped me.

Dr Hamilton told me that he would do everything possible to get me moved to Park Lane Hospital. I had a good think about this. I was now in a position that I had never been in before.

I wanted so much to pull the roof off, but I also wanted so much to move from this hell-hole. I had that chance if Dr Hamilton was being truthful. Was he for real, or was he giving me bullshit just to get me down?

It was decision time. It upset me to think that they had so much power over my life, but I had to take this chance. I went back to Hamilton.

I told him that if he was lying to me, I would get my revenge one way or another.

'I give you my word, Micky,' he said.

So I climbed down ... and not one tile was damaged. They put me straight behind double doors. Hamilton stayed away from me for days.

It was all a lie.

Doug was a staff nurse. A big strong man, he was a typical rough-and-ready guy. I liked him a lot as he stood his ground. I told him to tell the doctors that from now I was on a hunger-strike – 'til death or 'til they move me!

Doug said, 'Don't do it, Micky.'

But I was determined. Eighteen days I starved myself. I survived on just tea and sugar. My muscles disappeared, my whole system was fucked.

Doug talked to me all the time. He even came to see me on his days off. Doug told me if I started eating, Hamilton would see me. He convinced me it would be OK. I started eating and on the eighteenth day I saw him. He told me Dr Malcolm McCulloch, the Superintendent from Park Lane, was coming to interview me with the prospect of a move. And I was actually told that same day by a senior person that I would move to Park Lane. I felt that I had won.

I had beaten Broadmoor and survived. Four-and-a-half years of my life had been wasted in that place. Four years of that was spent on Norfolk. It had been a hard battle, but one that I was proud of. You don't get anything in this world unless you fight for it. Obviously, I can look back now, all these years later, and I can see two sides to it.

Lots of other things have happened since I left. There was a big TV documentary on drug control in Broadmoor, which exposed a lot.

Dr Hamilton died of cancer in his early 40s. I would not wish that on anyone, but he was a liar and I still deeply regret not doing that roof.

My mate Peter Lovesey survived Norfolk and went

back to Parkhurst. He was released and died within weeks of having his freedom. Poor George Shipley was, the last I heard, still in Broadmoor. Ronnie Kray plodded on there, doing his time like the man he was.

His death hit me like a sledge-hammer blow in the back of the head. That sad day will forever be etched on my memory. It was 17 March 1995, a little over ten years after I got transferred from the asylum. I woke up like any other day, ate my porridge, and then went into the exercise cage for my hour. I completed my press-ups, squats and sit-ups. The air was fresh and the sky was clear. Even the sun shone. But it turned out to be the darkest of days.

When I was out in that yard, under that lovely sky, I lost one of the greatest friends I'll ever have. I'll try to put the record straight once and for all. Since Ronnie's death, all sorts of maggots came out of the woodwork, going on and on about how mad and bad he was.

Ronnie Kray was a special man. He had the biggest heart of any villain I've ever known. There won't ever be another like him.

A week before Ron's death, he sent me £25 through his friend Stephanie King. Ronnie always looked after me. When Ron liked someone, it was total loyalty. I can close my eyes now and drift back more than two decades to the time when Ron walked into my cell at Parkhurst. I knew from our first ever meet that he was going to be a special friend. He had a handshake like a grip of steel, eyes that were full of strength and he conducted himself with dignity.

When Ron spoke, people listened. I learnt so much from him. He never spoke of crime or violence. He was always polite and respectful and he lived by a code of honour right to the end.

The reason that I feel I know Ron so well is simply that we both suffered mentally. A confused mind can and does tear a man to pieces. Paranoia is something that I wouldn't wish on any man. Prisons and asylums are full of paranoid people. Ronnie was very ill – Parkhurst made him ill. But once he went to Broadmoor, he settled. In the 15 years he was there, he had very few problems.

For most of the 26 years that Ron was locked away, he helped other people. He would read a newspaper and if he heard that some kid had cancer or an old lady had got mugged, he would straight away try to raise some money to help them. He would paint a picture or write a poem or organise a charity do, all to help the sick. He gave away thousands. He despised child abusers and people who took liberties with sick people. He looked after so many; he never stopped helping. That is why Ron was so special and why he was loved by so many different people from all walks of life.

Ron always got upset when he heard about my constant battles against the system. He used to write and tell me to slow down or I'd never get out. He was one of the few people who understood me.

Ron is now free and with the only woman that he really loved, his dear old mum Violet.

There were other inmates who helped me get through those depressing years in Broadmoor. Some I've already mentioned, but I'd also like to give a heartfelt thanks to Charlie Smith, Dave Wright, George Heath, Mickie May, Michael Smithers, Michael Martin, Steve Shore, Aubrey Cunningham, Jock Smith, Ron Greedy, Danny Clark, Walter Prince and Eric Davies. In spite of what I've told you about Broadmoor, there were some members of staff who I found to be truly decent men, who I came to respect: Barney Wright, Roger Russell, Trevor Pimm, Clive Mason, John Turner, Dave King, Dave Bevan, Mel Evans, Stuart Elliot, Tim Frampton,

Doug Mephum, Terry Griffiths and Les Mephum. Some doctors treated me OK – Dr McGrath and Dr Shaw. It's not worth mentioning all the evil bastards I came across in there – I would have to start another book! But they know who they are. They won't forget me – and you can be sure I won't forget them. May they rot in hell.

I left a big part of myself in Broadmoor. On summer days, the old boys of Broadmoor will surely tell their stories about my roof protests. It's how institutions come alive. Stories like those keep the loons happy! They know that one of them fucked the system. My deepest regret is that I never made it over that infamous wall. That would have been the ultimate slap in their faces – but it was never to be.

You should have seen the send-off when I finally walked out of there! As I was led out of Norfolk House, the loonies were at the windows, shouting and waving little Union Jacks. I couldn't believe it! The flags were obviously given to them by the staff. I couldn't work out what they were shouting at first, but I picked it up ... 'Good riddance to bad rubbish'. I saw the funny side of it all and shouted at them, 'If I come back, I'll do your roof again and you won't see telly for weeks!' It was a good way to go.

Leaving Broadmoor to go to Park Lane top-security hospital was, without a doubt, the nicest feeling I'd had for ten years – pure ecstasy. It was 16 June 1984. Big Roger Russell was the nurse in charge of the escort; he was pleased for me. By the van there were a few officials waiting for me to go, and if I ever reach 100 years old, I will have more spunk in me than those boring old farts!

It seemed like no time at all before we arrived at Park Lane. This place was a miracle. It was situated in a little place called Maghull, near Liverpool. The whole design was different from what I was used to.

It had only been open a year or so; the whole place seemed incredible to me. It had an indoor swimming pool, gymnasium, squash courts, tennis courts, bowling green, a massive library, education classes, and the food was superb. It was like nothing I'd seen for the last ten years. They put me straight into Hazlett Ward. The first thing that hit me the moment I walked in there was the full-size snooker table. They showed me my cell ... it was like a furnished bed-sit! It had a built-in wardrobe, dressing-table, bed, curtains, carpet, and a push-button radio on the wall. There was a sliding door which led to a bathroom with my own toilet and sink. It was a shame to call it a cell. I had never seen anything like it. For the first time in years I actually felt relaxed. The whole atmosphere had given me a fresh new outlook on life. I was seeing myself in a new light.

My doctor was Chris Hunter, a man I gained a lot of respect for. He stuck his neck out for me and gave me a lot of trust. After all I'd done in the past, he never once judged me. This was a complete new start. Now it was up to me. Chris took me off all the drugs. I ate better and I slept better. I felt altogether better. I began my training. I took up running, swimming and went to the gym. It was great. The staff were decent. My visits were nice ones – even my parents could see the change in me. I was finally smiling my way through – getting to the end. My confidence was coming back.

Stevie Booth was there as well. Rampton sent Steve there soon after I left. He looked fit and strong. He had done something that not only touched me but all my family, he changed his name to Peterson. He truly wanted to be my brother. As I tell you this story, he is still locked up.

Even in this place I had my bad days, but I got through them. I controlled my aggression. Some days I would just go and bang up in my cell – it was no big deal.

The big day at Park Lane was the Sports Day. We could invite people from outside to come and enjoy it with us. I made a list up for myself and Steve – we had more coming than anyone else. The sun was blazing and we all had a great day. There were no problems – the lunatics behaved. The staff were all surprised by me. They'd been told to expect a madman.

I felt I was truly changing. Violence had been a big part of my life, but it now made me sick to think of what I had lost. Violence had cost me ten years. Boxers were paid to knock people out, but I smacked people and got locked away. Enough was enough. It was time to think seriously about my future ... before I ended up like old Jip Carter in Rampton.

I was now preparing for another mental health tribunal. Everything was in my favour. Even Dr Hunter thought that I ought to be released. He recommended an absolute discharge in his report. A date was being fixed, my tension was rising.

It was going very well – then the day came that I came face-to-face with Gallagher once more. He had now changed his name to Morrison. At first I didn't realise that it was him, but I soon recognised his eyes.

I looked deep into those eyes. I watched him tense up. I noticed the scars on his face, the scars that I had given him back in Hull Prison in 1975. I had a strong urge to attack him again.

Instead, I smiled. This completely confused him. This was my ultimate test. I knew he had nothing to lose, not even by killing me. I, however had my whole future at stake. Even though I knew he'd killed four people, I couldn't chance it. We both walked away.

Even now, I wish that I had poked his eyes out!

I was later called in to see Dr Hunter. Morrison

(Gallagher) had complained to his doctor that I should not be allowed near him. I was praised for my conduct; it proved that I was trying to change my ways. I'd passed an important 'test'. Unfortunately, the next one was set to be a disaster.

Every morning I would jog four miles around the grounds. It cleared my head and prepared me for a brand-new day. I was only weeks away from the tribunal. I might be just weeks away from release. Chris Hunter explained it was a 50/50 chance that I'd get an absolute discharge. If I didn't get it this time, then it was almost certain I would get it at my next tribunal in six months' time. So, either way, I would be out in weeks, or months ... as long as my progress continued.

One morning I went out as usual on my daily jog. It was cold and wet, but I loved running in the rain. The wind and the rain on your face is really refreshing – something I miss so much now. I ran past Tennyson Ward when I heard a wolf-whistle. I stopped, then I heard it again. Some fucking idiot was taking the piss out of me! I went over to the Tennyson dining room window to see who it was. It was Mervin Horley, a well-known homosexual from Broadmoor. I went mad. I tried to hit him but I hit a steel bar on the window instead.

That made me flip. I was ranting and raving. My head was completely gone. I went back to my ward, brooding. The old thoughts were going through my head once again. Steve came over and told me to calm down – I had to think of my tribunal. Later, I was handed my mail. I had three letters from outside, and one from inside. The letter from inside set me off once again. This was a test I couldn't pass. Fuck the consequences. Horley had written me a filthy letter, saying that he wanted to do things to me, how he loved oral sex and that he dreamt about me. I felt sick. It disgusted me. My head exploded. All our mail was supposed to be censored, so how come I got this load of filth?

I smashed a sauce bottle and prepared my plan of action. I would run past his ward as they came out to go to the occupational therapy workshop. I was going to ram the broken bottle into his neck, drag him back to his ward and take him to the day-room where I would barricade myself in. At this point, I can honestly say that I didn't really know what else I was going to do to him. All I knew was that he would never insult my name again.

The plan was set for the next morning. It was a very stressful day for me. I was about to throw my life away again. But, my mind was set – nothing could or would stop me now!

I started my run. I was spot on time. As I was coming towards Tennyson Ward I saw a dozen loons and six staff come out. As I got closer, I pulled the broken bottle out of my tracksuit. I spotted Horley wearing a big, heavy, brown coat. No one suspected a thing. I sped up my pace; my adrenalin was pumping. I was about 20 yards away when Horley smiled and blew me a kiss! I couldn't believe it! I was on him in a second. I grabbed him around the neck. Some of the staff tried to stop me, but I waved the bottle around and told them all to stay back. Somehow Horley worked his way free out of my grasp. I panicked – I was losing him! It was now or never. I let him have it there and then. I smashed the glass straight into his ugly face.

His screams were like an animal. He fell to the ground. Staff were shouting and the other loons were screaming. One of the staff shouted into a walkie-talkie. I dived on Horley again and kept hitting him with the bottle. Blood was everywhere. I left him lying there on the ground. He was picked up and rushed to hospital. I heard later that the overcoat had saved his life.

The staff all circled me. It was over. I had no reason to fight with the Park Lane staff, so I dropped the bottle. They walked me to my ward, where Chris Hunter was waiting. My clothes were put in a plastic bag. I washed the blood off myself then sat down with Chris to talk.

I told him about the letter. He was amazed. Obviously the censor had made a serious blunder, but that didn't warrant my actions. Chris was as devastated as I was. He told me straight that I was back to square one. There was no tribunal on this earth that would release me now.

I was back to being a madman! I felt terrible. I had let everyone down, including myself. I was totally destroyed. The next day I smashed a whole room up, terrifying all the staff and loonies. The day after that I attacked a fat loony (a known sex-case) and took him hostage, just so I could phone up my cousin Loraine. I was completely gone in the head. I had lost all hope.

Nobody knew what to do with me. Even Chris Hunter was at a loss. I was finally sedated and charged by the police. I was then moved from Park Lane. The special hospitals had had enough of me. I was a lost cause. Nothing more could be done for me here. I was untreatable.

Park Lane is now known as Ashworth Special Hospital. Before I move on to my next establishment, I will take this opportunity to thank all the staff and patients who helped me through the seven months I was there. A special thanks especially to doctors Chris Hunter, McCulloch and Gough, as well as my fellow inmates Steve Peterson, Big Phil Baxter, Ron Greedy, Chris Reid, Steve Roughton, Sid Earnshaw, Jimmy Handsbourgh, Andy Doughall and Lenny Doyle. Chris Reid is now out and doing well for himself, standing tall after 23 years of hell inside. He's a loyal pal who still writes to me and visits when he can. As for the rest of the boys – good luck and keep dreaming, 'cos when you stop it's all over.

Life really is like a circle. Eleven years after I first entered Risley Remand Prison, I was back. It was 1985.

The Principal Medical Officer there was a Dr Lawson, a Scotsman. He ran the hospital wing. He said, 'Behave yourself and you'll be OK.'

I told him that I wasn't going to stay in his hospital – I wanted to go up on the wing. He told me that it was difficult to move me at that stage as clinically I was still insane and the Home Office was unsure of where to put me or how to deal with me. If he were to put me on the wing and I killed or hurt someone, there would be a public outcry. They would ask why I was in a prison and not an asylum.

For four days I brooded in my cell. The atmosphere was tense. I was verbally abusive to all the doctors and screws; bitterness was again creeping in and hope was fading.

I was a bit of a celebrity at Risley, as everyone there was fresh in from the streets. Out of my window was a great view. I could see all the visitors coming and going. I also saw the cons going to and from court. It was really weird to be able to see all this. The people seemed to have really strange clothes on ... I was obviously behind the times. I was now into my eleventh year and fashions alter.

One day I was looking out of my window when a load of cons were marching by on their way to the gym. One stood out from the rest. He remained in my head – his whole presence struck me. He was badly scarred (he looked as if he had been burnt) but it wasn't that that struck me. He had this aura of a special person. He was a proud young man, a man I felt drawn to, a man of respect.

I didn't see him again until Dr Lawson let me up on

the wing. He warned me that I would be on strict
observation. If a screw even thought that my
behaviour was strange then I would be sent straight
back to the hospital wing.

I was made up to be out of that hospital. Frankly, I
was sick of being a lunatic.

They moved me into B Wing but I only lasted a
couple of days before I chinned a con in the showers.
He was a bit of a flash fucker, mouthing it off, so I
stuck one on him. They moved me to another wing –
the same wing as the mysterious guy that I'd seen
walking past my window weeks before.

I kept an eye on him. He interested me. I am a
great believer in fate. Certain people are meant to
come into your life. This guy was meant to come into
mine, I was sure of it. I could feel a closeness towards
him. I started to go to the same gym class as him. I've
spent very little time in prison gyms, owing to my
years of punishment in solitary, but I can go into a
gym and bench-press more than anyone can work up
to. I noticed that this guy had no fingers at all on one
hand, and only half fingers on the other. This guy had
suffered terribly, whoever he was. He wasn't like the
others. They were loud, boisterous, all trying to be
something they weren't. This guy knew how to
conduct himself.

One day in the recess I was washing and I spilt
water on him. He was cool. He said, 'Easy, pal.'

Many wouldn't have dared say a word, but he said
it with confidence. I've chinned a guy for less – but he
was special, a man I respected. That was our first real
encounter. Soon after, we were like brothers. I learnt
all about him. He'd actually got burnt as a kid. His
name was Mark Lilliot. He has proved his loyalty to
me ever since. He's a man that I love and respect. God
bless you, Mark!

I met a lot of cons in Risley who helped me along.

Andy Vassell was a diamond to me, one of the best Manchester lads I ever met. Andy was a friend of another great friend of mine, Jimmy Hayes. There was also Sonny Carroll, Austie McCormack, John Dillon, Big John Carter, Billy Symes, Ticker, Dominic Gallagher ... all good lads. But Mark Lilliot was my special pal, a soul brother.

Violence exploded within me as usual. There was one guy whose name I could never forget – it was John Lennon! He was a Taffy who later got a life sentence. I smashed him over the head with his Roberts rambler radio and stabbed him in the neck with a knife. I lost 120 days for that and served a few weeks in the block. Then there was a lanky Scouser who owed me a bottle of pop for weeks. I opened up on him with a cluster of left hooks, uppers and crosses. He never knew what hit him. It turned out that he was a filthy sex-case, so I'm not a bad judge!

I trained hard in Risley and prepared myself for what lay ahead. I was charged with GBH with intent on Mervin Horley. A Miss Walker visited me from the Liverpool Probation Service. She was only a small woman and she'd been asked to do a report on me. I liked this woman from the first time I met her. She was fearless, spoke her mind and called me a 'bloody idiot' (but in a nice way).

She wrote me an excellent report and stayed in touch. I got quite fond of Miss Walker, in a respectful way. I love fearless people! Ted Saxton was my solicitor. I couldn't have had a better man at the time. He did a brilliant job. He got two independent psychiatrists to do reports on me. Both agreed that I was not suffering from any mental illness and could not understand why I had spent so long in the asylums. Even Dr Lawson's report found against any insanity. He actually said that I was a psychopath who refused to accept I had a personality disorder, and therefore there could be no suitable treatment.

So it was looking like I was going to get another prison sentence. The question was – how long? Ted explained that it was necessary for me to go through with the tribunal, as I still had the life section hanging over my head. The only trouble with this was that I was appearing in Liverpool Crown Court on a charge of violence – and this was before my Mental Health Tribunal. To me, this was crazy. How could a judge sentence me if I was supposed to be a madman?

I could smell a rat ahead! What would stop them sending me back to the asylums when I had completed my fresh sentence?

My court day arrived, I said my farewells to the lads, and off I went.

I pleaded guilty at Liverpool Crown Court in May 1985. My mitigation was all the stress I was under – and the blunder by the censor. I'd simply lost my senses.

Judge Temple, I was told, was the fairest judge on Merseyside. As it turned out, I could not have had better. I was expecting five to eight years at least. He sentenced me to three – a good result in anyone's eyes.

I was soon being escorted into Walton Jail, Liverpool. They were waiting in force – a dozen or so hospital screws. It had started once more.

They told me immediately that I was going over to the hospital wing. I didn't want to, so I started to argue with them. A senior screw stepped in and stopped an incident. He told me that I was going to that wing just for a few days, to see how I behaved. He told me not to make it hard on myself. If I did what I was told, it would only work out in my favour. It made sense to me.

A dozen screws escorted me over to the hospital. Trouble was in the air. I could smell it, taste it. Once inside the hospital, they marched me in silence to the strong box. One of them told me to strip.

I asked why I was being put in the box, then they all piled on to me. They cut off my clothes with scissors and carried me inside. I felt bad, hateful and, quite honestly, mentally ill.

I remembered that ten years ago, in this very place, I had sworn to get my revenge on them. I knew now that revenge would come very, very soon.

I lay on the floor for the days and nights I was in there. All I had were two blankets. I rubbed my own excrement all over the walls in protest. The doctor told me through the closed door that I must behave myself or I'd never come out. It was a very bad time for me. I felt trapped.

A little later, one of the night screws came to my door. He explained that the governors and doctors didn't know what to do with me. This screw was a decent man. He was telling me the truth. I asked him why it had come to this. He told me it was my reputation. He told me to stay cool, to play along with them and I would be out of there very soon. He wanted to pass me a sandwich, but there was no hatch in the door. I said, 'Cheers, mate, it's good to know that you're not all scum.' He asked me if I was all right, said goodnight and went.

The next day, the doctor came to my door to ask how I was.

'Lovely, doctor,' I said.

I was out of the box later that day. After some food, I was called to the doctor's office. He explained why the staff had been so difficult towards me; I was a danger to the system and was not to be trusted. He asked me what I would like and I told him that I just wanted to get rid of my 'loony' label and be treated like an ordinary con.

I learned that my tribunal was to be held in Walton. He agreed it didn't make sense to sentence a man who was already on a mental health section. And he said that if my tribunal was not successful, then I could be transferred back to the asylums after my three years was up!

This was all I needed to know. Now I was 100 per cent sure it was time to fuck this system once and for all!

He agreed to put me on a wing and he chose H Wing, the long-term wing.

I lasted days before a bust-up. It happened in the bath-house. I was naked apart from a towel around my waist and I was collecting my clean underwear from the hatch. A flash con told me to 'fuck off'. I chinned him through the hatch – only to have my arm grabbed by another con. I was pulled through this hatch and half-a-dozen Scousers started laying into me. I fought back for all I was worth, but six against one is bad odds. One lunatic had my thumb in his mouth, biting me.

I kicked out, punched and butted. For a while, I was actually getting somewhere, but they had me down. The bells were going. The joke of it all is the fact that I was the only one to be taken to the block for this incident. My thumb was bitten down to the bone, one of my eyes was closed, my mouth was ripped and my body was a mass of cuts and bruises. The doctor came down to see me to give me a tetanus injection and patched me up. He asked me what happened. I told him that I had attacked myself!

A week later I was back up, but not allowed to go to the bath-house. I had to have my bath in the block.

Then, when I awoke one June morning with the sun shining through my cell bars, I knew that this would be *my* day. It was to be a very special day.

I had sworn revenge ten years ago in this very jail. My time had come.

CHAPTER SEVEN

My word was my bond. Today was the day!

I jumped up on my table to look out through the bars. It was a bright day and I was ready for my walk out on the yard. The only difference was that today I had no intention of coming back! Two hundred of us would be going out to walk around in a circle, but only 199 would return. Fuck 'em all!

At 10.00am we all marched out on to the yard. I was smiling as I went over to Andy Vassell to say goodbye. He thought that I had flipped. I shook Dominic Gallagher's hand and wished him well. He

looked at me as if I had lost my head. Off I ran. I dived
on to a sentry box. The screw inside started blowing
his whistle; the cons were cheering. I then dived on to
a pipe and swung over on to a cell ledge and went up
another two storeys. Soon, I was five floors up. The
gutter was old … would it hold my weight? I reached
out and grabbed it. It felt a bit dodgy. I looked down at
the cons being taken back in. There were screws
everywhere; they all looked up, wishing and hoping
that I would fall. I could see it in their faces. By now
all the cell windows opposite me were full of faces.

'Go on, get up!' they shouted. They were all banging
their cups on the bars, singing, 'There's only one
Micky Peterson, only one Micky Peterson!' A good
hundred of them were watching, singing. I reached up
again, grabbed the gutter and pulled myself up. I'd
made it!

I'd fucking made it to the top of the world, and the
cons in Walton Jail loved me for it! The screws hated
me for it. I'd made fools out of all of them. For three
days I demolished the place – slates, timber, windows,
skylights – on four wings. It was great!

Lots of cons were moved out to other jails, so I'd
done them a favour. The Scousers passed me up food,
drink, blankets. Some even got nicked for it. That's
the sort of men they are – solid! They're a very warm
breed of people. When they take to you, they love you.
Despite my kicking, I have always liked them.

The 'Mufti' came up with their shields and
helmets but I made it clear – come near me and I'll
jump and take one of you with me! I'll grab the first
one of you and jump off! The crazy thing was – I
meant it. I was double-fit and strong at this time. My
press-ups had paid off. If I had to turn this into a
death mission, I would.

Over the wall, I could see a school playground.
They were all jumping up and down shouting at me,

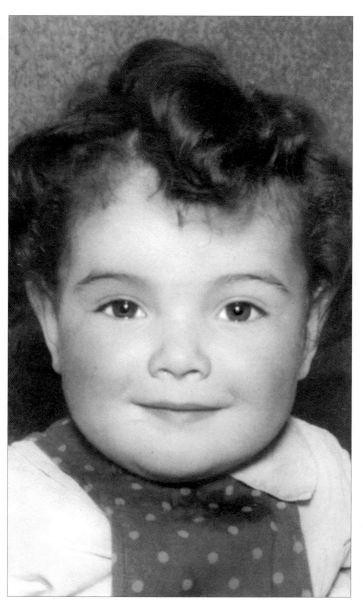

Me as a little boy.

Some of my family shots: playing up with my older brother John
(*top*); me posing for the camera aged 6 (*above right*); my Dad, Joe,
aged 19 in the Navy (*above left*).

My big brother and my Mum in July 1956.

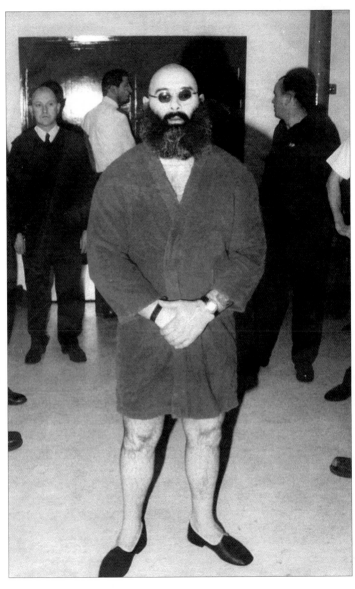

A police picture of me, taken in February 1999 immediately after I released my hostage Phil Danielson.

Working out during my residency at Hull.

Top: The first time I met my son in 22 years. I'm wearing the green and yellow suit that all maximum-security prisoners have to wear. My famous beard is looking good here.

Bottom: Me and my cousin Loraine.

With my dear old Dad shortly before he died.

Top: I was sent these instruments when I let it be known that I wanted to be a musician when I got out. I worked hard on a piece which I called 'Broadmoor Blues'!

Bottom: Playing pool on a visit from my brother Mark.

Top: I don't see the outsides of prisons very often, but here's a rare picture of me on my release from the Scrubs.

Bottom right: With my mate Eddie Clinton in January 1993, during one of my brief spells of freedom.

Bottom left: With a couple of the other inmates of Hull Special Unit.

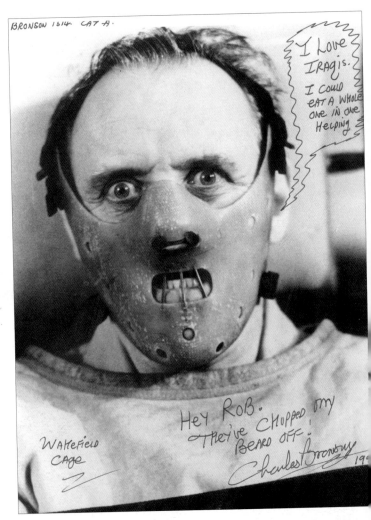

One of the few other people to have been in a Hannibal cage. The speech bubble says, 'I love Iraqis. I could eat a whole one in one helping'. And I could, too …

During one of my brief spells on the outside, I became a prize fighter. It was then that Charles Bronson was born ... These shots were taken at a benefit fight for a Leukaemia victim.

Top: Sweet revenge! On top of Walton Jail in the summer of 1985.

Bottom: The two Michael Petersons, father and son.

young girls of 14 and 15. They really made me happy
as they were shouting for me! At night, I found a spot
where I could just lie down peacefully. I thought about
my whole life, past, present and future. It was a total
disaster. Was I born to be mad? Would I ever live a
normal life? It's weird but I feel very emotional when I
am on these roofs. It's certainly a place to sit and
think. It's the next best thing to freedom: air, stars,
sky ... much better than being in a stuffy cell. I
thought about the cowards down below in the hospital
wing who'd beaten me up, and I thought about the
treatment facing me. I couldn't escape what I now
was. I was a victim of my own notoriety. The system
had my life sewn up.

I was surprised to see Dr Gough and Nigel Hughes,
the charge nurse, both from Park Lane. They were
standing on the top landing, directly below me. I could
see them through the hole in the roof. They shouted up
to me about my coming tribunal, and that I shouldn't
make things worse. Dr Gough was an Asian
psychiatrist, a lovely human being who I respected. I
had a couple of dealings with her at Park Lane when
Dr Chris Hunter was on leave and she was good to me.
And Nigel Hughes was one of the best staff I've ever
met. Both were concerned about me and had come to
try to help. As we spoke through the hole in the roof,
the cons started shouting abuse at them. I told them to
shut up, which they did out of respect for me. After
several discussions, I decided to come down subject to
the following conditions: one, that I would be allowed
to see my brief, Ted Saxton; two, I would not be beaten
up; three, a tribunal date would be fixed, and four, I
would be given fish and chips and tea – and lots of it!

Once all these conditions had been agreed, I came
down. They put a ladder up to a skylight and I
climbed down to Landing 5. If looks could kill I'd be
dead now! Dozens of screws escorted me to the

punishment block. I was given a hot bath and treated for cuts and splinters. I was then put into the strong box and given my fish and chips and hot sugary tea. It was lovely. I saw Ted Saxton and a date was fixed for the tribunal. I was charged by the police over the damage to the roof – it totalled £100,000.

Days later, my lovely mother came to see me. It was a great visit. Then Dad and my brother John visited.

I lost my head soon after. I pulled a sink off the wall in the recess and then started to smash up the block. I just seemed to lose control. I'm certain that I was having fits. The screws restrained me, put me in a body-belt, and slung me in a van. What waited was a human gauntlet.

I'd never had a reception committee like it. From the van to the strong box at Armley Prison there was a long line of screws, all eyeing me up and down. Even the Walton screws with me looked tense. There was no need for this show of force. After all, I'm only one man! Once inside the box, the cuffs came off. Then came the body-belt. A struggle began, but I was a beaten man. They left me wrapped up like a Christmas turkey. Blood was all over my chest, coming from an eye wound and my bleeding nose. My whole body felt bad internally. I was strapped in a body-belt and had ankle straps on. I couldn't fucking move.

The sad thing was, some of the cons actually slung batteries at me from their cell windows. I had done them no harm. It should have been the screws they were throwing them at. Obviously, I slagged them off. A couple came to their windows and asked why I was cuffed up. When I told them, they said that they would be seeing the maggots who had been throwing the batteries at me. Soon, I was given some respect.

Ted Saxton visited me. For him it was an experience he would never forget, for me it was an everyday event. They took Ted's pens off him – they told him that I might use them to harm him or take him hostage. He told them that he was a friend of mine and that I would never hurt him, but they said I was very disturbed. They cuffed me up, led me through the jail, and let me see Ted in the hospital wing. I was in a cell behind a cage door; he was outside. I couldn't even shake his hand. Ted told me that he had never seen anything like it.

For 28 days I was refused library books. I couldn't even slop out or collect my own water. It was a bad month, one of my worst ever.

I lost a lot of weight. I lay awake, hungry, every night. Every day when the Governor came to see me I would complain about my treatment but he'd just say, 'You shouldn't climb on the prison roof then.'

At times like this, the only thing that keeps you going is knowing that sooner or later they have got to move you. Another thing that kept me alive was the thought of the past years – if I'd survived all that, then I could survive this. That's how I coped. Sadly, some can't. They end up hanging themselves. I see it as murder. The system has pushed them too far. They just can't take another day, another beating, so they lose faith. It's tragic, such a waste of life, but it happens all the time. Brutality is rife in prison.

If I'm ever found in jail, hanging by my neck, you can be sure it won't be my own doing. I wouldn't give them the satisfaction. The only way I will die in jail is either old age, or I'll be murdered. End of story.

The day they opened up to say I was being moved was a victory for me. This box had been a tomb for a month. My head felt heavy and fuzzy and I was weak. Once I was out by the van I took a deep breath of the fresh morning air. It was like the food of life to me. I turned and spat on the prison in full view of the Armley screws. They were filthy scum.

I was soon back at Walton Jail, Liverpool. The van

pulled up outside the block. I was taken in and immediately locked up in another strong box. This time I was fed through a hatch in the bottom of the door. Again, I could not slop out. It was an empty, soulless way of living. Nothing to wake up for; no nice thoughts, no sweet smells, no sense of touch from a fellow human being. Life was shit! I had finally got myself into a trap and there seemed to be no escape.

I had heard voices shouting to me but I was just too depressed to shout back. I didn't know it then, but Kenny Goodhall and Tommy Curliss were in this block. They were both telling the Governor to let me out of the box and give me a break or they would start performing. The Governor soon let me out and I was put in a proper cell.

Life started to look up. There was a screw in this block called Lee. He was an absolute diamond. When he was on he always gave me extra food and sometimes a newspaper. He was a good man. Even in piss-holes like this there are decent screws. Kenny and Tommy were good to me, too. We all went out in the cage together for our exercise. They are two good lads – plenty of bottle.

My pal Fred (The Head) Mills came down to see me. Fred's a Geordie, ex-Broadmoor, some say a nutcase but I say a gentleman. Fred's one of the old school, a true survivor. Why is he called 'The Head'? Well, he's got a head-butt on him like a donkey! It's lethal! Fred's been around a long time – couple of years here, couple of years there. Last I heard he was out, which pleases me. He's totally fearless – one guy I'd like to have beside me in a war!

I was soon taken back to court and given another year for the roof … added to my three years. This was a good result. Then my Mental Health Review Tribunal was ready. This was to be the first tribunal held inside Walton. There was a proper judge, Home

Office doctors, and also doctors that my brief Ted Saxton had got me. Miss Walker attended. It went on for four-and-a-half hours, and still they couldn't decide whether I was a psychopath or schizophrenic. They couldn't even agree why I was ever in a hospital for the criminally insane. I gave seven years of my life to the asylums – and here I was, listening to faceless people mumbling on about what I was supposed to have been.

Let's be sensible about this. I'd been certified mad because of my violence. I was still violent – and they were now certifying me sane. Where's the sanity in that? Isn't the system just as crazy?

I was given an absolute discharge and obviously I was made up. I now had a four-year sentence with a date of release. It still felt endless but I was elated! I thanked Ted Saxton, Dr Clarke, Chris Hunter and, of course, Miss Walker. The rest were faceless people who meant nothing to me.

Lee, the block screw, was made up for me. In fact, several Walton screws told me it was about time they took away my 'mad' label. I asked the Governor if I could now be trusted up on the wing, but he looked at me as if I *was* mad!

'No way,' he said. He told me I would be moving shortly but wouldn't say where. However, it was still a great day, a victorious day. My sanity had now been handed back.

What I didn't realise then was that I would be forever regarded as ex-Broadmoor. It's like a scar, a cross you have to carry for the rest of your life.

The day I left Walton, so did Kenny and Tommy. They went in a van together; I went on my own, cuffed to two screws. I slept like a baby all the way to the Island. I couldn't believe it when I realised I was on the Isle of Wight. The slippery fuckers will stop at nothing. They had spiked my tea.

In reception at Albany top-security prison, they told me that I was going up on B Wing. I was well pleased. This was the break I needed.

Albany was used at this time to house a lot of disruptive cons. Most didn't like the thought of serving their time on the island – it was too much hassle for their wives and kids to visit. But it suited me! I couldn't wait to fry an egg, to play Scrabble with someone, to get in the gym. Just fresh air on my body would be nice. Fuck the blocks.

So I arrived on B Wing. I was determined to try, but I suppose I'd been on my own too long. I found it hard to mix. Years of isolation affects a man.

The first day I punched a con in the table-tennis room. He knows why I hit him. All I will say is, he's a fucking rat. I can't say any more because it involves a good friend of mine. I went into the telly room after I hit him. Jennifer Rush was on – 'Power of Love' – I'll always remember it. She had the voice of an angel. The song has always been a favourite of mine, but I could hardly hear it. There were a dozen or so cons in the room all shouting about something. I slung a chair against the wall. I was upset. My head went funny.

We were all banged up in single cells. Big Albert Baker was directly above my cell. Albert's an Irish prisoner. A lot didn't like him because of his political views, but I respected him because of the way he conducted himself in prison. He was solid, a big strong man. We were close buddies. The next day I went out on the field for my exercise. I had a run and it was lovely but I was knackered – I hadn't run for so long. Albert gave me some eggs and tomatoes to have a fry-up later – but later never arrived.

At lunchtime we were all banged up for an hour. While I was lying on my bed, my door sprang open. I was more amazed than anyone.

'Right,' they said. 'You're away.'

They told me not to argue. The van was waiting.

I shouted to Albert, 'They're taking me.'

I went peacefully, double-cuffed, and without an inkling as to where we were going. I actually didn't care. I knew I was a marked man all over again.

The van backed up to the doors of the block at Wormwood Scrubs. The screws were all waiting. They took me to a cell, made me strip, then left me. Later, the Governor arrived to tell me I would only be there for a few weeks. He didn't know where I would go next – it was up to the Home Office.

I was feeling depressed, with dangerous thoughts in my head. But Harry Batt was also in the block and I'm pleased to say he lifted my spirits. Harry got nicked with my old friend Sammy McArthy. Harry sorted me out some fruit and got me some sweets. We went on to the exercise yard together and the hour a day there passed really quickly.

Harry's about 20 years my senior and he told me all the old stories of how the East End used to be. Believe me, the East End people are the salt of the earth. I love them to bits! They're a warm breed. Harry and people like him remember the old days when people were safe to leave their doors open and when men were men. Respect was earned, not bought. God bless you, Harry! I survived two weeks with no problems, then the van arrived and I was off!

Wandsworth block never seems to alter. If you toe the line, there's no problem. Basically, they leave me alone – they know what I'm like by now. I've been there often enough. I play along with the rules (to a limit) but I've always been given respect at Wandsworth. Prison Officer Wells is an old screw who's known me for years. There's no better screw than Mr Wells. He's straight, he tells you the facts, he puts it on your chin. He can be as tough as the next man but I've only had good deals from him, and I've known him over 20 years now.

Christmas was on us again, but it was my worst one for a long time. My good friend Tony Cunningham hanged himself on 15 December. It upset me so much. For a while I even thought about what it would be like to hang myself, and whether or not there really was another, better world beyond. For days I had a vision of myself swinging from the bars. Those next few weeks were terribly morbid. I was on exercise with Noel Travis and Tony the day before he did it. It was a terrible blow for Noel and me. One minute Tony was laughing and telling jokes, the next thing we knew, he was dead. A young man, with all his life ahead of him. He was only serving six fucking years! It still upsets me to think about it. But prison life carries on as normal. I got over Christmas and started 1986 with a new move.

Going back to Parkhurst gave me mixed feelings. This was the jail where I'd been certified insane. I was back on C Unit.

I soon heard that Taffy Jones (the screw I'd cut) had died of cancer. I wouldn't wish this on anyone. I was really quite shocked. And another screw who I well respected, Arthur Pyke, had died. He was a lovely old boy who treated us all well. Old Tom Cotton was still there. I liked Tom. He always gave me a newspaper, and was a happy-go-lucky sort of screw. Kenny Pugh was also still there. I liked Ken. For a man in his late 40s he was super-fit. Every day he worked out on a punch-bag – he'd been a good boxer in his day. He always conducted himself properly with me.

C Unit had altered a lot – it was now double-secure – but I knew a lot of welcome faces there: Eddie Wilkinson, Andy Dougall, Phil Cartwright, Jim Donnley, Neil Adamson and Ian Doram. I got into a nice routine. I mostly hung around with Eddie, as we go back years. We came through a lot together, and we're still coming through it. Eddie had had a bad accident at Maidstone. It happened in the gym. He was rushed to Guy's Hospital with a blood clot but he still suffered severe paralysis. Eddie limps to this day and suffers a lot of pain.

I tried to make his life that little bit better for him, which is difficult in a place like C Unit as most of the cons on there are 'Broadmoor material' – paranoid, psychotic.

Eddie could look after himself, but I made sure I cooked him an extra bowl of everything. I also made sure that no fucker upset him. A week or two passed and life wasn't too bad, but I was very stand-offish with the screws as a lot of them were a little bit too friendly for my liking. They were false. They tried to push themselves on me – and I wasn't having any of that. Sue Evershed was the psychologist on our unit. I liked Sue from the start; I could see that she was sincere, she really cared about us. Anyway, I only lasted a month. One evening, after we were all banged up for the night, I heard this commotion coming up the stairs. It stopped right at my cell door. The door flew open. 'Right! Pack up. You're away.'

What gutted me most was that I had just ordered a chicken to cook for Eddie and me. I went to Eddie's cell, looked through the hole, and shouted, 'I'm away, Eddie.' He was so upset he started kicking his door. 'Bastards,' he shouted.

Eddie is such a good mate, he takes it all to heart. Weeks later, I heard that he'd gone into the office the next day and attacked a screw over my move. That's how much of a mate he is. He loved me as a brother, and he knew that I had done absolutely nothing wrong to warrant a move. I was gutted.

It was the first ride that I'd had on the ferry at night-time. The screws in the van weren't a bad bunch

– they gave me sweets and orange juice. I asked them, 'Where to now?'

'Winchester.'

The van pulled up right outside the block. I wasn't even allowed to see the other cons. This punishment block was only small. Even the exercise yard was covered over with a steel net, so it was very claustrophobic. But the block screws gave me no trouble. I pulled the Governor to ask if I could have a medicine ball and a gym mat for when I went out on my exercise. This was the beginning of my legendary medicine ball! Most block jails now supply me with a ball – I'm the only con in the country allowed one. If you don't know, these balls are stuffed leather, bigger than a football and quite heavy – they're designed to be thrown and caught as part of an exercise routine. I devised some great exercises with those balls and it helped me through a lot of soul-destroying months. The bigger and heavier the ball was, the more I liked it. They come in various sizes, from 8lb to 18lb.

Winchester was a good block to get my thoughts sorted out, as it was quiet. The only problem was the cockroaches. They came under my door in armies every night. My bed was only four inches from the floor so I found them in my blankets, in my clothes – the fuckers were everywhere! Still, this is prison life. I guessed I wouldn't be there too long.

Sure enough, four weeks later I was cuffed up and on my way. The van headed towards London but I never bothered asking where we were going. Personally, I didn't give a fuck. I saw each move as a way of trying to break me down. There were to be a total of eight moves for me in 1986 alone. All these moves were unnecessary, unjust and totally frustrating.

I was back in the Scrubs. Again, the van pulled up to the block door, same old routine as before. They put me in a cell and – lo and behold! – Reg Kray was in the very next cell. They took him back to Parkhurst in the same van that I'd just arrived in! Reg had only been at Wormwood Scrubs 28 days, but being the man Reg is, he took it all in his stride. This was, in fact, his first time back in a London jail since 1969. Reg actually held the record of being the longest-serving con in Parkhurst – 17 years. He came to my door to wish me all the best, and he was off!

On the other side of me was 'Joe the Greek'. Joe is just 5ft 2in and weighs 10 stone, yet he is one of the most dangerous men in the penal system. He was always up to something. Violence was his speciality. He put 60 stitches in a screw's face at Bristol. Joe has since been extradited back to Greece. The system could never beat Joe, he never gave an inch. To me he was a giant – his heart was strong. God bless you, Joe!

Up above me was Roy Walsh. Roy got life back in 1973 for bombing the Old Bailey and Scotland Yard. He is another man who would never back down. I'd met him years back and he hadn't changed a lot. He was always good company and never moaned. I, however, *had* changed. The years I'd endured in the asylums had rubbed off on me. I was still trying to come to terms with myself.

I requested to see the Number 1 Governor. As I was marched into his office by the screws I could see him sitting behind a desk. I felt strange, unwell, confused and dangerous. I leapt over the desk and began to strangle him. My brain just went. Screws were on top of me, the bells were ringing and more screws came. I started shouting. They put me in a body-belt and carted me away to the box.

My head was in pieces. For two days, I was in a state of severe depression but a screw called Mr Patterson, who I have a lot of respect for, got me thinking straight again. I was let out of the box but days later I tore the recess to bits. Sinks were flying, urinals, doors, the lot! I punched my right fist through the 'unbreakable' glass. It slashed my wrist and my arm. Blood was pissing everywhere, shooting out like a fountain. I ran about shouting things that I can't even remember – I was once again on the edge of insanity. If I'd had a gun I would have shot the whole block up.

I felt myself getting weaker. Mr Patterson calmed me down and I was taken over to the prison hospital and sedated. They stitched me up but I would need proper surgery. The rest was like a dream. I was in agony as I was put in the van. My arm was burning up – it felt like a million toothaches all at once. The screws in the van were very tense. I suppose they thought that I was going to lose control again. I was drowsy when the van pulled up at the Portsmouth ferry. I couldn't believe it. I was on my way back to Parkhurst where I was told a surgeon was waiting for me. I felt bad.

Micky Connell, a hospital screw, was the first person I saw as the van pulled up outside the hospital wing. Micky is the only screw I really talk to in Parkhurst. He's a real man who's had a lot of bad times but he always jumps back up. That's why I respect him. Micky's not a bully or a liberty taker, he's straight to your face.

I got cleaned up for the operation and put my dear mother's cross and chain on my ankle. As they wheeled me down to the operating theatre, one of the screws said to the surgeon, 'He's got a cross and chain on his ankle!'

'Yes,' I replied, 'and it's fucking staying on!' The surgeon said that if I felt better with it on then I could keep it. He then explained what he was going to do, including a skin graft. There was a piece of skin missing from my thumb and this was what was giving me the most pain. As the drug hit me and I was on my way out of this world, I smiled knowing that my mother's cross and chain was with me. God bless you, Mum!

I woke up later in a cell in the hospital wing. I had plaster of Paris on my fist and arm. I was in pure agony. Pain-killers were written up for me and then a doctor came to see me. I told him that I was not staying in this hospital because of all the bad memories it carried. He said if I didn't stay there, I would have to go in the block.

So my next month was spent in the block, a very depressing month. My mind was forever racing, looking for ways to fuck them up. Twelve years had now passed me by, and had obviously taken their toll. Maybe, subconsciously, I never wanted to get out. Then the van arrived once again, and I was on my way!

I was always put in cell number 13 at Wandsworth. It was the same old routine as I entered the block – even Prison Officer Wells was there to meet the van. He always seemed to be on duty every time I arrived.

Cell 13 looks out on to the caged exercise yard. I must have paced up and down 1,000 miles in that cell over the years. Some days I would pace from breakfast until supper, non-stop, wondering about where they would send me next. But that just caused me a lot of anxiety and stress, so nowadays I try not to think about tomorrow – just take each day as it comes.

Whenever I'm back in cell 13, I mostly stand by the window in the evenings, watching the planes fly over, their red lights flashing on and off. I've never been on a plane, but I imagine all the people flying off to distant places. Families with 'normal' lives. Actually, I've never been abroad. The furthest I ever got was the Isle of Wight on the ferry! At night, from cell 13, you can see the prison yard illuminated by floodlights.

Rats scurry about looking for food. I've seen these rats, standing feet away from me, just staring.

Some nights I'd have a chat with some of the boys above the block. They would tell me all the latest. Some nights I just used to sink within myself. Why was I Britain's most complex con? Why me all the time? There was really no answer. It's just a vicious circle I'd got caught up in. I was stuck in the centre of this machine and it was impossible to work my way out. I truly believed at that time that I would never get out. I thought I would die in jail.

The crazy thing was, I didn't give a fuck if I did!

Wandsworth Jail is always full up, and there is always someone in a similar situation to yourself. I've met real characters in this block: Alan Byrne, Chris Haig, Winston Silcott, Tony Steel, Alec Bray, Dominic Noonan and Frankie Fraser. So many. If you don't hit Wandsworth block, then you ain't done any block. Wandsworth is the block of all blocks!

Some people, of course, never go into a punishment block at all. These are model prisoners and I say good luck to them. We all have to get through our time one way or another, and I've spent a fair amount of my time on the road in prison vans! Guess what? The van turned up … I was on the move once more!

The move back to Parkhurst block was a bad one for me. I saw it purely as taking the piss. But Tom Cotton, the block screw, kept me cool. He'd apparently been told to tell me that it wouldn't be for long, but I still wasn't too happy. This was a blatant piece of psychological crap to upset me. They eventually put me up on M Wing, which pleased me a lot.

M Wing – for those of you who haven't been there – is like a little unit with only 25 cons. Everyone was settled, so I went on there hoping to get some serious time done. The Terrett Brothers, Charlie and Martin, were on there, as well as my pal Micky Hallett.

Freddie Sewell was also there. I'd known Fred for years. He'd been in longer than I had; he shot a cop dead in Blackpool in 1972.

I started to get myself into a nice routine. I kept myself pretty much to myself.

Reg Kray had moved to Gartree in Leicestershire, so, for me, Parkhurst would never be the same again. I plodded on for a few weeks – then I snapped!

Ray Baron upset me. It didn't take a lot, but it cost me a lot. He came out of the TV room. I spoke to him and he totally blanked me! I shot into his cell after him. He got cheeky so I gave him a slap and walked out and left him on his arse. A pal of mine saw me come out of his cell. He asked me what was up, so I told him the mug had upset me. He told me, 'Don't be silly, go and see if he's all right.' Like a fool, I did.

Baron was lying on his bed, pretending to read. His mouth was swollen and I noticed his foot was moving up and down (a sure sign of nerves). I sat down on the chair.

'All right?' I asked.

'Yeah,' he answered. Then the rat pushed his table over and started shouting. He was doing it to create attention to get the screws in. I grabbed him and gave him another slap. I told him, 'Shut up!'

It was too late. Screws were all over the place! I told them that we were only playing, but Baron told them different, so they took me back to the block. This was to be my last time on a wing until my release. The slap on Baron cost me loads. It kept me as a high-risk Cat A prisoner – and it also kept me in solitary until the very day I was released. The block was now my life.

The van arrived and away I went. Ray Baron had fucked me up all over a silly slap!

I was now getting sick of this game. I was all too often waking up not knowing where I was. I was coming to Wandsworth far too often lately. I told Prison Officer Wells that I was not happy. He told me to calm down as I wouldn't be there that long. The Governor wanted me moved as soon as possible.

My moves were dictated by head office. All Cat A inmates come under the jurisdiction of the Home Office. I had become a pawn. They picked me up and moved me when they wanted to. They had taken the Ray Baron slap seriously. A silly fucking slap and they were turning it into a serious incident. They must have been convinced my head had gone again. PO Wells told me to cool it and give it a few weeks, which I did. I trained in the exercise cage every day. I trained in my cell. I was basically ticking over nicely – until some arsehole upset me!

It happened in the caged yard by D Wing. I was jogging around happily when – Bang! – a stick hit me on my skull. I looked up and saw mops raining down on me from the top recess landing. Three or four actually got me in the face. My head was cut, so was my eye. This rat aimed each one, and I must give him ten out of ten for accuracy. I grabbed some concrete and started throwing it at the windows, but it was useless. The screws took me in. A doctor was there but I fucked him off. I was banged up in my cell and I was fuming. Whoever had done it either had a vendetta against me or was just an evil toe-rag.

I sent word up to some faces up on D Wing. Within a day, I had the con's name. This con knows that I know who he is – end of story. I believe he did it for his mate Baron. I'll catch up with him later – in or out. My head and face soon healed up and I carried on training. On a good day I was doing 2,500 press-ups. I would do 30 or 40, write them down, and at the end of each day I would count them all up. Fitness is how I buzz.

There's no excuse in prison – you can't but keep fit. It's the perfect set-up. A regular diet, no late nights, plenty of rest, no sex – and take it from me, forget smoking and drugs. It's just not worth it.

I'm the king of the press-ups and sit-ups. I've already said I once did 25 press-ups with two men on my back, and I've squatted with three men on my shoulders! I've been making prison fitness records for as long as I can remember. Show me another man – a man half my age – who can pick up a full-size snooker table. I can. Show me another guy who can rip out 1,727 press-ups in an hour. I can. And I do it even though I have to eat stodgy prison shit. People outside eat steaks, but I have to eat porridge and a lot of bread – I've no choice. I drink loads of water to cleanse my system. If I can do it, others can.

I once went eight years without using weights, then I went into a gym and bench pressed 300lb ten times. I'm 5ft 11in, I weigh 220lb and I feel as strong as I did when I was 21. I've been through hell in the prison system – but I must be doing something right! There's something deep inside me that pushes me on. I'm a solitary fitness survivor.

Sometimes my strength has been my downfall. I was getting restless after that rat lobbed those mops at me. The prison chaplain came to my cell door and I dived at him. I was depressed; I wanted a hostage. But he was fast, he slammed my door and ran. The screws piled in to see what I was up to. The van arrived. I was on the move again.

Now they were taking the piss! This was a fucking liberty. I told the Governor at Parkhurst to either move me from the block or take the consequences. He told me I would only be there for a short spell, until the Home Office decided a move.

George Leedum was in the block. George is one of Britain's longest-serving lifers. We all love George. Sadly, I upset him one day. The night before, I sat up all night and caught a dozen or more cockroaches, stuffed them in a sock and tied a knot in it. The next day I went to George's cell and said that I'd got a present for him and I would leave it behind the recess door in a sock. Poor old George went fucking berserk. He slagged me, banged my door ... he got so upset. I felt terrible. I later got him some sweets and tea bags and said sorry. Fortunately, he forgave me. God bless you, George!

Parkhurst is always full of colourful characters. The greatest oddball I ever met in Parkhurst was Ronnie Abrahams, also known as the Screaming Skull. Ron got life back in 1966, and as I tell you this story he's still inside. He is what you might call a little strange, but I love old Ron. He weighs seven-and-a-half stone, wet-shaves his skull, and spends his time in and out of the blocks. Some say he's a fucking nuisance, but I'll say this about Ron: he once took a terrible beating off some Cockney mobsters. He got his jaw broken and his ribs busted, and he just took it – kept his mouth shut. I've known 'faces' get a slap and then cry about it, so Ron's 100 per cent in my book. He's always good for a laugh and all jails need their characters.

Ron's one of my heroes – a born fighter! Incidentally, he got his name, the Screaming Skull, through me. I would pick him up on to my shoulders and run around. He used to scream at the top of his voice and because he had a shaven head he got the nickname. I pray that he'll be out some day. Ron killed somebody a long time ago in a domestic family tragedy that I won't go into. But the reason Ron's done so long is simple – he's a loony, and I love a loon!

Anyway, getting back to the cockroaches. I collected a shoe-box full of them and put some cellophane over the top. There must have been a good hundred of them. I put some breadcrumbs in to feed them. It took me a fortnight to catch the fuckers – all night long! I could see and hear them scratching about in the box.

Eventually, I pulled the Governor about the vermin in the block. He said it couldn't be that bad. Little did he know what was about to happen next!

I threw the box all over him. It was a blinder! I've never seen a Governor move so fast. I was on my way after that, who knows where.

Yep, back to Wandsworth block. Prison Officer Wells was as disgusted as I was. It was now obvious that somebody in the Home Office was taking the piss! The Governor in Wandsworth was also fed up with it. I was moved in less than a week, back to Albany on the Isle of Wight.

As soon as I arrived in the block, they told me that I would be there for two months and then I would be moving on. Two months suited me. It's not a bad block. At least it's clean and the food's half-decent. Plus, I got the medicine ball. I looked upon this as a training period, to prepare for my next test.

There are always good guys in the block at Albany. We have chats out of the cell windows, a bit of a sing-song. We keep each other happy. It's what life is all about in jail – helping each other along.

I used to have my explosions. But I can't blame the Albany screws. They did nothing to upset me. They fed me well and gave me my medicine ball and mat, so I had no complaints. John Flowers, the prison chaplain, was also a good man who I respected. He often phoned my mother up to let her know that I was OK.

One day, in the cage, I was on one of my work-outs when I had a seizure. At first, it was thought to be a stroke. The right-hand side of my body was paralysed, my face screwed up in pain. I was terrified. I crept back to my cell, with some help, and then they helped me on to the mattress. I could hardly move by this time. The doctor was rushed in. He said it was an anxiety attack caused by built-up tension. My whole system had collapsed. It frightened the life out of me.

Apart from that, my two months soon flew by with few problems. My mind was now racing. Where would I be going next?

Before I left, a con hanged himself. He was only cells away from me and it upset me badly. I could actually smell the death for days afterwards. I started again to imagine what it would feel like to actually do it. My two pals, Ronnie Johnson and Johnny Heibner, were either side of me, both on punishment. They got me over this period. Days later, I was on my way again.

Again the van pulled up by the block at Winchester Prison. I felt OK to be arriving there as it gave me solitude, peace and time to think. A lot of cons there either knew me or had heard of me, so many of them used to make up little parcels of magazines and books and give them to a block screw to give to me. Those little parcels used to make my whole day go right. It would make me feel wanted, not forgotten.

It's the same when I get a letter. It can make a bad day turn good. I still look forward to letters now. When they arrive, just after 11.00am, I read them. Then I read them at night again, poring over every word, imagining exactly what my friends who've written are doing and going through. I suck up and savour every ounce of freedom, every mention of the outside world. It's like enjoying a bowl of fresh strawberries. When my friends on the outside send me photos, it makes a big difference. I can picture them in my mind's eye, laughing and having fun. I feel I know them better. Bear in mind, they can go out any time of the day or night and see and do things I haven't done in years. They can see the real world; they can have sex; they can have a pint of beer; they can stroke a dog. They can experience the wind and the rain on their faces.

I don't even have a fucking window to open.

I've told you, but it's worth saying again – my philosophy has always been 'It's nice to be nice.' Basically, I'm a nice guy, but sometimes I lose all my senses and become nasty. That doesn't make me evil, just confused.

I'm a strange person, very complex. It's largely what prison has turned me into.

Winchester treated me decently. My only problem was that a scumbag called Rogers was in the block. Rogers stabbed to death Rocky Harty in Parkhurst's kitchen. This fat slag Rogers was already doing life for killing his wife, and then he killed Rocky over a measly pork chop!

This murder almost caused a riot, so they slung Rogers down there out of the way. I hated the fucker. He later got another life – fat twat.

My van arrived. It was a week away from Christmas, my thirteenth inside. I thought the Home Office might have sorted me out a decent move seeing as it was now the time of goodwill. But the evil rats picked the worst block again. I was now truly pissed off!

Prison Officer Wells was there once again to meet me at Wandsworth, so was the Governor and a dozen screws. Cell 13 was ready and waiting for me. I was told that I would be held there over Christmas, and that I would be moving in the new year to a good jail – but I had to behave myself.

Christmas in Wandsworth block is no fun. There's no TV, no films, no mixing, crap food. I couldn't have been in a worse block over that period. The only guy who made it for me was my good friend Alan Byrne.

For our Christmas treat they let us in the same cage together for a walk. We had a good chat. I sang a few carols through my bars that night. We had a laugh. Alan got nicked in 1985 for an armed robbery where a guard got killed. Alan and Dick Trump got life. I believe that they are both innocent men. It's a really tragic case, but Alan fights his way through. It's one of those cases that will eventually come to light. Good luck, Alan.

That Christmas was a bad one. We had nothing – just 23 hours locked in a cell, every day. They say that behind every door is a dream. My dream was to get out for the next Christmas. I knew that I couldn't keep sane for much longer. I *had* to get out!

Three days into 1987 and I was off again, this time to Gartree top-security prison, Leicestershire. A Governor was waiting for me in reception. He told me that I was going into the block so they could decide what to do with me. I went peacefully. The very next day, the bastards told me that I would remain in the block until my release – which wasn't until February 1988!

What the fuck was going on?

They told me the score. The Home Office had decided that I would remain in isolation indefinitely. So Gartree gave me a deal. If I behaved myself, they would give me some lost remission back ... so I could be out in 1987! Also, I would be allowed to go to a gym class. And, as time passed by and if I behaved myself, they would consider other privileges. They asked me to think about it. I did and I agreed to try it. I had to, for my own sanity. I could, after all, be out very soon. This block was only small and not used much. Cons used to come down for the odd day or two, then would go straight back up on the wing.

There were a lot of cons that I knew in this jail: Reg Kray, Rooky Lee, Ron Brown, Biffo, Paddy Hill, Charlie Tozer, Dave Bale, Billy Adams, Patsy Flannigan, Micky Ahmed, Paul Sumat, Ron Mcarthy, Steve Nordane. Lots of good guys. And all of them pulled the Governor to get me up on the wing, but the

Governor told them the same as he told me – it was down to the Home Office. Some were not too pleased.

It was clear they had no intention of taking me off Cat A. This was serious, and it ultimately denied me the chance of staying free. I was to stay Cat A until I was to be released.

No rehabilitation, no chance of learning about the outside world, the world that had long passed me by, the world that I didn't really understand. The fuckers were going to send me out on to the streets with no lifeline.

Cat A is the highest category to be on. You are classed as being a danger to the State and public.

The other cons felt that I was being hard done by. Taking into consideration how many years I had served, surely I should be allowed to mix with people before I was set free? Surely I would not be kicked out from isolation in a top-security prison straight on to the streets? A lot of the cons were very upset over all this, as it really was a liberty. But I was still a 'madman' in the eyes of the system – and that was final!

The block had a small exercise yard, 20 yards by 20 yards, and every day I jogged my hour away. Rain, wind, sunshine, I didn't care. I still ran … every day was one less! I even sang some days. I ran 20 times one way, then 20 times the other. The screws fed me well, and every afternoon I went to the gym for an hour. It was great. The gym Prison Officer was Lou. I rate him as a real gentleman. He was always decent to me, and let me get on with what I wanted to do.

In all my time at Gartree, I had no problems. But the best thing was, there were other cons in there with me and they were all great lads. Some of them bought me fruit and mags. Some I knew from the '70s on other sentences.

When I saw Micky Ahmed, I was sick he was now

doing life. He looked so well, hardly changed. I was proud of the fact that he was facing up to it like a man. A life sentence is no fucking joke, you've got to be a man to get through it.

Big Billy Adams was in the same gym class as me. He can bench press 400lb. I've seen nothing like it. The man's a mountain!

Weeks were flying by with no problems. Barry Rundeau came down for a spell. He'd tried to escape from a prison van and almost did. I liked Barry a lot. He was a solid man. He got life when he was 19 years old. He'd stabbed a guy at a football match. Some days, Barry trained with me in the cage. He loved it. He was 27 years old – and, boy, could he do some sit-ups!

A couple of years later, Barry cut his own throat and wrists and bled to death. It was a sad day for everyone who'd known him. I cried, as I loved the lad. I know of a lot more that wept. God bless you, Barry.

Over the months, I saw a lot of cons come and go in the block. I made it through to April with no problems. All was going well. The Governor was more than happy. I suppose it was a feather in his cap. Then my door opened early one morning. There were lots of screws. 'Sorry,' they said. 'But you're moving.'

I went mad. They told me to calm down. They said it would only be for a week or two and then I would be coming back. They said that I had to be moved because the exercise yard was having a cage put on it and it was going to be very noisy. I was gutted! I didn't want to go. I felt betrayed.

Why should I have to go? It was a sad day. I believed that they had lied to me and set me up. I've been lied to and lied to and lied to. All I've ever asked for is the most basic level of decency – an inkling of understanding, of respect.

But it was all shit. I was bitter and angry. I left a

very unhappy man. We travelled all the way in silence, seven screws and me, all the way to Leicester Prison.

They were waiting for me, a team of them. One cocky rat said, 'What's he been up to?'

I said, 'Fuck all yet. Why? Do you want a busted nose?'

He soon shut his mouth! Once in the block, the Governor came to see me. He told me that I was only there for a very short time and I would be returning to Gartree as soon as the cage was completed. This made me calm down. I was given gym class there as well. Everything carried on as it had done in Gartree.

Fred Low was here. He's a good lad. He got life for robbery, so he said he wasn't doing life for nothing. He stabbed a con to death and got a second life. He was now in there for cutting a con's face in Strangeways. Fred's a problem to the system. Many fear him, but I like Fred a lot.

Fred's never getting out. He knows that. He spends his time building dolls' houses, and bloody good they are, too. Fred's now doing three life terms – he likes to stab people.

After a couple of days, I knocked out a con in the gym showers. He was a sex-case. I hit him so fucking hard I thought I'd killed him. When he came round I told him, 'Come back and I'll put a lace around your neck.' We never saw him again. I was in Leicester for exactly ten days when the van came for me to take me back to Gartree. I was made up. It was one of my better journeys – a van ride I enjoyed.

I soon got back into my old routine. Another couple of months passed by and I was then allowed to go to the playing fields for an hour every weekend with the other cons. This was magic. I saw Reggie Kray, Rooky Lee, and all my old pals. Reg looked in great shape, fit and well. The move here had done him good. I saw my old mate Sid Draper, who I hadn't seen since 1975 in

Hull Jail. I ran a lot to build up my stamina. I was in superb shape. My pal outside, Paul Edmonds, was given a discretionary visit to see me. He told me that he had a prize-fight for me when I got out, if I wanted it. Fucking right I did!

It would put some money in my pocket – plus I reckoned it would rid me of years of frustrated madness. I promised Paul that I would keep on training and would be ready for the big day! The Board of Prison Visitors gave me 180 days remission back, which took my release date forward to 30 October 1987.

I had just a few months left to do. The end was in sight; my fight was almost over. I just had to keep my head together. My parents were a strong influence on me getting through those last few months. They visited me as often as they could to support me. My Uncle Jack was another great strength to me at this time, as were many cons. Even the Gartree block screws were as good as gold. Some days when I lost my head, they could have nicked me – but they kept me going forward.

I knew how close I was getting when they came and measured me up for a suit. The Governor allowed me up to an art class, twice a week. I was almost home and dry.

Then it happened ... something that I didn't need at this time! A mysterious letter arrived from a woman called Kelly-Anne. She was a friend of my Uncle Jack. She had been in his flat when one of my letters arrived. She asked who I was, and it began from there. She asked Jack if she could write to me, so I got this letter. I wrote back to her, and the relationship began, a relationship that would cost me dear. I learned a lot about her just through her letters. Her life was tragedy after tragedy. It seemed that the men in her life had abused her and beaten her. Her four children had been taken away from her and put into council care. On top of all this, her latest boyfriend was now beating her up and she was pregnant again. It was everyone's fault but Kelly-Anne's. She was the sweet and innocent and the world was bad to her. But her letters touched me like no others had before. My problems felt so little compared to hers. But I should have asked myself, 'Why did she write to me, a man who has served 13 years in prison?'

Some of her letters made me depressed. She was telling me how her boyfriend was pulling her hair out and smashing up her flat. Yet here I was in a prison cell; I couldn't help myself, let alone her! I felt trapped in a situation I had no answers to. A pal in the block told me to dump her. He said I needed to sort out my own life, not hers.

I thought about this, but I felt strangely committed to her. She was like a magnet. I tried to keep a level head, but I kept having visions of her being beaten up … Poor, sweet Kelly-Anne …

The time flew by. It was now a month to go. My parents wanted to collect me on the big day. So did some of my mates, but it was only right that my parents did. This was their dream as well as mine. A dream that they thought would never come true. We had all survived it together.

My last week was dominated by my reflecting on the past. I felt a strange feeling of loss. Thirteen-and-a-half years is a lot of time to lose. I was now a 35-year-old man. It was as if time had stopped in 1974. I was going out into a world that had left me behind. I had hardly any money, no roots, no trade. It was like leaving school to enter the real world. I was still a Category A prisoner and still isolated. Yet, within a week, I would be mixing with millions of people. This was one of the most difficult weeks of my entire life. Now was the time to face reality. The nonsense had to stop; I had to start my life all over again. I was obviously buzzing, but I was confused at the same time. The days felt like weeks; hours seemed to drag on and on.

I made it to the last couple of days. Big Billy Adams sent me down a farewell meal, a nice fry-up. Then on my last night, Rooky Lee sent me a roast chicken meal down. They are two solid men who I will never forget. That last night must have been the strangest in my life, as it was the night I thought I would never see. It was here at last!

My years had been spent living out of a cardboard box, in which I kept letters and photographs, toiletries, a Bible, some pens, my address book and bits and pieces that I had accumulated during my time inside. I went through it all that night. I re-read some of the letters, I studied the photographs. To anyone else this was a box of useless junk, but to me it represented my life for almost 14 years. Normal men of my age needed a house, a garage or a shed to store their treasures. I needed my cardboard box.

Obviously, at moments like those, it gets to a man. I looked at my son's photo and he was still three years old. That hit me so fucking hard. I knew what I'd done in the past, but I'm only human. I can get as emotional as the next man. I was so eaten up inside that night. I couldn't sleep. I paced my cell thinking of Mum's face and how Dad would feel tomorrow. I thought of all the cons I would be leaving behind. Then I sat there and tore up all my possessions. Even now I can't tell you why I did it, but I ripped up photos, letters and everything that meant so much to me. I was walking out of that jail a lost soul.

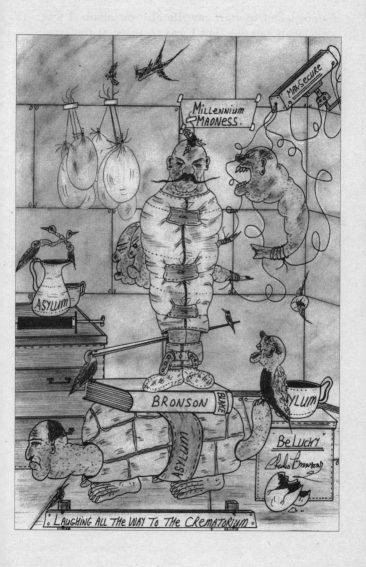

CHAPTER EIGHT

My cell door opened and I raced out like a greyhound. My mind was racing, too – at 100mph. I washed and shaved – fuck the porridge! I'd had enough of that shit! I was ready to go!

The block screws walked me over to reception. I had to walk past B Wing and H Wing – and then it started up! The cons were all there at their cell windows, banging, shouting and singing. What a send-off! I spotted some faces. There was Rooky Lee, Roy Walsh, Ron McCartney, Ron Brown. I gave them something to remember. I stuffed an old towel down

my back and I started to run up and down shouting,
'Esmerelda!'

I thought it was a fucking laugh, but with me I
always go too far! The dogs started to get excited and
almost went for me!

Bear in mind that Gartree is a top-security prison
and high-risk cons, such as Category A prisoners
like me, don't usually get released from there.
Ninety-nine per cent have to be de-categorised and
are then released from less secure jails. I made it to
reception. I put my black suit on, a white shirt,
black tie, black shoes. I looked like I was going to a
funeral! But I looked smart. Black is my colour, I
love black. I put my rings on (which I hadn't been
able to do for thirteen-and-a-half years). They gave
me about £50. Fifty fucking quid! What could you do
with £50?

Fuck it! I had £200 of my own, but that's not the
point. How far would I be able to go on £50? What
start is that? What would have happened if my
parents hadn't been meeting me?

There was a block screw called Steve. I shook his
hand. He was a real gentleman, he always treated me
decent, and he wished me good luck. I was then
walked to the gate by four screws. I looked through
the hatch in the gate and saw my old dad, pacing up
and down. Mum was sitting in the car with my Auntie
Eileen. Both looked nervous.

I shouted, 'Oi! Dad!' He looked over. 'They won't let
me out for another six months!'

Dad looked stunned, then the gate opened and I
ran into his arms. My old dad had tears in his eyes.
We had a big hug. Mum took a photo, and I had tears
in my eyes as well. Dad and I just couldn't stop crying.
All the pain was coming out. Happiness was entering
our world again. Mum started to cry, so did Auntie
Eileen. We'd made it! I was reborn.

As we drove away, I turned back to see the gates I had just come through. What a sensation!

They say in jail that you should never look back – or you'll come back.

We drove to Aspley Guise, which is in Bedfordshire and where Auntie Eileen lived. My Uncle John lived there, too, running the village pub. As we drove on, I realised that I wasn't in handcuffs. It was a strange feeling. I had really made it! After a nice meal at Eileen's, we all went for a drink in Uncle John and Auntie Julie's pub, which I really enjoyed. Then me, Dad and Mum set off for home.

My parents had moved to Wales, ten years earlier, to run a pub in Aberystwyth. Then they took on a club, and now they were retired. Everyone knew them there and they loved the place, but it wasn't my home. They had done well; everyone respected them in the town, but I knew I would not find my roots there. I loved my parents very much, but the town was strange to me. I stayed three days. They wanted me to stay longer, so I could adjust, but I felt I had to move on and make my own way. There was nothing for me there: no work, no future. I didn't want to sponge off my family, so I had no choice but to move. Those three days will remain in my head for all time. I couldn't have wished for better parents.

That's probably why I had to leave. I just didn't know how to cope. I was confused; I felt the danger signs coming on. I felt embarrassed – money had changed, there were new coins that I didn't know. I couldn't even use a phone. I was a fucked-up man! I was too proud to own up to all this, so I kept it bottled up.

I did do one thing that I had dreamt about so many times. I ran along the sea-front the first morning that I woke up a free man. It was sheer bliss, the wind and the sea spray in my face. That one moment spelt it all out for me – *freedom*!

So for three days we enjoyed each other's company. It was strange for us all. Mum and Dad were 14 years older so obviously they had changed a lot. So had I. We had to get to understand each other again. I watched Mum use her microwave (I had never seen one). I watched Dad use the video. I was lost. I still can't use a video, even to this day. I couldn't even begin to believe how my life had changed. I slept on a mattress with a continental quilt, I ate with real cutlery on real china plates, and I went for a pint and held a real glass.

This was crazy. One day my life was plastic – the next it was real. I believe that no man should be released the way that I was after so many years. I needed rehabilitation, a half-way house, where I could learn about life outside. This is why I feel so bitter against the system. They didn't give me a chance to survive in the outside world.

They kept me isolated and then slung me out to get on with it. Maybe they just wanted me to explode, then they could lock me away for good. We will never know. Still, fuck the system. I was out and I was on my way to face the world – alone!

Four days after I walked out of Gartree, I was on the train to London. As I waved goodbye to Mum and Dad, I could see the concern on their faces. But it was too late now. I was on my way. I had about £250 and a suitcase to my name, but I felt prepared for anything. I just hoped that I wouldn't lose control and do something stupid.

I started off the journey in a compartment all to myself. I felt it was best that way – no hassle, no aggravation. But after several stops it was full up. The world was now upon me. This was to be my test.

I felt like I was in a small room completely full of people – and all looking at me. I ended up by a table with an old boy opposite me. A woman in her early

40s sat next to me, and a young girl opposite her. It turned out that they were mother and daughter. The mum was taking the daughter for a job interview. I got into a conversation with grandpop, who was going to London to see his grandchildren (he was on his own, like me). We discussed boxing. He was telling me about all the old time greats: Louis, Marciano, Dempsey, Robinson. We compared them with today's boxers … we had a great conversation going. I bought them all tea and biscuits and the young girl had a Coke. I got chatting to the mother and daughter.

Then I fucked up. I unintentionally upset everyone.

The young girl asked where I was going. I replied, 'I'm off to London to kill the Queen!' (Obviously it was a joke.) I only said it for a laugh, as lots of people say, 'I'm off to London to see the Queen.' You have to bear in mind that I was dressed all in black, plus I was wearing sunglasses. They took it seriously. I'd probably frightened them so I took off my shades, smiled, and said, 'I'm only joking!' But it was just making matters worse. It was now embarrassing. The danger signs were obvious. Sweat dripped down my back. This was the first sign that my head was starting to fuck up.

I said, 'Excuse me,' and went to the nearest toilet. I had a strip wash to cool myself down, then I went to stand by the carriage door, with the window open, taking deep gulps of air. I knew that I had to clear my head – fast!

I was now dealing with real people in the outside world. Nice, decent, law-abiding people. I had to watch myself. After all, I was an ex-loony and saying things like this could send me back into the asylum.

I went back to my seat. They had all gone. They had obviously moved away from the nutter to a different compartment. What if they had told the guards and they had phoned through to London? The cops could be there, waiting for me. Fucking hell. I felt terrible. I was worried and confused, and also upset with myself, for the rest of the journey. I was in a state of anxiety. (If you are one of those three people I upset on the train, I apologise. I hope you understand and can see the funny side of it now.)

I do actually like our Queen! I've been lodging in Her Majesty's establishments for over a quarter of a century, although some of the hospitality hasn't been very good, I have to say. Stodgy food, plenty of rats and cockroaches. It's got to be better at Windsor Castle or Balmoral!

When I arrived at King's Cross Station, I legged it so fast London never knew what hit it! I went to St Pancras Station next door and put my case in the left luggage. Now I was free, no bulk to hold me down. I felt ready for anything or anyone. London is an insane city, so one more loon wouldn't make any difference!

Back at King's Cross, I clocked the pimps with their little white hookers. I watched them for a while. It's for all to see how they exploit those girls – they treat them like dog shit. I got a headache just watching them. They parade about like snakes in the grass. They're not villains, they are just leeches. I had to move on as I was getting upset.

My first call was south London (a friend). He let me down. Second call was east London. I did well there. A fight was fixed. I was going to have a prize-fight and I was going to enjoy it! I saw a few faces, had a few beers and, before I knew it, two days had gone – so I hit the road.

I happened to walk past a big toy shop and something told me to enter it. I bought a water pistol. It was as big as a Python Magnum. It even resembled one, although close up you could obviously see it was a toy. I shot into a toilet and pulled the muzzle out of the end. I swear now it could be passed as a real gun.

Now was the time to test it. Madness came over me. I don't know what possessed me even to buy the fucking thing, but I was buzzing with the fight coming up. I felt starved of excitement. I needed to venture out – I needed some danger. I thought that as long as I didn't hurt anyone, so what?

I stuffed the gun into my waistband, did my jacket up, and started my walk through London. There were millions of faces all over me. They were coming from every direction like ants – human ants. I decided that I needed wheels. I wanted a drive, I needed to get out of London. I'd collect my case later. Right now I had plans!

I hung around a multi-storey car park until I clocked this suited guy walking towards a Mercedes. I followed. I had the fake gun in his back before he knew what was happening.

'Don't fuck about, just get in and open my door.'

Once we were in, I gave it to him straight.

'You do as you're told and you'll be all right. Now drive!' I told him to head north, for the M1.

He had some tapes in the car. I told him to put on U2. 'In the Name of Love' came on, and I had the greatest buzz that I'd had in years. This was living!

He got to the M1 and then he started to ask questions. I told him to shut up and drive. When we got to the Luton turn-off, I told him that this was where I wanted to go. We drove into Luton. It looked so strange. It was a long, long time since I had been here. I saw a road I recognised so I told him to stop. This was when he started to panic. I told him to shut up and listen. I told him that he was safe – just drive off and forget me. I never saw a car move so fast in my life!

I made my way to my Uncle Jack's flat in Marsh Farm, an estate in Luton. He was one man in my life who understood me. Jack had been a loyal friend to me. Just like my dad, he was made of solid stuff.

Jack was born in the East End of London in the 1920s, but he came to Luton after the Second World War. He was a respected man all his life, had lots of friends in various walks of life, and he loved his drink! Uncle Jack was always immaculately dressed and had the greatest self-respect of any man I knew. Since he and my Auntie Eileen had split up in the '70s, he'd lived alone on the twelfth floor of a block of flats.

When I knocked on his door that day, it was as if I'd lit up his whole life. 'Come in, son,' he said.

There were tears of happiness all round. I had a nice hot bath and a shave. I felt great. Then she walked in … Kelly-Anne, seven months pregnant. It was the first time that we had met. She had a nice face, not pretty, but I would say attractive. It was her eyes that hit me. Strange eyes. She could look directly at a man without so much as blinking.

There was a lot of anguish and pain in that young face of hers. I had already been affected by her letters. But I knew by the end of that day that we were not going to make it together. She was a chain-smoker (I hate smoking) and she drank like a fish. Unless she cut down on the fags and booze it was a no-go situation. I weighed it all up very quickly. She was one of many who went for a drink with Jack; it was good company for him. But for a man just out of jail, it was pathetic. So I kept a fair distance.

Kelly-Anne did help me a lot. She sorted out my dole money, helped me choose some clothes, cooked me some lovely meals, and she was good company for me – when she was sober. But her lifestyle was not mine. I needed excitement, not a fucking drunk to take care of.

I trained hard in all the gyms that I went to. I sparred, did weights, swam, did some running. I felt great! I cooked great big pots of stew that would last me three days. Oh yeah – at last I was living! I got rid of all my madness and aggression when I worked out.

Then I met Hilary. She was a divorcée with three children. She trusted me and really helped me a lot. I rate Hilary as an all-time friend. We laughed a lot during our few weeks together. I loved her kids, and they loved me, but I started to drift away. I became confused. This was a commitment that was just too heavy. I had to escape the pressure. It was a magic time for me, but we both knew it couldn't last. It was short and sweet with lovely memories. Hilary and I remained good friends and her kids still love and respect me. They took me into their hearts and loved me as I had never been loved for so long.

Now I was ready for the prize-fight! It was to be held above a pub – obviously I can't say where, because it was illegal. I won. It was so easy it was untrue! I hit him with 14 fucking years of hell inside me. I got paid £500, a lot of money when you've got fuck-all.

It was all down to Reggie Kray that I took up the fight game. A few months before I was released from Gartree, Reg asked me what I was going to do when I got out. 'Fuck knows, Reg,' I said. 'Probably rob a bank or wrap somebody up.'

I was going out into the unknown, but Reg offered me words of advice. 'Look, don't be daft,' he said. 'You'll just end up back inside. Go out and win! Why not take up prize fighting?'

The Number 1 Governor gave me a discretionary visit. I was still Cat A, and all my normal visitors had to be passed by the Old Bill and security. Paul Edmonds came up to see me; he was a top promoter for the unlicensed fight scene, and is now sadly dead. I'd last seen him in Parkhurst when he was doing ten for a bank. 'Right,' he said. 'Fancy it, do you?' And that was it! Paul became my boss!

I was 14 stone, solid, fast, fit, 35-years-old … in the prime of my life. I didn't smoke, booze, or take drugs – and I had 14 years of madness inside me that I needed to release. Everyone knew I was lethal and very much insane.

Unlicensed fights in the '80s were a big thing, especially around East London. The two best known were Roy Shaw and big Lenny McLean. But there were so many others who, like me, were only known by their fighting names. We chose to fight under aliases, mainly for tax reasons.

My gaffer Paul Edmonds chose my name … Charles Bronson. I don't think I've ever even seen a Charles Bronson film – contrary to popular belief, I certainly don't hero-worship him!

I actually wanted to be called Jack Palance after the great actor, who in his early years won prize money boxing. But Bronson it was – and Bronson stuck.

Professional boxers take weeks to prepare for a fight, but I took hours. That room above the East End pub was rocking, full of ex-cons laying a few bets. My opponent was the 'Bermondsey Bear', an awesome sight – black body hair, shaven skull, toothless and covered in tattoos. But he was nowhere near my level of fitness. Just looking at him, I knew it was money for nothing! He was all show – growls, eyeballing, swearing. I had to hurt him badly. As I looked at him, I pictured every stinking screw that ever stuck the boot in my head, every bad prison doctor, every slag governor. I fucking hated him!

I said to my corner men, 'I'm gonna kill this fat c--t. But first I'm gonna make him scream.'

The crowd wanted a good fight, and they got it. Ding, ding! I ran out and smashed a right into his ugly face. He slung a few punches, but they all missed. I caught him a peach in the ribs and heard him wince. Then he kneed me in the bollocks and pain shot through me like a red-hot poker! I felt sick, dizzy. The c--t had kneed me in the bollocks! He nutted me, and dug a thumb in my eye. Ding, ding! The bell saved me because I was dazed, confused.

He had done all the damage he would ever do to me.

Crack! I nutted him so hard his nose split open. Then I opened up on him: 20 or 30 shots to the head. Ten would have done! As he fell over I fell on top of him. I had lost it completely. I was actually putting my whole weight on his windpipe. Guys jumped in, pulling me, hitting me – trying to get me off him. Luckily for him, they did.

I arrived back in Luton and it wasn't long before I met Alison. She was 18 years old. I was twice her age! She was my angel and I admit I went overboard. I'm no oil painting and here I was with a girl so pretty, so lovely. I was in love, but I couldn't leave her alone. I was suffocating her; I was too much for her. I probably frightened her to death with my obsession for her. I used to let her sit on my back while I was doing sit-ups every day. I made her laugh and every day she made me laugh. Then the bombshell dropped; she was seeing someone else, a bloke on a motorbike. I told Jack that I was going to shoot the fucker's legs off, but he talked me out of it. He told me to grow up and not to be so silly. Jack told me that she was too young, and that she had to decide for herself.

I was so depressed I stayed in the bedroom for days. Only one person saved me – Kelly-Anne. She talked to me, made me feel better. She was like a sister to me. Then out of the blue Alison came back. She was drunk and drugged up. She broke my heart. Jack was also hurt to see her like that. I wanted to go and kill the bastard for getting her in that state. I hate drugs. I stripped her off, bathed her, combed her hair, put one of my shirts on her and put her to bed. She was sick everywhere. I was so upset I smashed my fist into the wall and cracked all my knuckles. I had another fight coming up in a few weeks. I didn't need all this shit!

My next fight was, in fact, a charity one at a big theatre. It was unlicensed, but it was for a young leukaemia victim. There were six fights on that night and I was on fifth. I won again. Jack came to see it and he loved it. I made £500 but I donated £200 to the kid. He died a year later, but that night raised enough money to send him on a trip to Disneyworld in Florida. There was a lot of art work sold that night, donated by prisoners from all over the country. Reg Kray sent a painting, so did Ron. Harry Roberts sent a jewel box and I donated a painting myself. The Yorkshire Ripper sent a painting but the organiser Paul Edmonds smashed it up.

Paul put a deal to Lenny McLean – winner takes all – but Lenny didn't want to know. Others tried to get him to accept. I even said I'd put five grand on the table myself. But Lenny was settled at this time, doing well on the doors and choosing his opponents carefully. I was hungry for a fight, but he didn't need Charles Bronson. I can't blame him – nor would I put him down, because Lenny was a man of respect, a man I admired. But I'm gutted he didn't take up the challenge. It would have put me on the road to victory. Ronnie Kray once called me the 'un-crowned champion'.

My third fight lasted one poxy round. I got a measly £800. I fought a gypsy guy called Romany Ron, but I didn't even get into top gear. I was frustrated. I could have got thousands from a fight with Lenny McLean. I wasn't a fucking circus clown.

My next fight is not something I'm proud of, because I love animals. But at the time I had little choice – fight or go back to robbing. Looking back, the whole thing was pure madness.

It was in a warehouse – and I was up against a

massive, snarling Rottweiler. I can close my eyes now
and see that beast coming towards me. It was a giant
of a dog. The head on it was huge. It was snarling,
ripping. I managed to punch it in the mouth and as
my hand was in its jaws – as it was about to try and
rip my arm off – I just kept smashing my fist as far
down its throat as possible. As it was going down
there was froth coming out its mouth. It was a terrible
sight. But I knocked it right down and in one mighty
swoop I ripped out half its lungs.

I killed it. Not a nice thing, but when you're getting
paid ten grand cash, it's a lot of money when you
haven't got anything.

Christmas came and went and I decided it was
time to surprise Alison. I decided to get her a ring –
and while I was at it, I'd rob the jeweller's shop!
Well, I am a criminal, what else would you expect me
to do? Alison was worth more than the Crown Jewels
to me and I wanted to give her something precious. I
ran into James Tobin, a jeweller's in Luton. There
were three people in the shop, two men and one
woman. I got them all on the floor, pointed the gun
at them and filled the bag. I grabbed the cash, too,
and off I shot. Tally-ho! Happy New Year! It was a
piece of cake. I parcelled it all up, except one ring,
and delivered the parcel to a fence. My job was done.
I went to see Alison and put the ring on her finger.
Sweet as honey.

On 7 January 1988, my sixty-ninth day of freedom,
I went for my morning jog. It was a lousy morning,
foggy, wet and cold, but to me it was heaven. I had
just completed a five-miler, almost home, when – *bang*
– my life fell apart!

This big geezer in labourer's clothes was directly in
front of me. I went to pass him and – *crack* – he hit my
jaw. The next thing I was in a strangle-hold. Other
people were running about. It happened so fast. At

first I thought it was a little firm of gangsters, then the cuffs went on – these were cops!

'You're under arrest, Bronson, for suspicion of armed robbery.'

I was slung in a van and taken to Luton police station. 'Charles Bronson' was born. They had charged me under my fighting name, not under the name I was born with, Michael Gordon Peterson.

Fourteen years now I've lived as Bronson. I no longer respond to 'Micky Peterson'. I'm Charlie – and I quite like it. The cops did me a favour.

I was questioned for a day-and-a-half about the jewellery. They put me on an identity parade. Only one person picked me out. There was no jewellery found and no gun. There was nothing substantial to convict me – not yet! Someone unknown to me had phoned the police to say that Bronson had a gun. Now the police aren't silly. They knew that I was in town. They probably had a spy at my fights; they knew I was training.

Sixty-nine fucking days and I find myself back in prison, back on Cat A and back in the same stinking cell that I was in only months ago in Leicester Jail. The only difference was the name 'BRONSON' on a card outside my cell door. I was gutted!

I was double-cuffed in the van to Leicester punishment block. There were seven screws, plus a police car escort. It must cost the tax-payer a fortune to move me about. I was supposed to go to my local jail, Bedford, but they won't accept high-risk prisoners. Once at Leicester Jail, I went through reception. They hadn't decided yet what to do with me, but it wasn't long before they realised Charlie Bronson and Micky Peterson were the same person. They were gob-smacked! The Governor came over and decided to put me in the block.

So here I was, back in the block, with nothing but

69 glorious days of memories. Every single one of those days was like Christmas for me. If they had come into my cell at that moment and killed me, I couldn't complain. I had had the break – and fucked it all up.

I wasn't beaten yet, though. I felt I could walk this charge. The Governor came back to see me later to tell me that I was to remain in the block on good order and discipline for as long as I remained in Leicester. I was not amused. I told him he was breaking the law by doing this. I was innocent until proven guilty. Plus, I had just arrived here from outside so how could he justify keeping me in isolation? Surely I should be given the same chance as any other prisoner? He told me that it was because of my past. I told him that I was Charlie Bronson now, not Peterson. I was a new man! He went away smiling.

I wasn't smiling though. This was a very serious issue. I was back to being known as Danger Man, stuck in the block, and I'd done fuck all in jail to get there. How could this be just? I told the screws that if they didn't let me have some gym, then I would tear their block to bits. They did. Some of the screws said it was a liberty keeping me in the block for no reason. Everyone knew my past had been a bit crazy, but lots of guys have pasts that are not too clever – so why me?

A month flew by with no problems. I went to the gym with the other Cat As who were up on the wing. There were about six of them. Then Andy Russell arrived! Andy got nicked for hijacking a helicopter and helping my pal Sid Draper, and also John Kendall, escape from Gartree Prison. This was the first ever escape in England using a helicopter and it happened only weeks after my release from the same prison. Everyone was buzzing over it. Andy Russell is a great guy; he's got so much bottle it's untrue. He

even asked me if I wanted him to join me in the block!
He was prepared to come into the block just to keep
me company. This is the sort of man he is – loyal. I
told him that he had enough on his plate, and just to
concentrate on his forthcoming case.

The police dug up another two witnesses who
reckoned they saw me over the jewellery blag. I told
them, 'What a load of old bollocks!' I said if they
wanted another ID parade, they would have to do it in
the jail. They agreed. They picked out eight cons who
supposedly 'resembled' me. How they could do this, I
don't know. There isn't one con who looks like me. But
I went through with it anyway.

I must say that some of the cons they picked were
vicious-looking buggers! This was to be the first ever
police line-up in Leicester Prison. (I always set the
records!) The first witness walked past the line. He
looked terrified. Imagine it – the poor sod had
probably never been in a prison before, and here he
was, in the block (which looks like a dungeon), faced
with us lot glaring at him. These were all hardened
cons. The guy shook his head.

No identification.

The cops were gutted – I could see it in their faces.
The next one walked down the line. He stopped to look
at me and I glared into his eyes. He was only young,
about 25. I smiled at him and he carried on walking.
He even came back to look at me again. I looked hard
into his eyes again.

No identification.

The police were sick! My case was looking
stronger. Then the bombshell dropped, and I still
don't know why. Maybe she felt under pressure, but it
turned out that Alison, who was my number-one
witness, had retracted her statement and was
making another one. She was originally giving me an
alibi; now she was going to be the main prosecution

witness. She told them that I'd done the job, that I'd given her the ring, and she even told them what I was wearing on the day of the blag. She completely fucked up my case – and my head. OK, she was young, but I don't think she realised what she had done to me. I wasn't her motorbike boy going to Borstal with a slapped wrist, I was Charlie Bronson the fucking madman, an armed robber facing 20 fucking years.

Andy Russell was having a spot of hassle over some nonsense on his wing. He went on hunger-strike, him and three other cons. Andy's a pal so I sent a message up to him. I told him that I wouldn't go on hunger-strike – I'd sooner tie someone else up and make them do it. My plan was set. Fuck Leicester!

I went out on exercise and dived on to a gate. I pulled myself up. This was tricky stuff as it had razor wire on it. I got on to a ledge but I tore my right arm and left leg. Half the leg of my jeans was left behind on that wire. From the ledge I scaled a building and made it to a drainpipe. I was on my way up – 60 feet up!

This was where all my training paid off. I shot up that drainpipe like a squirrel with its nuts on fire! I got to the top, but now I was in trouble. It was impossible to reach the gutter as the pipe shot into the wall at least 6ft below it. I was trapped. I looked below; there were scores of screws and dogs, the usual riff-raff, looking up at me. I shouted down, 'You lot better move as I'm jumping!' The silly bastards moved out of the way. They really had pea-brains; they believed me.

I knew what I was going to do. The roof was going to come off. I was only feet away; I couldn't let it beat me now. I climbed back down to the ledge, which was only about 10ft from the ground. I found an air extractor and smashed it up, so I'd soon got myself a

piece of curved metal. Then I tore out the TV aerial
wire. I tied the wire around the metal and made my
way back up the pipe. Once at the top, I tried to hook
the metal on to the guttering, like a grappling hook.
Some would say it was a suicide mission, but what
was the big deal? I could only fall and die! The plan
worked. I tested my weight and had my last look
down. Then, to my horror, I saw a fucking screw above
me! He was looking down at me. I couldn't believe it!
He kicked my piece of metal off the guttering. Then I
saw another screw. The slippery fuckers had gone up
through the skylight to stop my plan. I was now well
and truly trapped. This was as bad as robbing a
security van full of forged notes – I was sick!

I had no choice but to climb down – but not yet. The
bastards would have to wait until I was ready. I made
it to the ledge and stayed there all day. It was pouring
with rain. I was cold, wet and hungry, and covered in
cuts and bruises. I felt at a total loss. I eventually
climbed down later that night.

The next day I was so depressed. I stripped stark
bollock naked and blacked myself from head to toe
with boot polish. Then I started to smash the granny
out of my steel door. They moved me early the next
morning. I left Leicester Jail as a black man.

On the way to wherever we were going, which was
via the southbound M1, I was bursting for a slash. In
the Cat A vans there was supposed to be a bucket for
emergencies as we were not allowed to stop. There
wasn't in this van; I was convinced that they had done
it on purpose. I had no choice. I flooded the floor of the
van. I will never forget the looks on their faces. The
van pulled up outside the gates of Brixton Prison, and
in we went.

I swear to God they just didn't know what to do
with me or where to put me, so they locked me up in a
holding cell until the Governor could come down to

sort it out. It seemed the choice was down to a hospital padded cell, the block or a top-secure special unit.

Personally, I didn't give a toss.

The Governor came down and told me that I would be going to the special unit. At that time – March 1988 – it was the number-one secure-unit in the country. It held 16 inmates, all for serious crimes. My crime was absolutely nothing to what these guys were facing. Just to give you some idea of what this unit was all about, there were four IRA terrorists, a cop killer, a drug baron (who was also an American Mafia man), a spy, several killers and, not forgetting the most remarkable villain I ever met, Valerio Viccei, master thief. He raided the Knightsbridge safety deposit boxes, taking them for £60 million.

And then there was little old me, in for doing a poxy jeweller's. And I was the one in the cage.

There were three cells on the bottom floor at Brixton. One cell, mine, had a 'cage door', an iron, meshed barrier inside the normal steel cell door. The reason for this is simple – they can open the outer door to feed you, but the inner cage remains locked. Your food is simply passed through a restricted hatch at the bottom of the cage. Human contact when you're caged up is out of bounds.

Micky Reilly was next door to me. He was facing a trial for robbing a bank. Mick is made of good stuff; he always cheers everyone up. On my other side was Valerio, known by some of his friends as 'Gi Gi'. The rest of the inmates were above us. Everyone on this unit was allowed to mix, to watch TV, play cards and so on. When I walked on to this wing, a lot of the cons thought I was a black geezer or a fucking lunatic!

Ronnie Easterbrook was on here. I knew Ron in Parkhurst back in the 1970s. He was now in a lot of trouble. He'd been on a bit of work when Tony Ash got shot dead by the police. Ron copped a bullet in the shoulder. A cop also caught a bullet. Ron's a good, loyal man and I was gutted to see him in trouble. He later got life.

Tommy Hole Sr was also on here. He was facing a couple of trials for robberies. I loved old Tom. I know his people from the East End, and I knew Tom very well. He was a man of honour. It was sad to see him facing so much, but Tom was one of the old breed – he got through it. He later got 23 years. Sadly, a couple of years later, Tommy walked into his son's cell at Parkhurst to find him hanging. It was one of the saddest, most upsetting days I can ever remember. I was in Parkhurst myself at that time. Tommy was only out a few years when, just before Christmas 1999, he was shot dead by some toe-rag in a London pub. God bless you, Tom.

After I scrubbed all the black boot polish off myself, I looked normal again ... well, as normal as a 'madman' can!

The lads used to come to my cage door and have a chat. We all got on very well. I couldn't see why Brixton wouldn't let me out to mix – neither could my mates. They all got together and asked if I could come out on the exercise yard with them. The rule was only eight at a time. Eventually, I was allowed out with the others. I mostly went out with Gi Gi, Micky Ridley, Perry Wharrie, Tommy Hole, Ronnie Easterbrook, Dennis Wheeler and John McCann. But we swapped about from time to time, so I ended up with them all. It was a giant cage with cameras set up on it. It was absolutely secure – it even had a steel net on top.

John Boyle, the American drugs man, got 20 years, but he walked on his appeal. John McCann and Finbar McCullen both got 20 years, and both walked out on their appeal. Perry Wharrie got life, along with Charlie Magee. Gi Gi got 22 years. Those were the type of sentences facing these men, but they were all gentlemen and a lot helped me along, for which I was grateful. Dennis Wheeler used to get a chair and come and sit outside my cage gate to have a chat. He gave me tins of salmon and chocolates. He really spoilt me. He was a lovely man and the slags gave him 14 years for a bit of cannabis – a fucking liberty. We all thought that it was a bad deal; after all, there was only 12 tons of it!

Gi Gi was another one who really kept me sane. Every day he would surprise me. He's one of those guys who's got a gift to be special. He's funny – and he's as strong as a bull. A smashing bloke. He used to wind up the screws with his Rolex watch. It was solid gold with a jewelled strap. That watch meant a couple of years' wages to a screw. Gi Gi once threw it in the bin for a laugh, just to tease them.

And he didn't stand for any shit from them. He always argued for his rights. That's why I liked and respected him. We used to play chess through the cage gate. I would sometimes nick a piece when he wasn't looking. He wouldn't notice for a while, but when he did he went mad! I'd swear black was blue and that I hadn't touched it.

Things were going fine for me at this time. Then, one morning, I lost my head. I ran out and picked up the scalding-hot tea urn and hit one of the Irish cons. The tea went all over him. Then I did him with a bucket. It was all over nothing but it caused a lot of tension. Violence in a unit as small as that one cannot be overlooked. One incident can lead to a dozen. The con that I hit was IRA, on a charge for something very serious. He later got 25 years. It turned out that I had built up the problem in my imagination. It really was fuck-all. I had been brooding over something that was totally unnecessary.

Time passed by. My Uncle Jack visited me with Kelly-Anne. He was so sad to see me back inside again. Kelly-Anne seemed very upset over it all. She had given birth to a little daughter who had been taken away from her. She'd also had all her other kids taken away as well, long before I met her. Her life of men and booze obviously went back a long way. She confused me so much; I could never work her out. One side of her was so sweet, the other so mysterious.

Alison was by now only just a memory. I blamed myself for giving her that poxy ring. It was a mistake that I would have to suffer for, I don't hate Alison for what she did – and if she ever reads this, I hope she has no reason to fear me over it. But, personally, I would go down for 30 years before I grassed on anyone.

I decided to plead 'guilty' to the robbery charge. There were two very good reasons for this. The first was to keep my Uncle Jack out of court – some slag had implicated him, which was totally untrue, but I didn't want him to have to go through all that shit. The second reason was Alison. I knew that she would go to pieces in court, and although she'd grassed me I didn't want to see her go through the ordeal of the witness box.

To plead 'not guilty' and be found 'guilty' carried 15 years. A 'guilty' plea would be half that. So I really had no choice. The only regret I have now is that I should have broken the motorbike boy's legs.

I was double-cuffed with screws all around me. I faced Judge Hickman at St Albans Crown Court. He was a small man with a large grey beard and in his gown he resembled Santa Claus. In court was Uncle Jack, Kelly-Anne and Jimmy Brookes, the landlord at our local pub. Jimmy, a fine boxer in his day, had been good to me. Most days he'd cook me up a nice big steak when I went down The Moakes pub.

It was 17 June 1988, my day in court. I spoke up:

'Today is the last day of my criminal ways.' That's all I said.

My QC, a Mr Major, spoke for me, too.

I sat watching Judge Hickman carefully. He seemed to be a man of great intensity. I tried to send him a telepathic message: *'Give me a break.'*

He said solemnly, 'We must remember that no gun was ever found and only one ring, but this crime was obviously premeditated. I have no choice but to send you back to prison.'

My mind was racing. How long? Just fucking tell me how long.

Seven years!

I went back down to the cells a very disappointed man. My QC came down to see me. He told me that seven years was a good result. If I was good, I could be out in four years and eight months.

I felt empty. Seven years for armed robbery is a result in anyone's eyes. I could have got 15 years, but I just felt that I shouldn't even be in prison at all. I needed help.

I was a fucked-up man. I was lost – and another seven years might finish me off.

Jack, Jimmy and Kelly-Anne were allowed down to see me. We were separated by a glass screen. Jack had tears, Jimmy looked gutted and Kelly-Anne looked oddly different. I saw something in her eyes that I'd never seen before. It spelt out faith.

'Be strong,' she said. I knew at that moment that I was going to make it, but I also knew that it was going to be some battle.

I told Jack to be strong and we both put our hands up to the glass and said our goodbyes. My head was throbbing. Now it was back to the cages of Lucifer. Plenty of porridge and plenty of cockroaches.

Jesus God Almighty, here we go again.

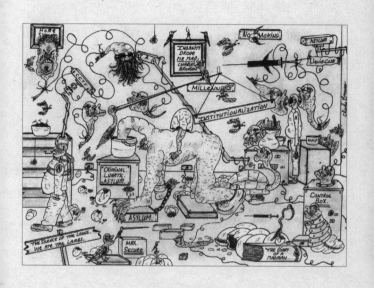

CHAPTER NINE

I swept into Wandsworth Prison to a hail of sirens –
I'm sure they must have mixed me up with someone
else! But for the first time in years they decided to
put me up on the wing with the rest of the Cat A
cons. Most had double or even treble the sentence I
was facing.

There was Wayne Hurran, 20 years; Kevin Brown,
17; Micky Reilly, 14; Steve Davies, 12; Jimmy
Saunders, 17; Dennis Campbell, 16; and Jimmy
Hampton, 15. However, they all kept their spirits up.
'Mad' Frankie Fraser was also back in. I used to see

him in the yard most days. Frank is a legend. He had once been very ruthless, but he stood out as the most polite man in any jail. Fortunately, he was only doing a three-stretch, so he soon got out. Not so long back he got shot through the face on the outside and survived. He was 66 years old and pulled through. He's the mean machine! Frank always calls me Genghis Khan – I can't think why, but if Frank wants to call me by the name of a famous warrior then he can. He's got a big place in my heart.

After two days, I got the arsehole. I picked up a screw and slung him out of the way. The silly bastard was standing in my way, trying to make himself look special and make me look silly. It didn't work. Here we are, a screw, 21 years old, called an officer, with a set of keys and a truncheon – it's power! But it doesn't mean anything to me. He only gets respect from me if he deserves it. Lots do get my respect, but pricks like this never will. They are basically idiots and they wind me up.

So after this I hit the block – what's new? They put me in a smelly cell with no windows. I slung all my clothes out the door, so they then put me in my old cell, number 13. The next day they put me back up on D Wing, where I had started. But violence was bubbling up inside me. I smashed my cell up, so I was back down in cell 13 again. The next day I found myself in a prison van. I believe now that my old friend Prison Officer Wells asked to get me moved. He's not a silly man. He knew I was unsettled and unhappy. I just couldn't come to terms with the fact that I was inside again.

On 24 June 1988 I arrived at Full Sutton, the newest top-secure jail in the country at the time. It was built on a marsh up near York, but for me it might as well have been on the moon. It was too far up north for me. How the fuck could my Uncle Jack get up there to see me? The jail itself was spotless. Every cell had a toilet and sink and it had the best prison gym in the country. The only thing was, it also had a lot of silly screws. Many were only used to working in local jails, and now they were in a long-term jail. They didn't have a clue how to run it. The cons that were in there were doing far too long to put up with their silly games, so obviously there were confrontations. A lot of cons (including myself) were not happy. I already knew many of them – Noel Gibson, Alan Byrne, Frank Cook, Albert Baker, Steve Waterman, and even Colin Robinson were all here.

I attempted to keep my head down but – guess what? – it didn't work out. My first explosion happened in the canteen. I wanted serving, but some screw told me to come back later so I punched his fat face in. Bells went off, dozens of screws came running ... I was bang in trouble!

I was put in the block where I remained for 56 days with no bed. I also lost 120 days' remission – not a good start. After I'd done my 56 days, they let me back up on the wing. The next one to get it was one of the Governors. I let him have a bucket of water all over his nice new suit. It was back to the block for me! When I was eventually allowed back up on the wing, the next to get it was a black con. I was talking to two friends of mine in a room when this con strolled in. It was his attitude that set me off, so I gave him a right hook! I was in trouble again. This whole Bronson reputation was now causing me a lot of problems.

I just couldn't settle, couldn't relax, even though I trained hard. Frank Cook asked me to move cells so I could be on his landing. Well, anyone would have thought that I'd asked to be moved to the Hilton Hotel the way that they acted. I told them to stick the move up their arse. They actually did move me that day ...

100 miles up the road to Durham. This was a big joke to them. It never made me laugh.

As soon as we hit Durham I saw the reception committee waiting. They took me to the punishment block and put me in a cage cell. It was filthy. A mattress was on the floor, it was freezing cold and the piss-pot stank like a sewer. I asked them to get the Governor and when he came down I demanded to know what the hell was going on. He said that I had been moved there for a month because of my violence. I told him that was a load of old bollocks – I'd only asked to move from my cell and instead I was moved 100 miles away. All he would say was that if I behaved myself then I could be moved from that cage. It was a fucking liberty to keep me in that cage. After all, I hadn't really been violent – yet!

My head was pounding. I had absolutely nothing, not even a bar of soap, to my name. I buried myself in the smelly blanket and tried to sleep. This was often difficult, because, being Cat A, a red light in my cell was supposed to be left on. (If a good screw is on, he turns it off.) On this first night it was off. I was in total darkness and I drifted in and out of sleep. I was hungry, cold and very depressed. All of a sudden, something woke me up.

It was a strange noise. At first I thought that I had imagined it, but then I heard it again. My fucking piss-pot moved – I could hear it scraping along the floor! Then I felt something brush past me. I leapt up in the air. There was no way these could be cockroaches. These were much bigger! I stuck my leg through the iron gate of the cage so I could kick the outer cell door. I shouted out, 'Put my fucking light on, quick!' The screw came running and, as the light went on, I could see them running about all over my cell – mice! A dozen or more of them. They must have come in to keep themselves warm. Those little rodents kept me company for the next two weeks. They were lovely little creatures; I became quite attached to them. I fed them bread and other bits of food. They were fast fuckers as well.

After two weeks, I was moved to a proper cell in the block. My old pal Fred Mills was there and he sorted me out some sweets and fruit. Paul Sykes was also in the block. The last time I had seen Paul was in Walton Jail in 1974. Fred and Paul are both right old characters. We all need people like them to cheer us up. Paul's a big Yorkshireman, hands like shovels. A man who clearly loved his beer, birds and fights. He once reputedly killed the prison cat, skinned it, and made a Davey Crockett hat out of it. The next two weeks flew by with no problems at all. Then the van arrived and off I went, seven screws and me. It was my thirty-ninth move in 14 years.

There was real tension in the block at Full Sutton. I was on 'good order and discipline' indefinitely but, despite my efforts, little things got to me. There was too much noise and certain screws kept trying to wind me up. In one day alone, I spat into three screws' faces. I did it to provoke a fight, as I felt that a good tear-up would clear the air. They were all watching me too closely. I couldn't relax or train and my sleep was being affected. The fuckers were getting under my skin! Christmas was days away. It's always a lousy time inside, but little did I know then that it was going to be worse for me than most. On 23 December my cell door opened.

'You're away, mate – you're moving right now. Come on, the van's waiting.'

I couldn't believe it. The day before Christmas Eve and I'm away! This was a deliberate move to upset me. I wasn't amused.

Two days later, my Christmas dinner ended up all over the wall. I tell you what – I don't recommend spending Christmas Day in a fucking dungeon with only cockroaches for company. I was the only con in the block at Armley over the Christmas period. The food was disgusting and I didn't even have a radio – evil bastards! I slung my dinner, as the dogs didn't give me half of what I was entitled to. I slept most of Christmas away in a state of depression.

Armley at that time had a lot of youngsters hanging themselves. There was a big inquiry going on.

1989 crept in, a new year. I was glad; 1988 had been a right stinker. I thought to myself that a move would be nice, just to get out of that hell-hole. My prayers must have been answered for once. I was off on my travels again mid-way through January – back to the block at Full Sutton.

One day, my spy-hole opened and a con shouted, 'All right, Charlie?'

It was Eddie Browning. A lot of cons didn't like Eddie because of his case. Eddie got life for the Marie Wilkes murder on the motorway. But I like to make up my own mind about these things. I read his case notes and became 100 per cent convinced of his innocence. I couldn't believe for the life of me why he was convicted. As it turned out, he was later cleared at the Appeal Court after a seven-year battle.

Colin Robinson was still there – and still at his swallowing game. This time he swallowed a blade. He was sent to hospital for another operation and then they sent him to Grendon in Buckinghamshire. Just after that, a young lad hanged himself in the block. It was all depressing stuff.

I pulled the Governor and told him he had better move me as I was getting very edgy. I was sick of the screws and they were sick of me. The time had come to move me on. Full Sutton and me had had just about enough of each other. The van arrived and I was off once more, this time to Long Lartin top-security prison in Worcestershire.

I have to say I wasn't happy about being put straight in the block. It was too intense. The screws were too close to you in this block. Cameras were watching us all the time and the cells and the exercise yard were claustrophobic. I knew that it wouldn't be long before I exploded down there.

Joe Whitty, the Governor, came down to see me. He was a Governor who I respected; he'd helped a lot of cons. If you fucked with him then he would come down hard on you, but he believed in giving every con a fair chance. He decided to give me a break and he put me up on the wing. He told me that it was all down to me to make a go of it. Joe Whitty was no fool. He knew what pressures I would be under; the screws would see me as a threat and some of the cons would not want me up on the wing, so I would be getting it from both sides. He told me to plod on and he would look into my progress as often as he could.

There were a lot of cons who I knew in this jail: Dave and John Anslow, Stan Thompson, Cyril Berket, Charles Knight, Alec Sears, Dave Bale, Albert Baker, Johnny Walker, Danny Foy, Steve Love, Eddie Watkins and Bubba Turner. They put me on A Wing and gave me a cleaning job. Long Lartin was a very laid-back jail, but it was also unique in that it had no 'Rule 43' protection wing. We all mixed together in here. Even rapists mixed with everyone else. I don't know why or how, but it seemed to work. At first I found it a bit weird, but I said to myself that as long as they didn't cross over on to my patch, then we would get on fine.

I kept my head down and trained twice as hard. I ate plenty and basically just did my porridge. I'd had no visits since court, but now I was nearer home. I sent Uncle Jack and Kelly-Anne a visiting order and they both came up to see me. Kelly-Anne looked good; she was dressed all in black. She wrote to me a lot after that visit. She told me she loved me and that there was no other man for her. It felt great to be close to someone again. It made me feel wanted, something I hadn't felt for a long time. She had put feeling into my life again. I called her my lady in black, and she swore that she had cut down on her drinking.

But after a few visits, I became confused. She always seemed to have plenty of money, yet she was supposed to be on Social Security. Where was she getting it all from? I think I knew in my heart that she had another man. She remained a mystery to me for a long time, but she did give me some nice thoughts and touching moments. I began to feel closer to her. It made me feel nice and, to some extent, contented, so I brushed aside the doubts that I was beginning to have.

At weekends I drank a lot of 'hooch'. It's what we called our secretly brewed prison beer. It was made with fruit, spuds, yeast, sugar and malt. It's rough stuff but it does the trick. We would all pile into one cell and drink buckets of the smelly stuff. Of course, you're not meant to brew-up, but all prisons do, and you can bet that a lot of Governors know full well it goes on. That hooch kept us happy – we'd all have a sing-song and the screws left us alone as long as it didn't get out of hand. So, at weekends, I'd have a few pints and then through the week I would train really hard to work it off. I have to say, though, prison hooch isn't without its hazards. It may be OK for cons, but not for connoisseurs! A few prisoners have actually gone blind through it and many get the shits. The problem is, it may have all sorts of dodgy ingredients – and if it is not ready to drink, it will ferment in your stomach. On balance, I'd say now to give it a miss. The odds are that the bad brews will outweigh the good ones.

Kelly-Anne had her own brand of poison. She soon came up to see me on her own and she was so pissed she walked straight into a table and almost fell over. It really hurt me to see her like that. In fact, it upset me so much that I just kept to myself for a week afterwards. I finally went over the edge. I was fed up with prison, fed up with myself, and fed up with life.

I thought that I would be better off in a strip cell – out of the way. My head felt terrible. I've always suffered headaches when I've been anxious about something, but this time I couldn't control it.

It was late one night. I got out of bed; the place was silent. I covered myself in black boot polish from head to toe. I was bollock starkers and black as soot. I then smashed a glass bottle over my head. The blood trickled down my face and neck. Fuck knows to this day why I did it.

Next, I secured the broken bottle on to a broom handle like a spear. Then I tied a red rag around my forehead and another around my right bicep. I lay on my bed, naked, waiting for the morning to arrive. The sooner my door unlocked, the better.

Long Lartin has electric doors. As soon as I heard that click I would be ready. My landing had 16 of us on it, but the whole wing held 90 cons. I knew that the new day would bring insanity at its best. I felt strange. My head was still throbbing. There was blood and black polish all over me and my bed. I thought about the outcome; would I hurt anyone? Would I damage anything? Would anyone try to stop me? I had no detailed plans. All I wanted to do was walk out of my cell with my spear. Long Lartin was about to explode!

My door clicked. It was time.

I walked out and headed straight towards the screws. One spotted me soon enough. His face turned white and he ran to the alarm bell. I began to run, too.

Then the cons spotted me. A lot of them legged it back into their cells. I was too confused to know what to do, so I bolted into the association room. I picked up the TV and slung it at the bars. It exploded. Then I tore out the lights and smashed about 40 chairs before tearing the door off its hinges. I smashed out the giant plate-glass windows. Some of the glass stuck into my feet and I even cut some of my body, but I was beyond caring. It felt great!

The cons were all shouting and by now the screws were dressed in riot gear. The wing was evacuated and I was in my glory. I ran into the next TV room and smashed up that one as well.

Nothing lasts for ever. It was soon all over. The riot mob came in and I was put into the strong box and given an injection. I slept for days; I was now a very depressed man. Pain had entered my world once again – mental pain – and I was close to the edge. The danger signs were creeping in. After a few days in the box, I came out to shower and clean myself up.

Joe Whitty, the Governor, had a slight problem.

I had to face the Board of Visitors for all the damage that I had done. That meant more lost remission and more punishment. I was getting sick of it and, to top it all, Kelly-Anne had phoned the prison, pissed-up, crying and shouting. I slammed down the phone and I told the screws that if she rang again they should tell her that I had been moved.

It was about this time that I thought about my life very carefully. I came to the conclusion that I was definitely not right in the head. Either I had to slow down and think, or I would be on my way back to Broadmoor.

Joe Whitty decided to give me another chance up on the wing. He was all on his own with this decision; nobody was looking forward to my return. It was at this time that a TV documentary was being made in

Long Lartin. I was asked by Danny Foy if I would like to go on it. I agreed straight away – what could I lose? Jimmy Boyle had been invited to join us. I already knew a lot of Jim's pals but I had never met him. Ron and Reg always spoke highly of him, as did many others. Jimmy had served his time and had made good his freedom. He always spoke up well for us lads, which we all respected. He got a life sentence and he served 15 years. Jimmy went through the system and got his home leaves and weekends out so he could prepare himself for his release.

Up to my 69 days of freedom in 1987, I'd spent one year less than Jimmy inside ... and I'd then got released from a top-secure jail as a high-risk prisoner. No preparation, no rehabilitation. Little, if any, hope.

Kate Akester also attended this televised forum. Kate was my solicitor at the time. I was asked to speak up, which I did. All in all, it was a very worthwhile cause, as it opened some eyes.

I upset Joe Whitty, though, as I held up some posters to say that the Birmingham Six were innocent – and so was Alan Byrne.

Soon after all this, a filthy rapist upset me. He was getting too familiar with me. I went into the showers with a pair of scissors and put them up to his throat. I told him that if he didn't move out of the wing that day I would stab him. He begged me not to hurt him and bleated that he would move straight away. I said to him, 'You weren't scared when you raped that old lady, were you?' With that I kicked him in the bollocks and left him in the shower. I had to fight a strong urge, because at that moment I wanted to kill him.

I could tell that I was starting to become ill again. The nonce moved that day. Nothing came of it.

Just after this incident, I decided enough was enough. I fancied taking a roof off! A roof was just my cup of tea. Perhaps I should have had a career as a steeple-jack!

Unfortunately they were not very good, the roofs at Long Lartin. They were all flat, only three storeys high, and very difficult to get up. So many people had tried this route before that they'd put barbed wire on the pipes and on the roof.

I spotted a way up but I knew I would need some assistance. I don't usually get anyone else involved in my plans, but this time I had no choice. So I asked. The con I approached wasn't keen, but he agreed.

Now this first stage was all arranged, I could work on the next part of my plan. I would need food, water, blankets and a rope. This protest was going to be non-violent, just a peaceful roof protest.

The only thing was, I hadn't decided what to protest about!

I was sure that I could think of something once I was up there. I thought about 'Free Nelson Mandela' as there were a lot of protests going on about him at the time, but then I thought, Fuck it.

I'd do one demanding: 'Free the Twins'. They deserved it. Yeah, I'd do it for Ron and Reg!

So my plan swung into action. I knew how I was going to get up and I had the material I needed – I just needed the break. I prayed that it would come soon ... it would be a blinder!

A bit later I was going down to the water boiler to fill my flask, ready to be locked in for the night, when I saw young Mark Barnes coming towards me. I could see that he was upset.

Mark was only 22 and to be crying in a long-term jail, where you mix with murderers, bank robbers and terrorists, just doesn't happen. (Not in the open, anyway.) I got him safely to his cell. I think he was very near to having a breakdown. I've seen enough in the asylums to know a breakdown when I see one.

Tears were pouring down his face. It was sad to see. This is what the system does to you. What the fuck was a kid like him doing in a prison like this?

I told him to pull himself together and not to lose heart. I believe he had girlfriend troubles. I told him to get into bed and said I would get him a cup of tea. I felt very concerned about the boy so I told Johnny Bowden. John was clever like that. He went to see the boy and then he went to see the Prison Officer in charge. I don't know what was said, but I made it clear to every screw that if Mark Barnes hurt himself that night they would have trouble with me. I went to my cell and banged up for the night, but my mind was still on that poor lad.

About half-an-hour after everyone had banged up, I heard a crash of glass and Mark crying out loudly. His cell was more or less opposite mine so I dived out of bed and shouted to him: 'What's up, mate?'

There was another crash of glass and more crying. Fucking hell.

I started to bang my door, then everyone was banging theirs. The screws went in and took Mark to the hospital. He had cut his wrists. I lay in silence for the rest of the night, just thinking about it all … not just about this incident, but about the whole fucking system. I knew that he was very near to a breakdown and if I had been a screw I would have taken him to the hospital before he had had a chance to hurt himself, not *after*. Any silly fool could see that he was upset. I really felt my head thumping against my temples. This was a bad sign for me. I jumped out of bed and smashed my fist into the door.

'You bastards, tomorrow you'll get it.'

I never slept all night, as I felt so bad. I felt tension, pain and anxiety – and my plans were being jeopardised. I felt that I had made a bad mistake by warning the screws that I would get them if Mark hurt himself. They might now put me in the block before the others got unlocked. It really surprised me when nothing like that happened. My door clicked open and I walked to Mark's cell. I could see the broken glass and the blood. This upset me more. There was tension in the air and I knew the screws were watching me. I stopped and looked them in the face and their eyes darted away.

Inside, I was fuming. I went back to my cell to collect my water bowl and I snapped. I shot down to the hot plate, where the breakfast had just arrived, and I picked up the porridge urn and hit the nearest screw with it. I punched the next one, and the rest of them ran to the office and locked themselves in. I then smashed up the whole recess. I pulled sinks off the walls, pipes off the walls. I went mad. I picked up a two-foot lead pipe and used it to smash up the hot plate. I broke a security camera and then I made my way down the landing where the known sex-cases were. I caught one of them in his cell and, as he ran out, I gave it to him over his crust. He fell on to the floor and crawled off. I then saw another sex-case and hit him as well. All the others were banged up, like the filthy rats they are. I wrecked their place as well.

The riot mob were standing by. Then the Governor arrived and I slung a whole urn of hot tea at him. Fortunately for him, he moved a bit lively. I didn't know what I was doing – I was completely out of control. I only found out years later the extent of the damage I had done that day.

When I had cooled down, big Albert Baker, Johnny Bowden and Johnny Walker all told the screws not to send in the riot squad. They took control themselves and walked me to the block. They were three good pals. When they had left, the screws put me in the box. I covered myself in a blanket and cut myself off from both worlds, the inside and the out.

This was it. I believed that this was now the end for me. I was convinced that I would soon be on my way back to the asylums, and that I would never see daylight as a free man again.

It felt as if I hadn't even been to sleep when they all piled into my cell. They put me into a body-belt and walked me to the waiting van. I was naked and on my way to the unknown. I asked them if I was going to an asylum.

'No,' they answered. 'You're going to Bristol.'

The van backed right up against the block door. The screws were there waiting and they took me straight to the strong box. I was still in the body-belt, hands manacled by my sides, and I was still naked.

That first night, a screw came to my door. 'Charlie, your wife Kelly-Anne has rung. She says she loves you.'

I shouted back at him, 'Who's Kelly-Anne? Never heard of her.'

He walked away. I thought about Kelly-Anne that night. I thought about her past, who she really was and what she was. I came to one conclusion: whatever she was, she was all I had – and maybe the only sanity I had left.

The Governor came in the next day. He told me that I was being moved to a proper cell. He took me out and I had a nice shower, clean clothes, food, tea and a nice clean cell.

I was obviously on good order and discipline in this block and kept isolated for the next two months. During this time there were no upsets. I wrote a lot, read a lot and thought a lot. The charges eventually came through from Long Lartin: two assaults on screws, two assaults on cons, as well as smashing up the place. All I had to do now was sit and wait until they dealt with me.

In all my two months at Bristol, I don't think I even had one bad day, though I must confess I was getting fed up in my last week or two. I wanted a bit of excitement ... but I fought the urge and won. On 7 July 1989, I heard a vehicle backing up to the block. I looked out of my cell window and saw the Cat A van outside. Nobody got out except screws, so I knew it was for me. Seconds later, my door opened and I was on my travels once again.

It wasn't long before I was lying naked in my cell. The screws at Winson Green block had told me I was not allowed to wear my overalls. I told them that if they took them away, I would stay naked. Needless to say they took them – so for two days I stayed in my cell, starkers. They came to me with a deal: if I agreed to wear pyjamas, then they would allow me to have a medicine ball. I agreed, and I got a nice big ball.

I used to work out with the ball for an hour in their strong box. It was a bit stuffy, but I loved it. No con had ever had a medicine ball in this Brummie jail before, so I was very privileged. I only spent two weeks there, but I was treated OK.

I got my medicine ball at my next stop, Winchester, and trained hard. My first week or two in the block went peacefully, then I hit a bad patch. I needed to escape the rut I was in. The exercise yard in the block was only small – more like a cage. Even the roof was a steel net which had a padlocked hatch in it. If I could smash the padlock off, I would be able to get up on to the roof. This would definitely cheer me up!

My plan seemed easy: climb up the pipe, grab the steel-wired roof, hang on by one arm and smash the padlock off ... get through the hatch ... and up I go!

It sounded simple enough, but it's never that easy. I needed a heavy instrument to smash the padlock, plus there were always a lot of screws out in the yard. I put my plan together one night, and the next day I was ready. I got hold of a PP9 battery and went out into the yard.

As soon as I hit the yard I was up the pipe and in seconds I was hanging on to the cage. The screws pushed the alarm bell and within seconds there were dozens of them below me. I managed to stick my feet into the gaps in the wire. I then got the battery out of my overalls and began to smash the padlock. I hit it so hard I cut my hand. It seemed like I was hanging on for ever. The bastard wouldn't snap!

Time was running out. With my hand cut up, and my other arm now 'dead', I had just enough strength to get down. It was a sad day, and a very embarrassing one for me. One that I would like to forget.

Soon after this incident, I really blew up.

It was a Sunday and I was reading *The News of the World* when my spy-hole opened. A con was at my door. He asked me for a light and I told him that I didn't smoke. He then told me that I was a tight fucker, and to give him my paper instead! This did it. I couldn't believe what I was hearing. I went to the door. It was a black con.

'Right, boy. I've got no matches, and this paper is my fucking paper, so fuck off.'

My head was throbbing now. He was an ignorant git. If he had asked nicely, I would have helped him out.

I was so upset. Violent urges kept coming over me. I couldn't get to him and this made me worse. I waited until it was time to slop out. Once I was out of my cell, I found him and poured my pot under his cell door. He went mad. I told him to lick it up – after all, bastards like him give me a bad name.

They moved him later that day but for a long time afterwards I was still mad about it … so out came the boot polish. I blacked up again.

I walked out for dinner, black as the ace of spades and completely naked. Everyone just stared in disbelief; no words were spoken.

Then I lost control. I slung some tables about and smashed my way into an office only to find a screw inside. I picked up a table and slung it at him but he ran out of the other door and escaped. I barricaded both doors and began reading my file. Then I tried to phone Jack and Kelly-Anne, but I couldn't get an outside line. Through the office door I could see there were a dozen screws, some governors, and the riot mob with their helmets and shields.

That fucker who upset me had a lot to answer for. This was all his fault.

I walked out with the phone in my hand and shouted out, 'It's for you-hoo!'

They all kept their distance. The Governor said, 'Go back to your cell, Charlie.' I walked back and closed the door.

Later they came in and injected me. I slept for a day-and-a-half. My head was becoming confused. I felt that it was time for a move.

By the time I arrived at Wandsworth block, in September 1989, I was the most moved prisoner in Britain. In fewer than 20 months I had been transferred 14 times. There seemed no end to it. Some moves were OK, others were deliberate attempts to annoy me. Visits were getting fewer and fewer and even letters were scarce. My whole world at this time was prison; I lived it, breathed it, and felt I would surely die in it.

Prison Officer Wells told me that I should start getting my head together or I'd end up going back to the asylum and never get out again. I did my training and I jogged every day. The next few weeks passed by peacefully. One good thing about that block was that there were new cons coming and going all the time. But I was always in cell 13 – it's now known as Bronson's quarters. Most nights I would cheer up the cons with a song. I'd get my chair and sing through the top of my door. They loved it. Some nights I used to think to myself, is prison all that bad? It was at such times that I had to check myself. That way of thinking had only one label – institutionalisation. Jesus Christ, I had to stop thinking like that. I wanted out! I did briefly get out, as I'll tell you later on. But more than 11 years after my first fears about institutionalisation, I am still locked away from the world.

It was still September 1989, and I was destined to have four more moves before Christmas. When I arrived at the block at Albany on the Isle of Wight, they put me in the block on good order and discipline. They told me that I would be here for two months and then I would move on. I was handed a medicine ball and a nice routine, so it was up to me. Albany screws always treated me with respect. I never had any trouble with them. They used to let my friend Sammy McCarthy down to see me from the wing. Sammy was the gym orderly for years. He used to be a brilliant boxer – he was British Flyweight Champion years ago. I love the guy. He was serving 18 years for robbery. He never complained; he just got on with it. He still weighs the same today as he did over 30 years ago when he won the title. I'd rate Sammy as one of the greatest men I've ever met. He would come down and see me on one of my bad days and leave me feeling happy again. A story from Sammy was like a breath of fresh air. Thanks, Sammy!

Every now and again an old injury would play me up. Some years back some screws cracked a vertebra in my neck, and every once in a while I'm in agony from it. On this occasion, I couldn't move it at all. They took me to Parkhurst prison hospital for an X-ray, then brought me straight back. It seemed to be in the winter that I suffered more and the doctors seemed to think that it might be arthritis.

Kelly-Anne came to visit. She looked well, but then it was rumoured that she had been visiting another con in another prison. If it's true it's always worse to be told by an outsider. Secrets are usually kept well hidden from the people nearest and dearest to you, but not from those who mean less. Anyone in a failed relationship will tell you that; the girl abandons the boy, he tries to work out why, but her girlfriends knew months before. I've often tried to keep the truth from my family. It would be hard for them to know what it is really like for me inside. I used to tell my mum that I spent my days watching TV and plays, that I was a great gardener and all the governors vied for my services, which is why I was moved so often.

With Kelly-Anne, I started to lose my trust in her. She was now more of a mystery than she ever was. I didn't need her lies. I'd had enough lies in these places; I didn't need them from outside as well.

I knew that I was coming to the end of my time there and it wouldn't be long before they moved me – I just didn't know when. The big day came on 22 November. The ferry ride was a bit choppy but I felt good. The New Year was only weeks away and things were looking up.

When I got to reception at Gartree, they told me that I was going up on the wing. I was made up! Christmas was coming up, a New Year was ahead, and I was out of solitary. What more can a con ask for?

Once I was up on A Wing, I met some old mates of mine. There was Ron Brown, Dale Roberts, Joe O'Connor, Dennis Campbell, Harry Roberts, Charlie Magee and Paddy Hill. I soon settled in. I went to a gym class, I ran at the weekends, I did my own cooking and had my pint of hooch.

The first incident occurred in the bath-house. I was having a bath and some loon came in and upset me by shaking his mat and covering me in dust. I pulled him about it, but he just laughed. I put a right hook on his jaw. A few days later, I heard that he was out to stab me, so I pulled him again. He denied it, so I gave him the benefit of the doubt and told him to move wings or I would stab him!

Then it happened. It was canteen day, the big day that we all looked forward to. It was my turn to go. I was going to buy sweets, stamps, toiletries and eggs, but as I walked over a screw grabbed my arm. I spun round and hit him in the jaw. Another screw pushed the bell. I was in trouble. Dozens of screws were running towards me like fucking lunatics. I turned and walked towards them … and they all ran past me! Obviously they didn't realise at this time that it was me. But as soon as they found out they came running back. They took me to the block; I was gutted. The screw got sick leave, and I got the block. My remission was taken and I was fined. It just wasn't worth the effort of smacking him. I should have learnt this years ago, but it seems I never will. Maybe I don't want to.

I spent my Christmas in the block with Steve Waterman who had just come down from the Leicester unit. It was good to be with Steve. Afterwards, I was put back on A Wing but it was never the same. The screws were now edgy. I could see it in their eyes – they were very tense.

Harry 'Hate 'Em All' Johnson arrived. Harry had cut George Ince in the 1970s for playing around with Dolly Kray whilst Charlie Kray was inside. He also stuck a mug into John McVicar's face. Harry was nicknamed 'Hate 'Em All' years ago … he hated every fucker! I met Harry in 1974 and I loved the guy. He was fearless; he would fight anyone. He was only 5ft 6in, but very stocky. Ron and Reg loved him, too, as Harry is a character. Unfortunately, the years inside caught up with Harry and sent him a bit crazy. I personally could relate to his strange ways, but a lot couldn't. In his later years, he lost more fights than he won, but for me 'Hate 'Em All' was a legend. He died soon after.

The inevitable had to happen; 1990 didn't last too long before I blew up. It started before breakfast when some fat, useless screw 'forgot' to open my cell. How can anybody forget a Cat A prisoner? I banged on my door. The fat twat opened it and I chinned him. He went down on the floor. Another screw pressed the bell and I hit him, too.

I was in trouble again ... big trouble! I then kicked the fat twat down the stairs and started to smash the wing up. Most of the cons were still in bed, others banged themselves up. I knew that I was going to blow up, but I went over the top as usual. I'm not sorry that I chinned the screws, but I shouldn't have smashed up the wing. My time was over at Gartree, maybe for good. I felt this time I would be certified insane again.

Once in the block, I learnt that Kelly-Anne had arrived to see me, but I was so depressed I refused to see her. I knew I was ill again. I knew that if I went on that visit I would lose control. It wasn't worth it.

The van arrived.

PRISON PRESS UP CHAMPION 1997

Certificate of Achievement

This certifies that

CHARLES BRONSON

Successfully completed One Thousand Seven Hundred and Twenty Seven Press ups in One Hour on The 30th March 1997 at H.M.P. LIVERPOOL

Special
Merit
Award

M. R. Blick   24/4/97
Signature   Date

M. Doyle   25-4-97
Signature   Date

R. Peak   25/4/97
Signature   Date

CHAPTER TEN

The cage at Durham hadn't changed since the last time I was there. These type of jails just don't change – they're brutal, dirty, smelly and medieval. I was getting a lot of unnecessary hassle from a small minority of screws and I knew that it wouldn't be long before I decked one of them.

After a couple of weeks there, they allowed me into a proper block cell. It was better than being locked away in a fucking cage.

Being caged is no joke, but it is funny-peculiar. Whenever I'd used violence against the system they moved me to the worst places – and I just got worse. So I found myself, in January 1990, in the Durham Cage, with the threat of what I'd have coming if I messed about. Didn't they realise? There was nothing more that they could do to me that hadn't already been done over the years – except kill me. I needed help ... and what I got was threats and incarceration.

Cliff Moody was in the block. He got life when he was 19 – he shot and killed a man. Cliff looked upon me as a father, and I used to spoil him like a son. I often bumped into him on my travels, as he was always being moved from block to block, forever on the move the same as me. Frankie Wilkinson arrived from the Hull Unit. His case was remarkable. He is an innocent man, yet he got life. Another man had confessed to the murder. It's a case that will never be buried, because Frank will never accept it. How can he?

One day, just as I was expecting, a screw went too far, so I punched his face in. The bell went. I was out in the caged exercise yard at the time, so they locked me in to wait for reinforcements. Frank Wilkinson was in the next cage, and he refused to go in until I went in. He's a loyal friend. We carried on with our exercise and when it was time to go in, there was a gauntlet of screws from the yard to my cell. I got back to my cell safely, only to find the Governor waiting for me. My door slammed shut.

Days later, the atmosphere was still tense. There was a screw who told me later that his idiot colleague deserved a slap. It turned out that the screw I'd hit wasn't too popular with the rest of his fellow screws, but it didn't do me any favours.

I went into myself for a spell after this because a young con called Hogan hanged himself. Jail deaths always affect me like that. What a waste of a young life. They just zip him up in a body bag and half-an-hour later the place is back to normal. Who gives a fuck? I do! I could smell death all around me. I knew I had to move or my head would go. When the Governor did his daily rounds, I told him, 'Move me, I'm sick of your jail.' I was gone in days.

I was glad to arrive at Parkhurst, but sad to hear that they were putting me in the block for two months. It now seemed that no place was prepared to accept me for more than a month or two. It looked grim, but I started to believe that it was all fate, that it was all meant to be. Mad Jacko was there then; it was always good to see him – he's always good for a laugh. The 'Screaming Skull' was also there. Nothing changes. Even the block screws seemed to stay the same. Tom Cotton was still there. He was a good screw who I respected a lot. It's sad that they can't all be like Tom – it would be a happier life for me as all these moves and all the violence is no way to live.

I worked out a routine and stuck by it for two months. I coped OK, but I had something planned, something that had never been done before!

On 30 May 1990, my door opened early. 'Come on, Charlie, you're away!'

I came out of my cell to slop out and clocked all the screws. It was going to be difficult but I had to take a chance. I gathered my stuff together and we left the block at about 7.30am. As we left, a dog-handler joined us. Shit! This could ruin my plans!

I made the break and ran as fast as I could. I leapt up on to a wall and straight on to a roof about 12ft high. I'd made it! It was now 7.45am and the cons were still locked up. I was directly under B Wing, landing three, so I gave them a wake-up call!

I started singing at the top of my voice, 'Please release me ...' Yeah! Set me free!

In no time at all, they started appearing at the windows. It was a classic! The Governor, security, they all turned up to hear my demands. I told them that I

wanted to see my friend 'Gi Gi' (Valerio Viccei). I told
them either they let me see him or I wasn't coming
down – and if they didn't hurry up about it, I would
strip the roof of all its tiles. It was agreed that if I
came down, I could see him before I was moved to my
next prison. But I would have to have the cuffs on. I
agreed but I made it clear that if it was all a trap,
then the screws would have a rocky journey in the
van. They gave me their word, so I shouted at the
cons, 'I'm going to see Gi Gi!'

I came down from the roof and I was allowed to see
my pal. He looked well, fit, strong and healthy. We
spoke about the future and I left feeling better for it. I
probably gave Gi Gi a memory for life; who else gets
on a roof to see a pal? With this I was put in the van
and away we went. This ferry ride was becoming a
recurring theme in my life. One day I have got to
make this trip unchained and free.

We stopped off at Leicester Jail for lunch; this was
another long journey. I think that I went as far as
they could possibly send me, all the way up north to
Frankland top-security prison, County Durham. By
the time we got there, my legs were stiff. They were
all waiting for me, but I also got a big surprise – they
told me I was going on to the wing. That made me feel
a lot better. They put me on B Wing. I knew loads of
cons in this jail but, sadly, as I stepped on to B Wing, I
knew that it wasn't for me. It was too intense, too
closed in and claustrophobic. I wasn't used to these
modern jails. The whole design fucks my head up.

They gave me a cell a door away from Micky Reilly.
He was hundreds of miles away from his wife and
kids, but he still found time to cheer me up. I started
going to the gym with him, but nothing ever lasts
with me. Some soppy screw upset me, so I told him to
stay clear of me. John Dunford also told him to fuck
off away from me before I got upset. But then the

screw did a stupid thing. He started taking down names! He fucking knew who I was but he still asked me my name! There is always one, and he was it. I had to stop going to the gym because I was getting visions of me killing him with a big weight. So I started training on the wing. I did press-ups, sit-ups, squats and some running. I ended up with half-a-dozen young cons training with me.

Unfortunately it didn't last. We got a bit out of hand and we all ended up over in the block. We'd been upsetting the other cons by running all over the wing, plus I pushed three screws out of our way.

Eventually, we were all let back on the wing, but I knew that I was heading for a brainstorm. Micky Reilly could see the signs, too. I missed Jack and Kelly-Anne, and I was too far away from home to have a visit. I was pissed off. For days I was on edge.

Brian Thorogood asked me what was up. I told him, 'Today's the day, Brian. I've fucking had my lot!' We all went out on the yard. There were about 200 of us, but I walked alone. I told the lads that I didn't want any company. Then I saw my target! It was a man with a beard, wearing a suit. He was walking towards me. I didn't know who the fuck he was – I had never set eyes on him before – but I knew he was for me!

I ran – faster and faster. Seconds before I grabbed him, he spotted he was in trouble. I slung him over my shoulder and legged it like hell. All 200 cons were cheering. It was total insanity at its best. I ran towards my wing, but I lost my hold on him and he fell and banged his head. The bells were ringing, screws were running … I was trapped. I grabbed him in a strangle-hold and shouted out, 'Anyone comes near me and I'll snap his spinal cord!' They all knew that I meant it, and I knew I was fucked up – trapped beyond return. But whether it lasted one minute, one hour or one day, I was King again!

I dragged him into B Wing. There were screws everywhere. I kicked open the office door and dragged him in. Still holding his neck from behind, I sat him in a chair. This was my day all right; it definitely wasn't his! My mind was racing at 100mph. I couldn't think straight. I had no demands, not yet anyway.

Andy Russell and John Dunford came in. They told me that the man that I had hostage was the Deputy Governor. I'd get more years and it just wasn't worth it, they reasoned. This was all going around my head and I decided that they were right. I had definitely flipped my lid. I let him go and walked out with Andy and Johnny.

The screws never came near us. We finished our exercise as if nothing had happened. After exercise I went back to my wing. After everyone was banged up, they came for me mob-handed and took me to the block. A few of my old pals were down there: Dave Andrews, Dave Taylor, and big Woody the biker.

Days later, the van was ready and I was on another long journey. I'm only glad that I didn't have to pay for the petrol or the ferry ticket! As soon as I arrived at Albany, they told me that I would be staying for about two months. They gave me a medicine ball and I got on with it. My routine was good here, so time just passed me by.

I got my first piece of bad news. Terry Jeffries had died. He had just completed a ten-year sentence, went outside and died a week later. It just doesn't make sense to me. Then Tony Steel and Paul Ross arrived from Parkhurst. They had both been up on the roof and got a good kicking for it. I made a statement to their solicitors to say that I saw their injuries when they arrived. I lost my head that day and smashed up the block. I demanded that they get a photo done of their injuries – they got it. Soon after that, I heard of two more deaths – Alex Kessen and Graham Young both died within a day of each other in Parkhurst. Alex had killed another con in the '70s in Maidstone and got life for it. He had been caged pretty much all his life. He was a lost soul like me.

Everyone I knew hated Graham Young – and they had good reason to – but I felt sorry for him. I'll explain why. I've lived amongst the insane for years. I can smell insanity, and Graham Young was one of the insane. He was sent to Broadmoor when he was 14 years old for poisoning his family, killing two of them. He spent 14 years in Broadmoor, then was released – only to poison his workmates. He was given life imprisonment. It was obvious to any rational man that Graham Young was mad. All that prison did was keep him drugged out of his head. His life was a constant daze. He was a very dangerous man but he should have been in an asylum, not a prison. I always felt sorry for him as I know the long-term effects of isolation. It's as painful as any form of torture. Years of emptiness killed Graham Young.

My time at Albany flew by with few problems, then nothing short of a miracle happened! I was called into the office and they told me to forget what had happened with me taking the Deputy Governor hostage at Frankland. I knew that I had to be careful from now on. This was a warning to me to slow up ... or else. I took note.

I was on the move right after that, but only a few hundred yards up the road. The psycho wing at Parkhurst was like a magnet to me. A lot of my old pals had moved on from C Unit, but others had taken their places. George Heath was now there, into his twelfth year and still on Cat A. A bloke called Cheeseman was still there. We didn't get on; he'd killed a young patient by the name of Alan Francis in Broadmoor. It was a senseless killing. In fact, most of the cons on this unit were ex-Broadmoor. This place was for the untreatable and the unpredictable. For me, it was like a trip back into the world of madness. Not a day went by when something didn't go on in this unit. You needed eyes in the back of your skull. Most of these guys were very dangerous. I stuck with George and another pal, Fat Joe. I made stews and curries. We lived well. I worked out hard; I was getting my act together and I felt a tiny bit of hope returning. I even watched a bit of TV, which is almost unheard of for me.

Big Chris Moody, all 21 stone of him, nearly landed me in trouble one day. He'd got upset over something and tore up a poster of Elvis Presley that I had given him. When I asked him why, he threw a punch at me. I ducked and punched him back. I watched him closely after that.

The screws there wrote out reports about us every day and most of them were crap. There were few screws that I spoke to. I didn't trust them and they didn't trust me. I wished that Mick Connell was there – he was one of the best screws that I had met. I pulled one or two screws on their own and told them that I despised their guts. I could see it in their faces that they wanted me off C Unit as they were afraid. I told them not to talk to me and I wouldn't talk to them.

On the exercise yard, George would help me with my work-outs. I'd run with him on my shoulders and squat with him on my back. He loved helping me keep fit. We were out there one day, when I had a run in with a con who told me he was going to grass someone up. I told him to fuck off away from me – I can't stand grasses. Later, he pushed little George Heath away from the water boiler as he was trying to fill his flask. I saw George was upset and asked him why. I steamed into this con's cell, 'Right you bastard! Try pushing me!' He went white. I smashed

him in the mouth and walked out. That was it for me
– another ferry trip awaited.

Prison Officer Wells was waiting for me once again.
Cell 13 at Wandsworth was ready. Sometimes it felt
like I'd never been away. It's a wonder that there isn't
a groove in the floor of cell 13. I've walked thousands
of miles in that cell. Sometimes I would pace that cell
for eight hours a day just waiting for time to pass me
by, wishing my days away. The only excitement was
the prison scandal – who'd pulled the big job, who was
in and who'd gone out. It's almost all there is to keep
you going.

I was well pleased eight weeks later when I arrived
at Full Sutton and they said I was going up on the
wing. It was the week before Christmas 1990 and I
could see some of my old pals again. Freddie Foreman
was now there, a lovely man and so genuine it's
unreal. God bless you, Fred. Eddie Richardson was
also there. Poor Eddie had just got 25 years but he
never moaned, just got on with it.

It was there that I met Peter Hale. Peter must be
the best artist in prison. He's also very heavily into
Buddhism. I learnt more from Pete than I've learnt
from any other single human being. We became like
brothers; we trained together, ate together and
painted together. I was privileged enough to see him
create some of his best paintings there.

Charlie Magee arrived, as did Kevin Brown,
Andy Dunford, Ray Johnson, Squeak, Billy Adams,
Dennis Wheeler, Elle, Roy Ivers, Alec Sears, Vince
Donnley and Roy Walsh ... a right good bunch of
guys. The jail was getting better. Big Albert Baker
was on my wing, so we always had a bucket of hooch
for weekends.

The first one to upset me was a con who pulled the
plug off our iron just for the fun of it. I gave him a pull
and told him to grow up. The next day he pulled the

TV aerial out and hid it. I hit him so hard his ancestors must have felt it!

Then I was walking around the yard with Harry Duggan when a pile of visitors, all official people, walked out to see our yard. They stood there staring at us walking around.

I said to Harry, 'I'm not having this. I'm not a bleeding monkey in a poxy zoo.'

So I ran over and grabbed a geezer by his neck ... and I had myself another hostage! I dragged him across the yard, out of view.

The rest of them ran in squealing, 'Rupert's been grabbed! Somebody help!'

I had this Rupert in a Japanese strangle-hold. I whispered in his ear, 'Don't stare at me and Harry again, it's not nice.'

I let him go after five minutes, and he promised never to gawp again. It turned out that Rupert was a trainee probation officer. I was put in the block and lost 120 days' remission. Governor Smith then sent me back on the wing as it was Christmas. I was being given another chance. Unfortunately, it was a phone call from Kelly-Anne that ruined my Christmas. She told me about some guy and I slammed the phone down. I went to my cell and banged up. I felt dangerous.

After Christmas, it was a crazy time. Full Sutton was like a madhouse; there was always something happening – fights, suicide, cell fires. There were some right old characters. It was quite exciting, and I actually saved a couple of lives. One was a con who'd slashed his wrists, the other was old Olly.

Olly was in his sixties, a good footballer in his day, but he had terribly bad feet. We'd sit down with a pot of tea and a slice of apple pie and swap stories, but one day his feet were so bad he was almost in tears. 'Chaz,' he said. 'I can't handle it any more.'

Fuck me! He showed me his feet – they were virtually deformed, big bunions and toes like sausages, all swollen. Poor old Olly, I thought. If that's what football does to you, I'll stick to boxing!

Anyway, I shot up to the office lively and asked them, 'Oi! Have you seen Olly's feet? Help the poor man!' They said he was down to see the chiropodist.

'Well, make fucking sure he is,' I said.

A few days later, I was playing snooker on D Wing when every fucker seemed to be shouting, 'Fire!'

I shot around and smoke was pouring out of Olly's cell. He'd been desperate and had set fire to it. No one had had the sense to kick the door in – so I did. It was wedged up, not locked. I ran in. Olly was coughing his guts up; I grabbed him, put him over my shoulder and ran around to a pal's cell, away from the smoke. The screws came and I told them, 'Don't worry! All's safe now.'

They said he needed to go to hospital.

'Fuck off,' I said. 'He will – when he's had a nice cup of tea!'

A week later I got an award from the Number 1 Governor, Mr Staples. But then I chinned a couple of screws and got moved again, back to Parkhurst, and was banged up in solitary.

I pulled one of the bosses there and pointed out that I'd recently saved a life.

He said, 'Yes, Bronson, I did hear. But it was probably you who set fire to the cell.'

You just can't fucking win, can you?

There were good times and bad times at Full Sutton in the months before I went back to the island. A con called Micky Jamieson hanged himself, which saddened me. It was at this time that I met Bob Mapplebeck who was a pastor. He was a lovely man and has since become a life-long friend. Bob was an outside pastor who came into Full Sutton to see anyone who wished to see him. I went to see him with Albert Baker and I must say that Bob is one of the greatest men I have ever met.

It was now 1991 and the years were rolling by. I was super-fit but I was really very much alone. I hadn't seen my parents since 1987. It was my own decision; I'd told them that I was fed up of seeing them inside, I wanted to see them next as a free man. I explained all this to Bob Mapplebeck, who really helped me with meaningful words of wisdom. I saw Jesus in a new light. I'd always believed in something, but I didn't know what.

All too soon I was back in the block, where my problems escalated. I'm not a defeatist, but I know I'm a born loser. I just won't learn. This time a recorded letter of mine went astray and I got very upset over it. I ran out of my cell completely naked. I'd been half-way through a shave when a screw opened my door and I just flipped. I shoved him on his arse and ran into the office. I slung another screw out and then barricaded myself up with the Senior Officer still inside. It was actually only then that I realised I was naked. The bells went and the screws arrived, but they couldn't get in. The SO let me make a call to Kelly-Anne, and she cooled me down.

The next time I blew up was when I was being unlocked for a shower. I walked out and – bang – I hit the screw. The heavy mob put me in the box. I later ended back up on the wing but I had a feeling that it wouldn't be for long.

I got back to my training and I hung around with Peter Hale a lot. We both started meditating. Pete taught me how to breathe, relax and be a better man. I felt that I was winning. I amazed everyone, even myself. Then … crash! It was all over. I was finished.

It happened on a Saturday night. Some cons were shouting and singing and I just wasn't in the mood.

I was trying to switch off from it all when somebody shouted my name. I still wasn't interested, so I ignored them. Then someone shouted, 'Bronson's a mug.' I shot out of bed and told them to say it to my face in the morning. Words were exchanged. I vowed that I would be ready in the morning – and ready I was!

There were three other cons involved. I told them to meet me in the dining hall and be ready for action. I shut my window and everything went silent. The whole wing heard this going on – and they all knew that I would be waiting for these prats. I slept very little that night. I was preparing for battle.

At about 5.00am I got up. Out came the boot polish, and on it went. I was black from head to toe. I then put on a pair of overall bottoms and tucked them into my boots. I tore up a sheet and made a bandana and a bicep wrap. I was ready, and I was looking forward to a real tear-up!

It was soon 6.00am. One-and-a-half hours to go. I started limbering up, stretching and doing press-ups and sit-ups. My heart was pumping. I felt better, fresh, alert and ready. I was ready to die! It wasn't long before it was 7.20am. I was like a greyhound waiting to sprint away. Then 7.25am. Come on, come on. My adrenalin was pumping … 7.30am … I could hear the screws unlocking and coming closer to my door.

As soon as my door opened, I ran out and punched the screw. He fell against the wall. I ran to the dining hall and pushed a big table against the door. The three cons always arrived from the other end of the dining hall – but they hadn't arrived yet!

I was ready to explode. The cons hadn't come. The screws came in. I picked up a broom and smashed one over the head. I hit another one in the stomach. My head was pounding. It wasn't the screws I wanted to fight, it was the three bad-mouthed scumbags who'd upset me.

Roy Ivers and Alec Sears calmed me down. It was obvious by then that the cowards were not coming and I was bang in trouble again. They took me to the block and put me in the box. I was a sick man again. I was sure that I was now going to be sent to the madhouse. As it was, the screws that I'd hit were decent ones. They'd always been good to me and now I'd repaid them by doing this. I felt bad over my actions. I was sure that they would now put me in the biggest hole possible; no fucker would give me a break after all this. I lost more time and got more punishment. Lots were upset that it had happened, especially Bob Mapplebeck and Albert Baker. But I was pleased when the van turned up for me. I needed to move away. I didn't care where to – a box, a cage – who gave a fuck any more?

They put me straight in the block at Parkhurst. Mr Marriott was the Governor and I rated him as a one-off. He'd done more for Parkhurst than any Governor has done in 20 years. I personally liked him as a fellow human being. I've met all the governors, the good, the bad and the ugly. Mr Marriott was definitely ugly, but a good man. Sadly, he later got sacked over the infamous escape of two IRA suspects in the mid-'90s and has now died. He and the Deputy Governor, Ken Rogers, were working on me going on to M Wing, as long as I behaved. I did control myself and made it up to the wing, where I met up with a load of my pals. There was Pete Pesato, Tommy Hole, Vic Dark, Keith Richie, Big H, Noel Gibson, Mickie Mo and Dave Andrews. I was also allowed to see Gi Gi for a visit every week.

Kelly-Anne visited and we had a photo taken. We seemed to be getting back together. I was also starting to get my head back together once more. The lads all helped me along and I really did well for a week or two. I really felt that I could make it. Then I just went strange.

Something crept inside me. My mind went from sparkling to being just sort of dull. I felt fed up with prison: it was beginning to eat away inside me again. I felt that the system was fucking me up. I'd get terrible feelings of bitterness and an overpowering urge to explode.

One night I sat alone in my cell, thinking. I was thinking about Kelly-Anne, Jack, Mum, Dad, my son and Loraine. I felt trapped. I had to get out of the cell. I couldn't breathe. I knew I was about to flip my lid.

I got on the bell and a screw came. It was big Dan Shepherd, a screw I'd known for years. He asked me what was up and I told him that I had to empty my pot, but he said he couldn't let me out as he had no keys. I went mental. I told him that I needed to get out desperately as I needed to go to the toilet. He went off and within half-an-hour he came back with a load of other screws. The key went in the lock and my door opened.

I ran out, smashed a bottle, and told them I'd kill any fucker who came near me. They all ran.

I had M Wing all to myself. Every con on the island was banged up – except me. I was unlocked and I was staying unlocked! Fuck Parkhurst, fuck the lot of them! I was the Governor again!

I made my way up the stairs to the top landing and I began to destroy it. I smashed all the lights, tore out the recess and smashed up the screws' office. All the cons were by now awake, shouting, screaming and banging on their doors. I could also hear other wings shouting and banging. This went on all night. I was having a riot on my own and it was great!

The heavy mob came in accompanied by Mr Marriott. I was sitting on top of a demolished office roof. We must have spoken for hours and it must have done some good as I came down. They handcuffed me and then took me to the block and put me in the box.

I stayed in the box for weeks and it was while I was in there that the saddest thing ever to occur in Parkhurst happened. Tommy Hole was on M Wing and his son had arrived in Parkhurst from Full Sutton while I was in the box. Tommy went into his cell only to find his own son hanging. It wasn't until I came out of the box that I found out about it. I was shattered, devastated. I had actually been in Full Sutton with the boy. I cried my eyes out that day. I sent Tommy a cross that Kelly-Anne had given me – it was all I had. I still can't get it out of my head, and I never will. They held a church service for Tommy and his friends, but it was the day my van arrived. I was on my way, sad and empty.

Was it all a dream? Had I imagined it all? The boot polish, Olly's cell fire, the death of Tommy Hole's son, and my explosion in Parkhurst? Maybe I'd been in cell 13 all the time. The same old, familiar cell. The same deal. Back in purgatory, back in Wandsworth.

The weeks flew by, and then I was hit by what seemed like a sledgehammer blow. It was something I knew, deep down, would come sooner or later. Perhaps I'd just escaped facing up to it until now. On 6 September 1991 my Uncle Jack Cronin died. I idolised the man. I'd promised him that I would one day be out to buy him a pint. I couldn't even do that, let alone say goodbye.

I didn't find out until the next day. Prison Officer Wells came in to tell me. It cut me up bad. I felt hurt and empty. Life would never be the same again. I asked the Governor to let me go to the funeral and my family bombarded the Home Office with requests to let me go. The answer came the day before Jack was buried. The answer was no. The reason they gave – I was too dangerous. This was a man who I had idolised all my life, and I couldn't even go to his funeral.

For days I couldn't eat, I couldn't sleep. I didn't want to do anything.

Something strange did happen, though. Hours after Jack died, I was lying in my cell when I felt something move. I focused my eyes. It was a bird, a starling, sitting on a shelf by my window. Now, outside my window was a cage with a small hole in it, so that is obviously how it had got in. I'd never seen one before in all the time I had been in prison. Was this an omen, sent to let me know that there was life after death? Was it Jack sending me a last message? God bless you, Jack. Please God, love him.

I pulled myself together. Kelly-Anne came to see me; she had taken it badly, too. She loved Jack as much as I did. We were both lost. My head was in pieces.

The next day I decided to smash the place apart. I'd get on the roof and wreck it. I'd do it for Jack.

Then I would jump off the roof and join him.

Once I got into the exercise yard, I jumped up on a window and pulled myself up to a pipe. From the pipe I climbed up until I got to a piece of tin which was like an umbrella bolted to the wall to try and stop people getting on the roof. I was convinced that I could smash it off. I hit it with my fists, my head and my shoulders for a good half-hour. It drained all my strength until I had none left. It was useless. I came down to scores of waiting screws. It was a roof that I had dreamt of pulling apart, but it wasn't to be. I was never the same after losing Jack and the screws knew it.

Fuck the rats in the Home Office. They are more ruthless than any criminal I have ever met.

Eleven days after Jack's death, I was ghosted off to Albany on the Isle of Wight, where I was put in a cell next to Micky Reilly. He'd just had a bashing in

Frankland Jail and was sporting a lovely black eye. But thanks to Micky I lifted out of my depression and got back into training. I was still very bitter, but when Charlie Magee arrived we all had sing-songs through our windows. We basically all kept each other going – that's how it is in the punishment blocks.

Kelly-Anne had booked up to see me but didn't turn up. This didn't help me at all. I started to think things, like she'd had a smash or some other bad accident. My head was starting to get fucked again. The screws knew it and next thing the van arrived. It was to be a long journey. They told me I was off to Hull – it was 16 years since I'd been there, watching the Humber Bridge being built and the seagulls swooping by. But on the M1 the van exhaust fell off, so we ended up at Leicester for the night. We set off again the following morning and eventually drove over the bridge that I'd watched being constructed all that time ago from my prison cell. Memories came flooding back – some good, some bad.

I was told I would be staying for a couple of months. I asked for a medicine ball, which I got. I was soon into my training. The screws were good as gold. Lord Longford came to visit me along with Julian Broadhead, a probation officer and a good friend. Lord Longford is a man I respect. He condemns no one – that's just his way. He's visited me all over England and I've always liked him. He once wrote a book called *Prisoner or Patient* and did a section about my life. God bless you, Frank.

Just after this, Michael Showers arrived. He'd just got 20 years. It was 16 years ago that I swapped with Michael in this very jail. Life is a circle. You always meet up again. Vince Donnley arrived from Full Sutton and he cheered us all up as usual. At nights he used to play his rebel songs on his harmonica. We all loved Vince.

Kelly-Anne visited me a few times … nice visits. But now it seemed that she couldn't visit me unless she'd downed a few vodkas first. I saw the last of her on Christmas Eve, our final visit. She'd come into a lot of money from her grandfather's death. I told her straight, 'You've fucked my head up once too often.'

All in all, I was plodding on and sorting out my life. The Board of Visitors gave me 100 days' remission back and everything was starting to go my way.

Next door to the block was the special unit, where some of my pals were: Paul Ross, Jacko, Fred Low. But unfortunately I never made it over there.

The van was waiting and they told me that I was going to Winson Green block, Birmingham. Fuck this! I was sick of the constant moves. I stripped off and put a white sheet around myself. I then put a cross around my neck and picked up my Bible. Yeah, sure I was going – but I was going as the Pope!

It must have worked because I never got to kiss the concrete outside Winson Green block. My Pope-mobile never arrived and I never got to wave to the crowds! Instead, I spent my Christmas in Hull block, which suited me. I couldn't wait for 1992. I was sure that it was going to be lucky for me.

On 24 January, the van arrived once again. I knew it was coming, as I'd overheard something. I blacked up from head to toe and when my door opened I ran out and smashed the block to bits. I was swinging about like a monkey, smashing lights, pulling pipes out. They came in mob-handed and I ended up in the box. I didn't want to leave. Why should I? I was happy in this nick. The screws were decent and I had my medicine ball. Fuck it, I was staying!

On 14 February, Valentine's Day, I got a big hug – from the heavy mob. The van had turned up. I refused to go even though the Governor said I had to.

I left Hull Jail in a wheelchair like Hannibal

fucking Hector, naked and strapped in a body-belt. They wheeled me out, picked me up and put me in the back of the van.

The Governor and screws were waiting for me at Lincoln. I was carried out of the van, still in the wheelchair, and pushed to the block.

Once we were in the block, I just said, 'Box.'

They put me in the box and took me out of the body-belt. I excreted on the floor and spread it all over the walls. I wrote in it, 'This is your life'.

I lived like this for a week or so until finally the Governor said that if I came out and behaved myself he would put me in the special unit. Tony Steel was up there and Fat Joe, two good lads. There were only five cons on the special unit and I reckoned that I could handle it so I came out of the box. I had a shower, got fresh clothes and breathed fresh air again. For a few days I was in the block with Cliffy Moody. It was great to see him again and I caught up on all the news.

A couple of unit screws came down to see me in the block to tell me what the score was. I was up there the next day. It was only a small place; it had a workshop, TV room, a multi-gym and its own caged exercise area. It was good to see Tony Steel again. He's one of the most violent men in the system but he's a diamond. A few weeks passed by with no problems. I trained with Tony and we both got fit. I got back into my art work and painted 18 paintings in one weekend.

I had a visit booked with Julian Broadhead. It had been agreed by Governor Pratt that he could come on the unit, but on the actual day of the visit I was told that he wouldn't be allowed up. They were testing my patience. I snapped, told them all to 'Fuck off', and went to my cell and banged myself up. Governor Pratt arrived, my door opened up, and I smashed him in the face, then banged myself up again. I was in trouble!

The heavy mob were called in. Tony Steel shouted to me, 'They're coming into the unit with shields and sticks.' They had banged up the whole jail, just to come and get me! Brave fuckers!

My door sprung open. I saw the shields coming at me … I never had a fucking chance. It must have taken them ten minutes to get my arms bent. Pressure points were secured – wrists, arms and neck – then they lifted me up and carried me out. To get me to the block they had to carry me right through the jail. I screamed out, 'Happy Christmas everybody!' I didn't care that it was February.

I could hear the cons banging their doors and shouting back, 'Happy Christmas!'

Once in the block, I was put in the box. They held me down tightly and struggled for another ten minutes before they got me into a body-belt. The reason for this was simple: the belt was far too small. Body-belts come in three sizes – small, medium and large – and these evil bastards put me in a small one. I'm nearly 6ft tall and over 14 stone. In no time at all my wrists started swelling and my fingers went numb. The belt was so tight it started to dig into my midriff. I crawled over to the door, just like a worm, rolled on to my back and kept smashing my bare feet into the steel door. I was raging mad and I wanted to make as much noise as I could.

People don't realise that prison is 99 per cent a law unto itself. I was pleased to leave this piss-hole. I knew that if I didn't, I'd do something nasty to one or more of the screws responsible.

Three long years had passed since I was at Long Lartin, but this time I was going to try harder as I had been told by an official that I was very close to being certified again. They put me on C Wing where I knew a lot of the cons. The first few days were great, but nine days after my arrival, and on a Saturday afternoon, I received a body blow like no other.

We had all banged up for lunch when my door was unlocked. A prison officer and a senior officer came into my cell. They said, 'Charlie, you've got to go down the block. A very serious allegation has been made about you.' I told them to fuck off; I wasn't going anywhere. I was fuming. What allegation? I knew that I hadn't done anything wrong. I was so upset, I spat at them. I told them to leave me alone and they left. It wasn't long before the heavy mob arrived with their helmets and shields. All hell broke loose.

All this time, the cons were banging and shouting, 'Leave him alone!' I put one screw out of my cell and the rest went out. The Governor now arrived.

'Come on, Chaz,' he said, 'you must go down to the block until we investigate.'

I asked them, 'Investigate what?'

So he told me that some con had made a very serious allegation concerning me.

This was a blatant fit-up but I knew that one way or the other I would end up down the block, so I went to the cells of a few other cons who I knew and told them that I had done nothing wrong to anyone. I walked to the block to clear my name. I was still not told what it was that I was supposed to have done, just that the police would be called in. I was even more baffled now. Something was seriously wrong. I wasn't a happy man. I started smashing the granny out of my door, demanding to know what the hell was going on. The Governor came back and told me that I would have to see the police. I told them that I would not see the police without a solicitor, so one was arranged.

I went up to the wing the next day, still not knowing what I was meant to have done. Most of the lads were out on exercise but the ones that were left were giving me funny looks. I'd had enough of this so I pulled one of them to see what was up. He told me the story – I was supposed to have raped a con! I couldn't believe what I was hearing. It just wasn't in my nature to do that sort of thing. All the cons knew that it was a load of rubbish, and it turned out that it wasn't the first time this con had pulled this shit. He'd done it twice before to other cons. This guy was a nut, a loony.

I pulled out a blade, sliced open my hand and I let the blood drip into a cup. I gave my solicitor my blood. He went pale. I said that if this con had been examined by the police doctor, then they would have samples, and my blood would prove that I had not been near him! I told them to fuck off and leave me alone. I later got a letter from my solicitor saying no charges would be pressed. The allegation was ridiculous.

I hope that one day I will meet this nutter. He should be in an asylum. I couldn't believe that the police were brought in when the toe-rag had done it twice before. It was obvious to anyone with half a brain that it was a load of nonsense.

This all unsettled my mind, but the cons were great – they all supported me. They even had a petition and more than 300 signed on my behalf. I did get an official apology from the Governor, but it wasn't enough for me. Two decades I'd fought against this system and look what I get, a filthy con slagging my name! I spoke to several cons very deeply about it. I wanted to get something sorted out; it was not going to end here.

A week later, there was another incident. This time a screw said that I'd strangled him. Again, I ended up in the block; this was a serious charge. The screw had been outside my door. I went outside to have a word with the screw and he fell over. I went to pick him up and I took hold of his neck. I got him to his feet and he ran to the landing shouting, 'Bronson's strangled me.' There were no screw witnesses but a dozen con witnesses.

I was on the verge of killing, so I'll take this opportunity to thank all the cons in Long Lartin who stood by me and supported me over that bad patch. Yes, it was a bad time which left a bitter taste.

They sent me to the biggest piss-hole in the country, the Armley block, but in this case they did me a big favour as my old pal was here – Brian (The Bear) Ismond. He was a block man like me. He never cried about it, just got on with it. Brian and I exercised together in the caged yard. It was good to see the old rascal! Brian's well-known in Leeds; we had a good chat and picked up on all the gossip. Lord Longford came up to see me and I asked him to see Brian as well, which he did. I could have happily stayed a month or two, but when the van comes, you're off. It arrived on 21 July 1992, less than a month after I'd arrived here. I shook Brian's hand and wished him well, as he had a court case coming up. The van sped off. I was on my way to another ferry ride. This was becoming ridiculous.

I was put straight in the block at Parkhurst, but I was told there might be a chance that I could go up on M Wing if I behaved. Danny Reece was there.

Many didn't like Danny. In fact, I've never met a more hated con. He was by then doing life for the murder of Ronnie Cook, a respected armed robber. Danny had a reputation as a bully and a grass (he'd turned Queen's evidence against a sex killer and the man got life). But I couldn't help warming to him. I'd first met Danny in Wandsworth and now he was the block cleaner, so I asked if I could go out on the exercise yard with him. We worked out together. Danny's as strong as a bull.

One day, Keith Ritchie came down on the block with a bag of goodies for me and the lads. He had sweets and biscuits but the screws wouldn't let him give them to us, so I stripped off and pressed the bell. I was going to run out, get in their office, and shit on the carpet. They must have known that I was up to something because they brought in the heavy mob. My door was flung open and in they waded. We had a rough and tumble for about ten minutes.

They love it ... well, so do I! But I can never win. They overpowered me and in the box I went.

I stayed in the box a week – not something I'd recommend for the faint-hearted. Danny Reece would put cheese rolls and milk through the flap in the bottom of the door. In all the prisons and all the blocks that I have been in, no block cleaner has ever done this before. Every day, Danny came to the hatch to shake my hand. He doesn't like to admit it, but he's got feelings. He's a tough fucker, but he loves me to bits!

Eventually, off I went to M Wing. There were loads of cons I knew were up there: Kevin Brown, Tony and Pete Coulson, Micky Reilly, Dennis Campbell, Vic Dark, Gerry Parker, Rupert Tibbs, Keith Richie and 'Big H'.

I ate well, trained well and slept well. Time was flying by and I was winning. Most nights I trained alone on the wing for a couple of hours. I was feeling good. Mr Marriott, the Governor, was obviously terrified in case I went off my head again, so he often came to see me and I assured him I was OK. Big H was a good pal to me, but then they moved him to Whitemoor. I missed him a lot but I was still allowed to see Gi Gi. Don Swinton, a psychologist, helped me a lot. He's a good man who I respect. My head was better than it had been for years. Then I had a brainwave! Years ago, in the 1960s, big Frank

Mitchell built a fish pond on some waste land down by our football pitch. I decided I was going to build one as well! At first they all saw it as a big joke, but a meeting was held and permission was given. My reason for wanting to do this was simple – in all my years away, I'd never done anything in prison but smash it up. A fish pond represented peace and tranquillity and a change in my ways. I was going to do my own design, a figure eight with a bridge. It was all in my head and was about to come to life.

They gave me a pick-axe, a shovel and a fork, and I went to work. The first day I dug deep, about eight feet. Some screws were looking worried. No, I hadn't knocked up a wooden horse in the workshop! They were just concerned that I was fit enough for the job. I assured them I was. I just wanted this pond to be the best fucking pond ever! I wanted to leave it for my fellow cons. It would live on and people would see that I had finally got my act together. It certainly wasn't for parole, as I never got fuck-all off these people. This pond was my own idea – and I felt great!

On the second day, Cliffy Moody arrived, so I let him help me. By the third day my dream had been shattered by a cowardly act.

I ended up in an outside hospital, St Mary's, with multiple stab wounds. They were all in my back, which says a lot. I won't name any names, but everyone there knew what happened. One con claimed he'd done it himself, telling everyone that he had stabbed Charles Bronson. But, as the surgeon said, there were two knives with different-sized blades. It happened by the half-dug pond. I was having words with a con and some others joined in. Some were men that I knew and respected and some were genuinely trying to stop a fight, but it was when I was being pulled away that I was stabbed in the back.

They all left me, blood pouring out of my wounds. I knew I was hurt badly. My breathing was painful but I still managed to walk back to M Wing. Poor Cliffy was devastated. I felt sure I was dying; I saw the faces of all my family passing by me as I collapsed in my cell.

Big 'Bill the Bomb' came running in. He stuffed up all the holes that the bastards had put in me. Bill saved me that day, as he once saved me outside. They put me on a stretcher and as I was being carried off M Wing, the face that I will always remember is big Dennis Campbell's. He was looking down at me from landing two. I shouted up to him, 'I stabbed myself, Dennis!'

Later, I fucked the police off. Ninety-nine per cent of cons would have tried to get compensation, or use it to get out faster. Not me. When I was brought back into Parkhurst I couldn't even walk. They put me in the hospital wing. Gi Gi was allowed to come over and see me; he was mad over it and so were a lot of others. He told me that a lot of cons feared me and that's why they'd done it. In my back was the only way.

After Gi Gi left, I had words with a screw. I smashed the hatch of my door and slung everything out on to the landing. As I destroyed my cell, all my wounds opened up. Blood was everywhere; the pain shot through my body.

They sent the heavy mob in to me – a man with holes in his body. I was bent up and put in the box. This was the same box in which I had been certified mad, back in 1978. It was still rotten and dirty – it hadn't altered in 14 years. I fucked all the doctors off; I wouldn't let them in the box. They spoke to me through the hatch and I just spat at them.

Mick Connell, a screw, came to see me. He told me that they were worried in case the wounds became infected. I told Mick that I was shitting blood. Then

Don Swinton came to see me. Through Don and Mick I took some anti-inflammatory tablets and put some antiseptic on my wounds. I was in a lot of pain.

Don did a deal with the doctors so I could be put on the high-risk landing. Once I was up there, I showered and let a doctor examine me. He prescribed some drugs and changed my bandages twice a day.

Colin Robinson was on this landing, so was Bob Maudsley. Bob had killed three cons – one in Broadmoor and two in Wakefield. It was good to see Colin again, but most of the others were a pain in the neck. One in particular was heading for a clump as he was upsetting me.

Mr Marriott came in to see me. I genuinely believe that he was a sad man over what had happened to me. For the first time ever, we were getting somewhere. He'd stuck his neck out for me and given me trust. I'd like to think that I wasn't responsible for letting him down this time. He told me that I would be moving on soon. They had no choice, no one knew who it was who'd plunged the knives into me. I wasn't very pleased about all this. I'd got stabbed in the back and I'd lost my pond – and it was me that had to be moved.

Bronson's quarters were ready! Again – amazingly – I was back in cell 13 in Wandsworth's punishment block. And Prison Officer Wells was there to greet me. I could barely walk and I was still in a lot of pain, but Mr Wells told me he knew what had gone on and assured me that I would not be here long. He urged me to keep calm as something was being planned for me in my favour. Two weeks later, the van arrived and I was on my way to the Scrubs. What awaited me?

I was put in the block on 23 September 1992 and was told as soon as I'd arrived to settle down as I would be seeing the Board of Visitors very soon. I was told I would be getting lost remission back and would be staying in this block until my release. I got 120 days back, which put me out on the street on 9 November that year! I had just a month-and-a-half to survive.

Lord Longford visited me and made arrangements for us to meet on the day I got out. We were to have a meal at the Grosvenor Hotel in London. My friend Mark Lilliot and his lady were picking me up on the day, so they were invited to lunch, too. James Nicholson, Number 1 crime reporter at the Old Bailey, came to see me to discuss some plans. James is a seasoned old hack and a good pal. He's also a good pal of Gi Gi's. Julian Broadhead came to wish me well, as did Sammy McCarthy and his daughter Jackie.

The weeks slipped by. I went out on exercise with a guy called Charlie. He was a lifer who kept me really cheerful. I was getting stronger every day. I did a few gentle exercises – nothing heavy. I needed my strength for when I got out and I certainly didn't want to tear my wounds open again. I bathed in salt water and every night I put salt on to my wounds. A couple of screws were also good to me. They helped me get by with no nonsense. I felt that they were pleased for me that I was finally getting out.

I now had only days left.

The night of 8 November was a long one. I paced my cell for most of it. I was really tense.

I felt an odd twinge of despair and doubt. Was I really going out into the big wide world tomorrow?

CHAPTER ELEVEN

When my door unlocked, I was out of my cell like a rabbit with a rocket up its arse! I was buzzing!

I had survived a long, hard battle. I'd bled for this day; I'd shed tears for it. And now it was finally going to happen.

They soon got me over to reception. It was great to put on my black suit. It felt lovely! They gave me £60, which is what I was entitled to. I shook the hands of a few cons in reception. They all wished me well. There were hundreds more hands I would have liked to shake throughout the prison system – mostly cons, some screws and a couple of decent governors. Prison was my whole life. Nearly 20 years inside now, apart from those 69 days in 1987. And none of it an easy ride. Sure, sometimes I'd made it bloody difficult. But I'd taken the medicine – and the fucking punishment.

I was ready.

The gate opened. It was a really dull, wet, rainy day, but I didn't care. Today was 'my' day. I'd made it!

Kelly-Anne had always promised that she would be there to meet me, but what the hell. Mark Lilliot was there and Jackie, as well as James Nicholson and a cameraman from one of the newspapers. It was a great feeling. Mark looked powerful – two stone heavier than when I last saw him.

We had a hug and off we went. We found a café first and caught up on everything, then James took us to the Grosvenor in Park Lane for a nice meal with Lord Longford. Old Frank Longford never turned up and it wasn't until later that we found out why. A terrible mistake had been made. Lord Longford was at the Grosvenor in Victoria! I got the wrong one; it was my fault and a total fuck-up – one that could only happen to me!

I felt terrible at the time because Mark and Jackie had driven 200 miles to be there. But it couldn't spoil the day. Nothing could do that. The sight of real life was heavenly on its own. Real cups and glasses, fresh, clean air, real people.

We drove to New Brighton, where I was going to try to settle down and make a fresh start, meet new people, shake the old lifestyle away and live like normal people do. I phoned Mum and Dad to tell them I was free. They were so pleased. I promised them that I would be home for Christmas. Mark and Jackie got me a place to live; I had my own kitchen, my own bathroom. I was made up. They had put loads of 'Welcome Home' signs up all over the place. They'd really done me proud. That first day out had really touched me. I now had a new life.

New Brighton. What a lovely place it was, such great people. Even the air felt magic. I couldn't get enough of it! I got a little job as a doorman in a club, only two nights a week, but it suited me just fine. Every day Mark and I would work out in the gym. I must have put on a stone of muscle in three weeks. I had good food, fresh air and exercise. All this was pure heaven. Bear in mind, it was only three months since I'd been stabbed. Now I was getting stronger by the day.

Mark's dog was a Bull Mastiff, pure muscle and power. Her name was Della and Mark used to let her stay with me every other day. I'd make pots of stew, with big lumps of beef in it. Della used to love my cooking – it often turned into a dog's dinner! I'd run along the sea-front with her, then give her half my meal. When people saw her they would freeze, but she was as gentle as a lamb. Dog's can sense real trust. Della knew I was the boss, but she also knew I'd kill for her. I loved that dog like a baby.

Mark and Jackie's daughter was a little angel called Chantelle. I had a lot of laughs with her. She loved my stews as well! All was going well until one night, when I was alone in my flat, I noticed that I was being watched. Outside my window across the street were two guys in a car. They were obviously cops. They looked it; I could smell them. I was under surveillance and I was overcome with depression.

It started my mind racing. I packed a few things and sneaked out the back way. I left Mark a note. I was going on one of my missions to find myself. You see, I felt totally empty now. A new life beckoned, and yet cops were across the street. To top it all, only days before, my mother's sister, Auntie Pam, had passed away. She was only a few years older than me and she was a lovely human being. Everyone idolised Pam. I made it my business to go to the funeral, which was to be held in Luton.

I arrived and made my way to Kelly-Anne's place – God knows why. It was like a magnet drawing me to her. But I'm glad that I went as she took me to Uncle Jack's grave and then left me there alone.

It was peaceful, tranquil, almost dream-like. Jack was buried in a lovely little graveyard out in the country, a couple of miles from Luton. His grave is by a tree and there are horses in a field nearby. It felt so right for me to be there. This was reality. It really hit me hard to be standing over his grave. This was the man who I had promised to see next when I was free, who I had planned to buy a pint, to thank him for his love and to celebrate my homecoming. I'd let him down. I'd failed dear old Jack. I felt really sad about that.

I went silent for days after. My mind was very disturbed. Kelly-Anne always found time to go to Jack's grave a couple of times a week. She was, in fact, tending five graves at that time – her mum's, Jack's, a bloke called Barney's, her grandad's and her uncle's. They had all died within months of each other.

I turned up at Auntie Pam's funeral and saw all my family. It was lovely to be with them again, but so sad to be drawn together in such a terrible loss. My mum took it really badly. We all went to a pub after but I felt terrible. I was not only upset for Pam, I was still grieving over Jack. We all said our farewells and went our own ways.

I promised Mum and Dad that I would see them soon, at Christmas. I then went to London for a few days. I was trying to find myself, but in reality I was lost in a crowd. I was walking about stunned, in terrible mental anguish. I was fighting myself. I started to get crazy urges to attack or rob. I decided to go back to Luton.

I walked slowly towards Jack's grave. I had to decide now – go back to New Brighton, or stay here, stuck in the past. I went back to see Kelly-Anne to try to express how I felt, but she clearly had her own problems. She couldn't even help herself get off the booze, so how could she help me sort my mind out? I told her that if she stopped drinking I would stay with her. But really we had nothing between us.

I left Luton a very sad and lonely man. This was my town, my past, and all it ever gave me back was grief. I headed back to New Brighton. Mark had been worried about me but I told him that I had got it all out of my system and I was here to stay.

Christmas arrived and I went home to my parents in Wales. Mark, my younger brother, was there. We felt like strangers; we knew nothing about each other. We even had our first pint together, as Mark was only a child when I left. But this Christmas was the best I'd ever had. Mum, Dad and Mark really made it good for me and I met some lovely people. It really was a nice Christmas. Even Ronnie and Barbara, who ran the Crystal Palace Public House, spoilt us all ... so thanks to everyone for that magical time.

After Christmas I went back to New Brighton. Then I decided to go on another mission. I made my way back to Luton, found a man in Kelly-Anne's flat, and broke his nose.

Days later, on 2 January, Kelly-Anne left the flat with her friend Carol. About half-an-hour went by, then there was a knock at the door. It wasn't the postman.

All hell let loose. Cops came tearing in with guns and bullet-proof vests. They piled on top of me. I was chained by my ankles and wrists and carried out to a waiting van. Once they got me down to the station, they questioned me about the guy's busted nose.

Later, they asked me about a wig, a gun and a

bank. Then they charged me with: (1) conspiracy to
rob a bank; (2) possession of a firearm; and (3)
grievous bodily harm.

On 4 January 1993, I appeared at Luton Magistrates'
Court and was remanded in custody.

Woodhill Prison was brand-new, a sprawling mass
of red brick and razor wire. No jail, not even Alcatraz,
is escape proof. But if you got out of this one you
wouldn't stand much of a chance without a pigeon's
homing-sense, or a damn good map.

Woodhill is on the outskirts of Milton Keynes in
Buckinghamshire, a 'new town' criss-crossed by a
perplexing array of anonymous roads, each
monotonously dotted with dozens of roundabouts.
They told me as soon as I arrived that I would be
going to the block – and once I was in the block, they
said that I was on good order and discipline. Don't
forget, I was only a remand prisoner. Something was
desperately wrong here.

I wasn't going to rob any bank and I didn't own a
gun or a wig! I admitted to the broken nose – big deal
– but I wasn't about to let anyone fit me up on
anything else.

So here I was, back in the block, back on Cat A, and
again the 'danger man'. For the first few days, I was in
shock. It was obvious that I had been set up and only
Kelly-Anne could have done it – but why? She had
made a statement to say that it was my gun and that
I had shot it out of her window. Her friend Carol had
also made a statement to say that I asked her if she
would drive a car, as I was going to rob a bank in
Harpenden. It was all pathetic nonsense. The broken-
nose guy made a statement to say that I punched him.
They were three filthy rats together.

Kelly-Anne retracted her statement a week later,
but why did she set me up in the first place? For the
life of me, I had no answers.

After only days of being there, I lost my senses and jumped a screw. I tried to turn him around so I could get him in a neck-hold … I wanted a hostage. But the screw I chose was too big and somehow he got free – so I just hit him. My madness had started again; I was losing control. I knew that I could never survive in jail as an innocent man. My only crime was breaking a nose; I should have been out on bail, and yet here I was, back to all this again! I was gutted.

I lay awake every night thinking of guns, banks, GBH … and more lost years. I was sure the judge would take one look at my past and give me 15 years.

I'd had 55 days of freedom and now all this. My lawyers, Maggie Morrissey and Tim Green, seemed confident that I would get a result, but I just felt so depressed. I couldn't get my head around why Kelly-Anne had done this to me. Was it police pressure?

On 9 February I was to go back to court. To protest my innocence I had decided to go there naked but Maggie phoned me to tell me to stop messing about. She told me to make sure I was dressed as two of the charges were being slung out. All that I had left was the GBH. The anxiety just fell from me. I felt relief. Even if I got two years I'd be happy. I'd just take it on the chin. As the Cat A van sped off towards Luton, I was buzzing. Once I was there, I met Tim Green, one of the best briefs in London. He told me not to worry, I shouldn't even get a sentence. The magistrates slung the two charges out of court and gave me a £600 fine for the nose. I walked out of court a free man! On 9 February 1993, somebody up there loved me.

I can't begin to describe how I felt. One day I was looking at 15 years for something that I hadn't done, the next I was a free man.

Now that I was free, I wanted to know why I'd been set up. I had told my family not to attend court, simply because I thought I would get another remand, so no one was there to meet me. I phoned Loraine and her husband Andy and asked them to come and collect me. They were elated. For five fucking weeks I had sweated and now I had to know why.

Someone had also set me up back in 1988 ... was that Kelly-Anne as well? If it turned out to be a man that had done this to me, I would pull his teeth out, but it's not my game hurting women. However, I still had to know the truth. It was driving me mad. Either someone had paid her to get me out of the way or she was an evil bitch.

That night I went to her flat; she was gone. She had left Luton. I found out later that she had phoned the court to see how I had got on, and as soon as she knew I was free, she left town. I didn't know where Carol lived, and Broken Nose had gone missing, too. I phoned Kelly-Anne's flat at least three times a day but there was no reply. I also went around there every night to see if there was a light on – but nothing.

She had to come back sooner or later. I had to know.

Loraine and Andy were a tower of strength to me, two of the loveliest people I know. They sorted me out a room in a friend's house. It was just right for me. Nobody knew my whereabouts – just how I wanted it to be. I kept my training up, I even got a little job, but at the end of each day I slept alone. I had no one to share it all with.

Sixteen days after I'd walked out of court, my world collapsed.

On 25 February 1993, I had so many guns pointed at my face I felt like screaming, 'For God's sake, just kill me!' If it wasn't for the guy sitting next to me, I reckon that I would be dead meat now.

I was in a car with another man, when out of nowhere armed cops were all over us. The car was a potential death-trap. There were guns pointing at our faces with cops at the other end of them.

I ended up back in Woodhill Prison in Milton Keynes and my charges were practically the same as before: conspiracy to rob a bank and possession of a sawn-off shotgun. I couldn't believe that this had happened again. I would either walk free or face more years of porridge.

I spent my time training hard in the block as I waited for my trial. I was now as fit as I was 20 years ago. As jails go, this was one of the better ones, but they still wouldn't allow me to be a normal con. I was still classed as Cat A. I plodded on with life. The screws there were a decent bunch; they let me go to the gym and I got plenty of food and a shower every day. I was also getting plenty of visits from Loraine and Andy – they are both priceless to me. But the thought of spending another two decades fighting the system brought me out in a cold sweat. I really felt by that time I had become a hostage to my own past. Every day I had to keep myself in check and fight myself to stay in control.

It was while I was on remand at Woodhill that I was refused a visit from a very good friend of mine, James Nicholson. James had been to see me on numerous occasions before, but for some reason the Home Office was being awkward and they refused it. This made me really mad. I was only on remand – I should have been allowed all the visits I wanted. And here I was banged up in the block, with the spectre of more and more years of isolation hanging over me. I was determined now to make a protest; I was pissed off, to say the least.

Before I really knew what was happening, the cell door was shut – bosh! I had myself another hostage! My adrenalin was already pumping; I'd just polished off 600 press-ups in the exercise yard. I was buzzing. And Andy Love was just in the wrong place at the wrong time.

Andy was the library screw and actually a really lovely fella. But he got me on a bad day. Bang! I blew up and carried Andy, who just happened to be on the seg unit, off to my 'flowery dell'. They brought in negotiators and a marksman; I threw a blanket over the window to stop him popping me one in the nut.

Andy was a model hostage. Sure, I threatened to snap his neck, but hostage situations are like that. It's like a game of chess; I make a move, they make a move. When I told Andy to be good, he said, 'No problem, Charlie.' We had some nice chats during the siege – all 14 hours of it.

Looking back, I was really craving company, craving humanity. I just wanted to chat to someone in my cell, to have a cup of tea with them. Maybe play a bit of Scrabble.

Isolation gets to a man after 20 years. I wanted to be with people, or at least have a little pet. I didn't want a budgie – they just eat and shit all over your cell. I wanted proper company.

That was my main demand – and, yeah, it was a crazy enough demand as it turned out. I asked for a blow-up doll! That's what I told the negotiators.

'Get me a doll!'

Just to talk to; to have a cup of tea with.

'Get me a fucking blow-up doll.'

'But you're worth more than that, Charlie. You need a real woman, a real human ...'

'Yeah,' I shouted back to the female negotiator. 'But I'm not allowed to have a fucking human, am I? I'm not allowed fuck-all, no one in my cell ... not a woman, a man, or a child. Just get me the doll.'

It was fucking crazy; madness at its best.

The negotiator said if I got a doll, every other con would want one.

'I don't give a fuck about them! I'm telling you what *I* want. It's not too much to ask. I'm not asking for a machine-gun, I'm not asking for a helicopter. I just want a blow-up doll. I want to marry her in Broadmoor asylum!'

'But what if you fall out of love with her?'

I thought seriously about this. My head was clearly flipped. 'Come that day, and I hope to God it don't happen, I'll sling her out of my cell and I'll never speak to her again!'

The negotiator laughed. I have to say it sounds funny now. But I was obviously seriously fucked in the head through years of isolation.

I was getting frustrated. These negotiators were upsetting me: they couldn't negotiate a bag of boiled sweets. And Andy, with all due respect, was starting to piss me off. He was boring me. Time was ticking by and I was pacing up and down. It was like being stuck in a lift with a stranger.

Andy asked for a piss. 'Yeah, go for it,' I said. 'But don't flick it more than twice or I'll kill you. And wash your fucking hands. I don't want germs in my home!' I told the negotiators to get a cup of tea for Andy. I wanted a T-bone steak, French fries, and Andy would have a fillet. (I reckoned I'd eat his!) 'And I want a fucking axe, a machine-gun, 10,000 rounds and a helicopter out of here!'

Then it happened.

'Andy, did you just fart? You fucking farted in my cell! You broke wind and polluted my atmosphere, you bastard.'

I felt I couldn't breathe with this man so close.

I told them, 'Fuck the axe, stick the steak up your arses. I've had enough. It's over. Open up and take him!'

I never got my doll.

They later charged me with two offences – the first, false imprisonment. Charge two read:

*Charles Bronson, at Milton Keynes in the
County of Buckinghamshire, on 26 May 1993,
with a view to gain for himself or with intent to
cause loss to another, made an unwarranted
demand of an Inflatable Doll, a cup of tea,
weapons and a helicopter ... Contrary to
Section 21 Theft Act 1968.*

The next day I was off to Winson Green and more
solitary. And then, within the month, I was shunted to
Belmarsh. There was a mob of screws waiting for me
when I arrived at Belmarsh special unit on 24 June
1993. This is the max-secure London jail where they
hold IRA and other high-risk cons.

Six screws took the van ride with me, even though I
was strapped up in a body-belt, unable to scratch my
own arse. In reception, I recognised one prison officer
from way back in Armley. We'd had words many years
ago, but apart from that I'd always found him fair. He
told me the second I walked into Belmarsh that I was
heading for the block.

This was part of their special Cat A wing. There
were 48 Cat A prisoners on there, and they could all
watch television, play football, tennis and pool. But
there was one person who wasn't allowed – me.

I always give it time before I kick up about
something. The block screws treated me fairly, but I
fell out with the unit governor. We had words and I
fucked him off. One day, he upset me so I started to
break down my cell door. Fortunately, nothing came
of it.

I got a bit of gym, plenty of exercise and more than
enough food. One particular screw, Mick Reagan, was
one of the best I've come across. He was only in his
late 20s, but a solid guy. He didn't stab you in the
back, but told it like it was – and to your face. If all
screws acted like him, prison would be a better place

and there would be half the trouble. He and several others went out of their way to make my stay comfortable. Mick slung the medicine ball at me. They even got a tennis net for me to play in the exercise cage. Basically, I was happy and contented.

They gave me a lot of trust. Bear in mind that I was Cat A and usually had at least six screws just watching me.

Right outside my cell was a surveillance camera. This was the most up-to-date and secure unit in Britain. Some doors even the screws could not open. It was like something out of a science fiction movie. Security was the Number 1 priority for cons and screws alike. We were all being monitored.

My only problem was not being allowed to go on the wings with the other Cat A cons. There were two that I had told to stay away from me if I ever got up there. One was a filthy rapist. He was a fucking disgrace to the human race. The other one was 18 stone and 6ft 6in of shit. He was up on trial for the murder and disembowelment of a prostitute. He had a history for rape but walked free from court.

I was getting my life back to normal there. I felt good. So, I couldn't go up on the wings – hell, that's show business. By now it was only weeks away from the trial. Loraine and Andy visited and brought me a nice suit to wear. I gave Loraine my wooden cross; she loved it. Days later, on my twenty-eighth day there, Ben, who was a senior officer, came into the block with some other screws. I knew by their faces that it was time for me to go.

'OK, Charlie, you're away.'

I was gutted, fed up and depressed. Why fucking move me again? I was convinced that this was the Home Office playing games. I stripped off and they put me in the body-belt – and that's how I left Belmarsh, trussed up like a fucking Christmas turkey.

A lot of the screws said that it was a wrong decision; they were genuinely concerned for me. Two in particular shouted out to me as I got into the van, 'Behave yourself, Charlie, and good luck.' It wasn't the screws' fault, but as the van pulled away from Belmarsh I felt betrayed. It certainly didn't help things to be tied up like that and have to travel 200 miles to a place I didn't want to go to. But nothing lasts, does it?

The last time I'd been in Bristol nick was four years earlier. I'd arrived trussed up that time, too. The only difference was a new gate-lodge at the jail. Again, they put me in the strong box.

An official came to see me and I explained that I wouldn't come out of the box until the van came for me. I would not wear any clothes, I would not slop out, wash or shave. Neither would I see anyone, including my solicitor. I asked him to phone Loraine and Andy to express my belief that I was being victimised by the Home Office. My trial was only six weeks away and they had moved me so far away from everyone. Bad thoughts were entering my head; I was feeling dangerous. But my mind was set: I would remain boxed up in what I can only describe as a concrete coffin.

A doctor called Brown, an old boy, kept coming to see me. It's no secret that I despise the fuckers. I shouted at him every day, 'I want some chocolate! Fuck off if you haven't got any!' Obviously no prison doctor gives cons chocolates, but lo and behold, he came one day with a big bar of fruit and nut! I nearly fell off the concrete floor! It just goes to show they're not all vets.

On the fourth or fifth day I started to hallucinate and my mouth was very dry. I was convinced that my food had been spiked. On the sixth day I got a bad cramp in my gut. I was sick and had the shits really

badly. Messages were starting to come in for me from
my solicitor. I had nothing; no books, no radio, no bed,
nothing. This was like the bad old days all over again.

My thoughts were all bad. I thought of taking a
hostage, but I knew it wasn't the screws' fault. My
mail was being redirected from Belmarsh and I got
letters from my brother Mark, who was out in Italy,
one from the Mayor of Luton, and one from Andy and
Loraine who sent me £20 so I could buy some sweets.

I started to sleep all day and walk up and down my
cell each night. I also sang a lot – loudly! I found that
it eased my tension. On the ninth day they came in
with smiling faces. 'You're away, Charlie.' This was
the breath of fresh air that I had been waiting for.

I refused clothes. They strapped me up in the body-
belt and off we went. As we got to the van, which was
parked outside the block, I noticed there were screws,
dogs and even a governor, waiting and watching.

I stopped and gulped in some of that beautiful air.
It was like food. Believe me when I say this: I really
love the world … to see flowers, animals and trees.
Even the sky is heaven. Anyway, I felt bloody good to
be out in the daylight, even though I must have
looked a right mess with over a week of not washing
or shaving. Two screws jumped in the front of the van,
four in the back – and me, the madman.

We drove through Wandsworth's gates at about one
o'clock and the van pulled up outside the block.
Bristol Prison had phoned through to this lot to tell
them what to expect. I honestly can't remember the
last time I actually passed through reception here. It
seems that I am destined to always arrive at the
punishment block and leave from it.

I jumped out of the van naked and in the belt to
face a score or more screws. Prison Officer Wells was
no longer there, he'd retired. I walked straight into
the strong box and told them that I was staying in

there until somebody told me what the fuck was going on. They uncuffed my wrists from the belt and left me alone. I was still naked and in total isolation. They brought me some food and a jug of water and told me that the Governor would be coming to see me soon.

Later, the Governor arrived to tell me that I had been sent there for my legal visits and then I was going to be moved on again. I asked them if they knew where I would be going, and he said that he thought it would be Woodhill as screws from there were taking me to the trial. This suited me fine, so I came out of the box and went back into my old home – cell 13. I showered, shaved and I felt like a new man again. I saw my face for the first time in over a week. I looked older, pale and drawn. My eyes were sunken. In nine days the system can destroy a man.

My next few days passed peacefully. On 5 August, Maggie and my barrister, Issy, were due to visit. Issy – Isabella Forshall – is a diamond. The visit was booked for the afternoon, but in the morning I was told that it had been cancelled because of a mix-up. All legal visits were supposed to be in the morning there. I saw the Governor and I told him that if I didn't get my visit, then 'FUCK EVERYTHING'. I would be going to my trial bollock naked, and I would tell the judge what he and his filthy scum screws had done to push me to this.

I got my visit. It now seemed that there was additional evidence. The police were now saying that I was waiting to hit a security van delivering to a bank. What were those police – fucking mind-readers? They were living in Disneyworld. My visit was held in the block, something that had never been known before. It was the first time that I had met Issy and she certainly made me feel a lot better. I gave Maggie a cross which I had promised her. It was made out of matches by my pal Kirk who was with me in Woodhill.

It was now four weeks from my trial. It couldn't be soon enough – neither could my next move. Maggie had been informed why I had been moved so much. They said it was because six screws were needed to unlock me and the prisons hadn't got the manpower to keep me more than a month. Don't they come up with some bullshit?

I just wished that the van would hurry up and come for me. I was looking forward to going back to Woodhill. It was as I was sitting in my cell thinking about all this that my mate Stevie Gillen came back from the Old Bailey. His trial had been going on for two weeks and that day he got 14 years. I shouted out to him, 'Be strong!' There is an end to everything – even if it's Hell.

Big Stevie Jarvis arrived. He was a good pal, one of the old school. Then his brother-in-law Ray Johnson arrived. The block was starting to liven up a bit, but I was once more beginning to get fed up. I'd had my legal visit, now I wanted my move. I wanted to go to somewhere better so I could get more gym and decent food. I was fucking starving – Wandsworth food was disgusting. On 12 August I spat in the Governor's face and told him to 'Fuck off'. I wanted to punch his face in. The next day I spat on his suit. The next day the Deputy Governor came to see me and got the same treatment. On Sunday night, 15 August, I decided enough was enough. I shouted to Steve Jarvis and Steve Gillen that in the morning I would be going into the strong box. I was now getting danger signs; bad things were in my thoughts. I wrote a letter to my lovely Loraine to tell her that I'd had enough. I also wrote to the judge at Luton Crown Court to say that I would be coming to my trial as a madman, unshaved, unwashed and in chains. I wrote to my solicitor to say that 16 August was to be isolation day. Fuck Wandsworth, fuck the system, and fuck my trial.

Monday, 7.30am, and my door unlocked and I walked out naked to face a dozen screws. The senior officer, who treated me OK, said that he would notify the Governor of my stance. I walked into the box and started to do my press-ups. Life was about to put me to the test again and I could sense this would be a long battle. They brought me my porridge and half-an-hour later they came to tell me that I was going – the crafty fuckers.

The belt went on and off I went to the waiting van, naked as the day I was born. This bondage lark was becoming a habit. Once in the van, I asked them where I was going. They replied, 'Belmarsh.'

I was stunned. I was supposed to be going to Woodhill. Now I was well confused. What were they playing at? It was only three weeks until my trial and I was still being fucked about. The screws in the van were a good bunch, so it was a pleasant journey – only one side of London to the other. But I felt more uncertainty.

So here I was, back in my old cell at Belmarsh. It was clean and I had more food as well as sweets and mags. I was still isolated, but it wasn't too bad. As soon as I arrived they told me that I would not be stopping. At the most I would only be there a couple of weeks, then I would be moving on to a jail in Oxford ready for my trial.

I phoned Loraine and Andy and I spoke to Andy's pal Les. He's a good man, a man of respect. I had some gym there and the screws were decent. I promised myself that over the next two weeks I would try to get my muscle back; over the previous month I'd lost a stone in weight. Roll on 6 September, the date of my case.

Two days before that, I was allowed to attend Del Coxen's service. It was a very, very sad occasion. Del had died there in his cell. He was 36 years old and as strong as an ox. He was a lovely man who I'd first met in Wandsworth Jail back in the 1980s. He was fit, full of life, honourable and respectful. I remember him talking to me out on the exercise yard. At the service were the other Cat As who were equally devastated by Del's death. Pete Pesito read out a nice farewell note and I said a little verse.

A screw read a bit out of the Bible, so did the Chaplain. It is a fact of life that we all have to go at some time, but 36 is beyond me.

The stress and anxiety eats away at us all. There has been a lot of bullshit written about how cushy we have it in prison. Maybe open prisons have it easy – sex, drugs and rock 'n' roll – but us Cat As have a very stressful way of life and so do our families. This service hit it home to me. It made me think. The flickering flame of the candle and the expressions on all the faces there that day told the same story. I'll be straight with you: whatever is said about us Cat As, there were a lot of tears in the room that day – mine included. God bless our mate Del, a man of steel.

The Woodhill screws picked me up at Belmarsh and brought me to Bullingdon Prison, Oxfordshire. It was the day before my trial and I was put in the block. This was one weird place – a local jail. The whole design of it seemed odd. It turned out that I was the only Cat A prisoner they had there, so it was a really big thing for them. They saw me as some sort of danger man. It was like I had two fucking heads – a freak. Out of the dozen cons in that block, I only knew one, Mick Green. Mick was a young guy, about 25. He was serving seven years. He'd been in Full Sutton with me when I took the probation guy, Rupert, hostage on the yard.

The other lads were mostly short-termers. They were all excitable, loud and disruptive, but they were a good bunch. It's funny, but I always meet the best guys on my travels through the blocks. These block boys are a breed apart – all fighters. I love them; they love me. It's how it is. Even though we live in the same units, only feet away from each other, I rarely get to see them. Their faces are hardly ever to be seen but their voices remain with me. Most of them spend a week or a month in solitary and then go back on to the wing. I am the only man who seems to be forever alone.

They told me that I would just be a lodger there. I would sleep there and go to court from there, but at the weekends I would be going back to Belmarsh. That all suited me. Every morning when I got into the van the boys would all cheer ... and every evening when I arrived back from court they would cheer me again. These were the original block boys, made of good solid stuff, and those cheers were a big boost for me. Thanks, lads!

We were 40 minutes late for the trial at Luton Crown Court. The Cat A van arrived at 10.40am. Issy, my barrister, and Maggie, my solicitor, were not too pleased, but it wasn't anyone's fault. We had hit traffic and even though we had an escort with flashing lights, and travelled some of the way down the hard shoulder of the motorway, we were still late.

After a quick chat with Issy and Maggie, I was led up to the dock along with Felix – the man with me when I got nicked – and six screws. Straight away, I noticed Loraine and Andy in the public gallery, and my aunt and uncle, Billy and Leila Cronin. There were also two friends of Loraine and Andy's who I had met while I was out.

But, of course, the one person that stood out was Kelly-Anne. She looked very smart, but it was obvious to everyone that she was very pissed. I could feel myself getting mad. She was not supposed to be in court; she was a witness. She was told to get out.

Truthfully, she was just a pain in my fucking head. Lord Longford was also there, as were Julian Broadhead and James Nicholson. After the 12 members of the jury had been sworn in, it was time to make our pleas.

For the first charge, conspiracy to rob a bank, we both pleaded 'Not Guilty'. For the second, intent to rob, we both pleaded 'Not Guilty'; and for the third, possession of a shotgun, I pleaded 'Guilty'.

The wheel of justice had begun to turn.

It was like a chess game. Move by move, we were the pieces drawn together by fate. Every single person in that courtroom was now a part of my fucked-up life. And now it was my life that was going to be played with. There were 12 members of the public who would decide my fate.

Jesus Christ, at that moment, I just prayed that they would believe my story or I was fucked – well and truly fucked. Here I was, the madman, facing ordinary people who couldn't even begin to understand me or my life and how it had been. What chance did I have?

This was going to be a battle, the fight of my life.

Off went the prosecutor, and in came the Crown's witnesses. No sooner had one cop given his evidence than another took his place. Issy tore into them like a vulture. Right behind Issy stood Maggie. She's fast, smart and misses nothing. I had a great team – the best – but would it be enough? I sat in the dock for three days, listening to all the Crown's evidence, and I can honestly say that most of it was a load of shit. They even produced a video film of a Group 4 delivery van which was taking money to the bank months before. It had no relevance to the case whatsoever as far as I could see. But it looked good for them, bad for us.

On Thursday afternoon at 3.00pm, I was called to

the witness box. Man, you should have seen their faces! My story – and what a story it was – knocked the jury sideways!

I wasn't going to rob any bank or Group 4 van – I was going to blow myself away. The man who was charged with me, Felix, must have been the most unlucky guy in the world the day we were arrested.

This is what I explained to the jury … Felix was driving along one morning when out I jumped with a shooter. I leapt into his car and told him to drive. He was now my hostage; either he drove me where I wanted to go, or I'd stick the gun in his face. He drove. There was never going to be a raid on a bank.

My plan was simple. Two shops up from the bank was a hairdresser's shop – and that was my target. Kelly-Anne used to go there every Thursday to have her hair done. Bear in mind I'd been trying to contact her for weeks with no luck whatsoever. By now I was totally pissed off. I wanted to see her to find out the answers to my questions. I was very depressed. I had no love in my life, I saw no future for myself, and I wanted her to see what she had done to me. I intended to wait outside the hairdresser's until she got there, then I was going to rush in and blow my head off in front of her. I wanted her to live with that. Me? I didn't believe then that I had anything to live for. Felix, who stood alongside me in the dock, was totally innocent.

All the time that I was in the witness box, I could feel Loraine's eyes boring into the back of my skull. She was giving me energy and strength. I felt her presence in that courtroom like the gentle breeze that a butterfly feels to help it along. I'd noticed that her youngest son was also in the courtroom. He was a good kid, just 16 years old, a cheeky bugger with plenty of spunk.

The next day, I went into the box again. I truly felt

I'd blown their legal machine to pieces. Felix was next in the box. It was hard work for him and for his wife who was in the public gallery. I could almost feel her pain. He was fighting for his future.

The following Monday, all the evidence was over and it was time for the summing up. All we had to do was wait; the sweat was now on. For me it was twice as bad as I had just heard the previous Thursday that my dear dad had fallen ill with lung cancer. Loraine and Andy had broken the news to me. I was allowed to phone home. I spoke to Mum and to Dad, who had been given three weeks to live. I went back to my cell in Bullingdon Jail that night, turned off the light and buried myself under a blanket. I broke up inside. I didn't know it then, but my dad turned out to be a true fighter to the last. He lived for a year and three days after being diagnosed, and enjoyed every moment of those final months.

By 4.30pm the judge called it a day; he needed more time to sum up. Issy told me later that day that if I was found guilty on the charge of conspiracy to rob, the judge was looking to life me off. My head was pounding ... a life sentence! So that night I lived in the hope I'd get a 'not guilty', but it was all down to the jury.

On Tuesday, 14 September 1993, the van pulled up into Luton Crown Court at 10.00am. I was tense. It had been a silent journey. Fortunately, the screws all knew me well so they left me deep in thought. I changed into my decent clothes and had ten minutes with Maggie and Issy before I was up in court at 10.30am.

Judge Rodwell finished his summing up. The tension increased. I felt numb; a life sentence was hanging over my head. I looked at Loraine, Andy, Billy and Leila. They all looked stressed. Then in she walked, the one and only Kelly-Anne. I stood up and

shouted at her, 'Go home. Get out of my fucking life.'
She left. I was taken down to await my fate. A lot
would have dearly loved to see me go free, but even
more wanted to see me put away for ever. The screws
who were with me in the cells were actually all decent
blokes. One in particular, Darren, had been with me
every day through the trial. He was a block screw
from Woodhill and he gave me a lot of moral support.

After three hours, the judge called us back into
court. The jury couldn't decide so he told them that
he would accept a majority verdict. The pressure
was turned up even more now, and it showed on
every face.

Issy and Maggie came back down to see me and we
spoke at great length. Issy looked very concerned; she
clearly takes all her cases very seriously. Everyone
wanted to come down to see me. Loraine came first.
We put our hands together against the glass screen
which separated us and I could feel her strength.
Then Andy and Bill came. Andy was wearing my ring
for good luck. Then it was suddenly time to go back
up. What would my fate be? Would the police finally
get their wish for me to be locked away for ever?

The courtroom was silent. All eyes were on the jury
foreman. My eyes were focused entirely on his mouth.

The 12 members of the jury found me guilty on
only one charge: 'intent to rob'. The main charge of
'conspiracy to rob' got a 'not guilty'. Felix was found
'not guilty' on all charges. I was glad for him and I
grabbed his hand and wished him luck, although I
knew all I had to look forward to was more years
of porridge.

Issy stood up on my behalf – a nice short speech. I
saw the tears well up in Loraine's eyes, and I saw
the look of despair on Andy's face. It was obvious
that Judge Rodwell didn't think that much of me. He
said that I was a danger to society and that prison

was the only place for me. He sentenced me to eight years for intent to rob and two years for possession of the shotgun.

It was all over. Time had stopped for me once more. I knew the clock of life wouldn't start for me again until – or if – I walked free one day.

Eight years! No man likes to be defeated, but sitting inside a court cell after receiving a sentence is the biggest fucking defeat of all. It comes no harder than that. The system had beaten me back into a stinking cage. I felt hard done by. After all, I was found not guilty on the main charge, so why give me eight years? It was all bollocks. My family was devastated. Loraine actually shouted at the judge in pure frustration. I looked around the court at the faces. It was like a bad dream.

I knew that I had a rough ride ahead. Fuck the system! The only good thing that came out of that day was the fact that Felix was going home. The rest stank!

On went the body-belt, and off we went. As we drove out of Luton, I sensed that it would be a very long time before I returned. But by the time we hit the M1, I was more positive. No stinking judge was going to destroy my dreams. I'd survive! We arrived safely at Belmarsh special security unit, a police escort with us right up to the gate. This Cat A unit was a prison within a prison, even having a separate 20ft wall surrounding it. Everything was treble secure: electronic doors, metal detectors, strip searches, cameras and a heavy ratio of screws. Being on this unit was apparently not enough for me, though. I had to be kept in the block section on my own. It was a fucking joke! All the other cons asked if I could be with them, but the Governor decided that I would remain in isolation.

Apart from all this, Belmarsh treated me OK. I got

plenty of food and my regular workout in the gym. There were also visits from Loraine and Andy, and the screws were decent to me. One screw in particular, Mick Reagan, was still a real gentleman. He went out of his way to put things right for me.

A week passed by without any problems, then I got a whisper that I was going to be moved. Parkhurst was mentioned, then Whitemoor. I didn't have a clue which was true, but I needed to know, or my head would go!

Then I found out. I was moving up north to Wakefield, one of the worst piss-holes in the system. It had been almost two decades since I last slept in that dive and, I swear to God, it was the last place that I wanted to end up in! I felt bad. My mind was racing; I was thinking bad thoughts.

I felt like tearing up the place, but Belmarsh didn't deserve that. This was the work of the Home Office. My name alone had caused this move. My eight years had begun, and they intended me to serve it the hard way!

I knew straight away that they had something planned for me because there was no way that Wakefield would let me go on the wing. It's a jail full of stinking sex-cases – 80 per cent are lifers and 50 per cent of them are very unpleasant. Wakefield is infamous for its monsters – and I wasn't about to serve my eight years with a bunch of monsters!

This was a bad move, and every screw's face in Belmarsh confirmed my anxiety. I was now a time-bomb. The body-belt came out and I was trussed up once more. Most of the screws were genuinely gutted, and they all wished me well. I left there a very bitter man.

The journey up to Yorkshire was a silent one. As the van passed Luton on the M1, I thought of Loraine and I thought of my sick dad. I felt that my world was beginning to cave in. It seemed that I was destined to walk the road back to insanity. I actually felt myself slowly going mad.

I've been on the edge of madness for as long as I can remember. I've always fought for my sanity and, at times, I've lost it, but I've always managed to get it back. The feeling that I had now was a strong desire to bury myself; a sense of complete defeat. I could not win. They would never allow me to be a normal con, and this move proved it. I started to fear myself, and believe me, this is the worst fear you can have. As Wakefield drew nearer, I went deeper into myself.

The only change that I immediately noticed as the van pulled up was the wall, which was no longer painted white. I watched as the gates opened, and as we drove slowly towards the special unit it seemed like I was going back through time to 1975. The van crept its way through another couple of gates. We stopped, and there they stood waiting, no less than 15 screws. With the six in the van, that made 21. Not good odds at all! I clocked the face of one screw who used to be at Full Sutton. The rest were distant, tense and ready to pounce. It's quite pathetic the way that they crowd a man. It may well intimidate a lot of cons, but for me it just fuels my anger. I'm well past being scared. There's only one man in the world who frightens me – and that's myself.

Their eyes were all on me. They asked me my prison number and, as usual, I told them that I was a person, not a number. They also asked me what diet I was on and I told them, 'Anything, as long as it's dead.'

I was taken to a cell where the body-belt came off. Then I was strip-searched and they led me to the cage. So here I was in Wakefield, an animal in a cage. Alone, naked and bitter. That cage was infamous. I could smell despair in there. It was a concrete tomb.

They had their rules – you must wear prison clothes and must at all times be properly dressed …

I had my own rule, which was 'bollocks to the rules!' On 25 September, a Saturday morning, one of the governors came to give me a copy of the reason why I was being kept in the cage.

> Information to inmate Bronson:
> You have been segregated under Prison Rule 43, good order and discipline for the following reason.
> You have been received on allocation to 'F Wing' because of your record of bad institutional behaviour during previous sentences and while on remand.
> This has included the taking of a hostage and threats to repeat that action.
> You are to be held at HMP Wakefield until directed by prison service headquarters.
>
> Issued by G Forester. 25. 9. 93.

All this hostage shit had happened long before, so I couldn't understand why they were taking action now. After all, I had behaved myself since then. The claim that I was threatening to do it again was a load of bollocks!

I wasn't allowed out on exercise for my hour's fresh air because I was refusing to wear clothes. And every time I slopped out there would be no less than a dozen screws watching me. The young screws chewed gum, trying to look hard. Really, it was quite pathetic.

The block was full up. Jon Jon Murray was here; he was one of the last to come down off the Strangeways roof after the riot there in Manchester. I couldn't see him, but we had a good chat most nights through my window.

The geezer in the next cell to me had problems. Most nights I could hear his cries creeping through the walls. He would sob himself to sleep. It sounded like he was in pain; this poor sod obviously needed help. If I could hear him, then so could the night screw. But they just let him cry.

I banged his wall and told him to pull himself together. I sung Louis Armstrong's 'It's a Wonderful World' and I told him that it was only a matter of time and everything would seem better. But he would never respond.

Then the nights became so silent. Had he ripped up the sheets and hanged himself from the bars? One night I even rang my bell to tell the screw to look through his spy-hole. I felt sure he was dead. This guy was bugging me.

The guy that was above me was a sad case, too. He was a pre-operative transsexual and a double-lifer. He had killed his boyfriend's lover and was now in the block awaiting transfer to Broadmoor. He kept on about a sex change, and how much it would cost him. I told him that if he got me a razor I'd do the operation on him myself, and I'd only charge him a couple of Mars bars! He didn't speak to me again after that!

These sort of guys actually put a bit of humour into our days. He was calling himself Natasha, and it seems that he was doomed to die inside – I found out later that he was HIV positive.

I made it my duty to write to Loraine as much as I could. I can release a lot of tension by writing a letter. She also wrote to me more; she understands what a letter means to me. I wasn't allowed any visits, except legal ones, on account of the fact that I refused to wear clothes. Julian Broadhead, my probation officer, booked a visit to see me but he was informed that I was too dangerous to be let out of the cage for a visit. But Julian said he needed to see me to make sure that

I was OK. He wouldn't give up and he eventually got his way.

Julian was allowed to see me but I was not allowed out of the cage. Julian sat outside the cell door and I was naked on the other side of the bars. My cell stank – it had been my toilet and my bed for weeks. I'd had no air, so obviously I had started to smell, too. I'd not even been allowed to have a shave. It was embarrassing.

I looked like a wild man, an animal … like an ape in a dirty Victorian zoo.

It was magic to see him and actually to have a visit, but the circumstances were totally demeaning.

There were a few occasions when violence almost took me over and I just knew that the screws were waiting. But the Governor said he'd been instructed by the Home Office that I should remain isolated until further notice.

I sat in the corner, covered in a blanket and holding a biro pen in each hand, ready for the screws. I was prepared to blind the first fucker who walked through my door. I was getting ill again. Had my time come to go back into the nut-house? Was I mad? Or was I being driven mad simply because the prison system didn't want me?

On 2 November the van arrived. I had spent 40 days and nights in that stinking cell with no clothes, no air and no real human contact. I felt bad, bitter and nasty. They secured me in the body-belt and led me off.

It was beautiful to feel the fresh air on my face. I filled my lungs with it; it felt like heaven. I shouted out to the lads, 'Stay strong!' as I climbed into the van. The electronic gate opened up slowly and the van drove off into Love Lane. As I was leaving that evil place behind, I thought to myself, May it rot. I was hoping that it would be the last time I would see

Wakefield. How wrong I was. I didn't know it then but I was destined to return, very soon, to my very own nightmare.

The screws at Frankland didn't seem to be taking any chances, maybe because the last time I was there I'd grabbed the Deputy Governor! I was put straight into the block. I was confused and bewildered because I'd been told I wouldn't be there long, but they hadn't told me what lay in store.

Eddie Slater, a lifer, was two cells away from me. Just beforehand, he had been up on the roof at Durham, protesting. Stevie 'Sawn Off' Galloway was also in the block. Steve is a Scouser, a lovely lad with plenty of bottle. He'd had a rough ride over the years, but always kept cheerful. A lot of my old mates were in Frankland at that time, but unfortunately I didn't get to see them. At least Frankland block was clean, and we had sinks and toilets in our cells and I could wear my own clothes.

My next three weeks passed with no serious problems, but my pal Eddie Slater lost his father and the bastards denied him permission to go to the funeral. That put a bad taste in my mouth. It made me think about my own dad. If he were to die, as it looked likely he would soon, would they allow me to attend his funeral?

Three weeks doesn't sound a long time, but believe me it is when you are stuck in no-man's land, not knowing where you are going next.

One day my door unlocked and I was asked if I would see an officer from the special unit in Hull Prison. I agreed – what did I have to lose? Sweet fuck-all. I spoke to the senior officer from Hull for about 30 minutes and he as good as told me that my move to Hull Special Unit had already been sanctioned by the Home Office. I felt a bit of hope run through my veins. For the first time since I had been sentenced, I

actually felt relaxed. At least I would be able to make
a cup of tea on that unit. I'd be able to mix with other
cons and work out in the gym. I could try to settle
down at last. I slept a bit more peacefully that night.

A couple of days later, the van arrived, the belt
went on and off I went. I shouted out to Eddie and the
lads to stay strong. This was going to be one of the few
journeys that I actually felt happy about.

It took just over two hours from Frankland to Hull.
As we travelled in the van, I truly felt now that I
could get on and do my eight years. This was the
break that I needed. It had to beat the blocks and the
dungeons. I decided I would give it a good go. This was
surely my last hope.

Hull gave me, in my first few months, the feeling of
being in control of myself again, a big step for me at
the time. It also produced one of those rare, magical
moments that are so cherished by long-term cons.

I'd arrived on the unit on 29 November 1993 and
settled down well. I did my own cooking, and I was
allowed to phone Loraine and Andy twice a week. But,
as often happens with me, a situation developed
where I ended up not talking to the screws on the unit
for three months. It wasn't a sensible way to go on, so
I put a deal to them – and I put it down in writing. It
turned out to be an absolute blinder! By now it was
Easter 1994, and Good Friday – which was also 1
April – was coming up. I told the screws, on a piece of
paper, that I would talk with them only if they all
stood outside my door on 1 April and sang 'O Come All
Ye Faithful'. That was my full and final demand!

I personally didn't believe that they would do it,
but to my amazement they did! Every screw on duty
that morning at 8.00am stood there in a line and sang
it for me. The other three cons on the unit, Paul Flint,
Tony McCulloch and Eddie Slater, just couldn't
believe what was happening! They were buzzing. It

was magic – and it finally buried the hatchet. I've a lot of respect for them for doing that. The reason I had chosen not to speak to them in the first place was because one screw had upset me. I won't go into it as it's personal, but he knows what he did, so I'll just leave it at that.

By now I'd learnt how to cook, I'd taken English and carpentry lessons, I'd done some paintings and a sculpture of a head. I got more certificates of achievement in four months than anyone else had in four years. Everyone was impressed – the teachers, the screws, the psychologist – but most of all I impressed myself.

I trained hard in the gym and helped the other three cons along, as I respected each one of them. They were only young, but all of them were good, dignified men. Karen Simpson was the unit psychologist. She was a lovely person and I don't think she realised how much she helped me. Our chats together were always positive and I rate her as one of the nicest people that I've ever had the privilege of meeting. She certainly gave me a lot of hope and good advice.

Roland Barber was another lovely guy. He was an outside cook who came in twice a week to teach us. He always cheered our days up. Then there was Lach Forbes, an outside carpenter, who came in to teach us woodwork. Lach's a diamond. He would come into the gym with us and have a laugh. He also made all the frames for my paintings. Then there was Steve Burgess, a hypno-therapist who came on to the unit twice a week to help us relax. Steve and I wrote a play for the radio together. I've a lot of respect for Steve, he helps so many people and he's also got a big heart! There were so many decent people there, like Ivor Man, the English teacher – such a nice guy. They all helped us. And one screw in particular was very decent. His name was Roy Kirk. Roy was only in his late 20s, and I've got to be honest, he's one of the best blokes I've ever met. He stands no shit, but he'll speak up for the cons if he thinks they are right. You couldn't ask for better.

So here I am, heaping on the praise. But then what happens? A man causes me to flip. All this good work was going on, and – for me – it turned to dust in seconds.

It was Easter Monday and the last three days had been magic. 'O Come All Ye Faithful' was still a big joke to us all. The unit was buzzing, alive.

It was about 9.00am, and the boys and myself were in the kitchen preparing breakfast. I was the porridge man; I used to make the porridge every day. Paul was sorting the eggs out; Eddie was making the tea, and Tony was having a fag. This was like any other, normal day. There were no upsets and we were all OK ... until a governor appeared. Adrian Wallace was the Deputy Governor of Hull and also the unit governor. When I saw him that morning in his blue, pin-striped suit, I felt the sweat running down my neck – and then I lost control of my senses.

I ran at him ... and in seconds he was my hostage. My insanity had broken free once more. Months of pent-up madness were pouring out of me. My eyes were bulging and my whole body ached for excitement.

I had Wallace in a Japanese strangle-hold. I screamed at everyone, 'Come near me and I'll snap his neck!'

Easter Monday was mine and this unit was mine. I was the Governor today!

I shouted to the lads not to get involved. Tony, Paul and Eddie all looked stunned. I shouted out to them, 'Cheer up, lads, Happy Easter!'

The screws started to crowd around. I told them to stay back. I could feel Wallace trembling. I dragged

him into one of the TV rooms and barricaded it up
with tables and chairs. I then took his tie off and tied
his hands up behind his back. The Hull siege (well,
my first Hull siege!) had begun.

I sat Wallace down on a chair in the middle of the
room and then grabbed his keys and went through his
pockets. His credit cards went flying; I ripped up the
bank notes. I went wild, kicking over furniture. It was
a crazy scene. Rock music was blaring out from a telly
I'd turned up.

'You're a bastard, a bag of shit!' I grabbed an iron
that was in the room. 'Don't move or I'll kill you. I'll
batter you with this, c--t!'

I demanded a couple of cups of tea for me and for
Wallace, and after a few minutes two steaming mugs
of cha were pushed through the barricades. I love a
cup of tea! Helps calm me down. I undid Wallace's
hands so he could drink his tea.

Then I used the man's radio to order them to shut
the whole fucking prison down. Soon it was Wallace's
turn to relay a message. I wanted the blow-up doll I'd
been denied at Woodhill – plus steak and chips twice!

I grabbed Wallace around the neck and walked him
along the corridor to the next TV room. I barricaded
the place up and told him I was going to sing 'I
Believe', the song I wanted playing at my funeral. (I
was sure police marksmen would soon surround the
place, and I have to say that, at that moment, I was
prepared to go out fighting.)

Sing it I did, at the top of my voice! Then I made a
mistake. I tried to get back to the other TV room with
my hostage. I loosened my grip on his neck as I went
for the door handle and I lost my balance and was
rushed by screws. Wallace started kicking me in the
face and body. I was overpowered.

I left Hull the same day ... stripped naked and
put in the body-belt. Once in the van, I felt

numbness to the right side of my face. I had a terrible headache that caused me to feel sick and dizzy. It was a good two-hour journey before the van drove into Leicester Prison.

The door opened and the seven screws and I jumped out. There were governors, screws, members of the Board of Visitors. And all saw my nakedness. They led the way to the steps that would take me to the punishment block. It was like some crazy dream. As I walked barefoot through the puddles outside, I thought about the past, the good times, the moments of joy. I just didn't want to face up to reality. But the screws' faces said it all. They believed I was a madman.

They took me to a cell where they took off the body-belt and gave me some food and a mug of hot tea. I can remember little else about that day. I drifted into a big, black cloud. All I could feel was the pain in my head. I couldn't eat the food they had given me – I couldn't even move my jaw up and down.

The next morning I awoke to the sound of the night screw getting ready to welcome the day screws. My jaw was hurting like hell. I had cuts and lumps all over my head and I think that the muscle in my right shoulder had been torn. I felt terrible.

As my door unlocked, I rolled out of bed to see the familiar face of a screw who I knew. He was a decent old boy and had always treated me OK, so I gave him respect. I told him about the pain I was getting with my jaw. He soon got a doctor over to see me. As you know, I despise prison doctors. But at times you have to give in. This was one of those times. He examined me and told me that I would have to have an X-ray. He also noted in writing the injuries to my head.

The screws in Leicester were no trouble to me. They gave me no shit and there was an element of trust between us. They allowed me to make a call to

Loraine. She was gutted when I told her what had happened. She always cheers me up does my Loraine. She made me promise to her that I would stay cool. She's the governor in my eyes, so I made the promise, gave my respects to her husband Andy, and hung up. As soon as I went back to my cell, I went to sleep. It was obvious that I was suffering from concussion. I remember very little of the rest of that day.

On 6 April, I heard my door unlock at 8.00am – I presumed for breakfast. But there were a dozen screws and a governor standing there. Before they said anything, I knew that it was time for me to move on again.

'What about my fucking X-ray?' I asked. The Governor assured me that I would have it done where I was going next.

'Where's that?' I asked.

'Wakefield,' he replied. 'But it will only be temporary.'

I knew that the Home Office didn't have a fucking clue what to do with me. They had helped to create me, and now they couldn't control me. They are such short-sighted, petty-minded, vindictive bastards.

The belt went on once again and off we went – back up north. I wasn't happy. My head was throbbing, my jaw ached and I was thoroughly pissed off. I stayed silent throughout the journey. I had no reason to slag off the Leicester screws in the van. They were only doing their job and they had done me no wrong. I did a lot of thinking during that journey. I wondered if I would ever be free again. I thought that if I didn't get a life sentence over the Woodhill siege, then I was bound to get one over the Hull one.

I'd been digging myself into a fucking big hole, and holes couldn't come bigger than this.

★ ★ ★

Wakefield Prison. The Hannibal Cage.

The whole of Britain must know by now about the 'Hannibal Cage'. It was plastered all over the newspapers. This cage was ten times worse than the last cage I was in, here in Wakefield.

It was total isolation.

Being locked in there could quite easily destroy a man. It is potentially the last bus-stop before total insanity – or death.

It was the only cage of its kind in the whole British prison system. The last convict to be held there was Bob Maudsley. Bob was jailed for life in 1974 for stabbing and garrotting his uncle. He later killed three cons. One was a hostage in Broadmoor, who he tortured and, when he was finally dead, held aloft to show the screws who had been negotiating for his release. Then there were two cons he killed in Wakefield. He reputedly cut open the head of one of his victims and ate his brains with a spoon.

For the three-and-a-half years since Bob had left, the cage had remained closed.

Now they had opened it up again – just for me. The cage was a living death, a total void. It has its own toilet and shower, so there is no human contact at all. All meals are put on a table ten feet away from the cage doors. When I was unlocked to collect my meals, there were never fewer than a dozen screws standing by. Once I counted 15. Thirty eyes watching my every move.

This procedure happened three times a day. It was the only time that I actually left my cell. I was not allowed any exercise, neither was I allowed any visits apart from legal ones. When my solicitor or probation officer visited me, they had to sit outside the cage door. We could not even shake hands. We had to talk through the steel net in the cage door. There are two doors to this cage. The outer one is solid steel and has an observation slit in it. The inner door is also steel, with the steel net across it.

The inner door has a 1ft-wide gap in the bottom, through which I was passed a cup of tea at supper time.

Sheets of bullet-proof glass form one section of the cell wall. Through these I could be observed 24 hours a day. My table and chair were made of compressed cardboard and my cutlery and plates were plastic. My bed was bolted to the concrete floor.

The walls are reinforced steel and concrete. The bars on the windows are solid steel. A steel cage is attached to the outside of the window.

I was forever pacing up and down, naked except for a blanket. I had a lot of time to think. The Cage is the end of the line. The silence is the madness. Fantasy becomes reality. There is nothing to look at, no one to talk to and no one to listen. You are the living dead. Dreams and nightmares, day and night, merge seamlessly.

You are empty, utterly empty. You are as lost as the coma victim who can hear what goes on around him but can only blink helplessly to an unknowing world.

To be stranded in a desert with no water, weak limbs and merely the faintest hope of survival is one thing. To be stranded without hope, yet surrounded by people who could really help, is another.

But I still had my dreams, however fragile they might be. To stop dreaming is to stop breathing.

On Thursday, 28 April 1994, the cops came to my cage door.

I was charged, through the bars, by Humberside Constabulary, with: (1) False Imprisonment; (2) Threats to Kill; (3) Actual Bodily Harm; (4) Criminal Damage; (5) Criminal Damage.

These five charges were the result of the Hull siege. At 15.35 hours the police walked away from my cage.

I'd made no comment, merely nodded and grunted. The cops had looked shocked to see me in such a medieval cage. As they left, I shouted out, 'Next time, bring me some pies.'

The outer door slammed shut and I was alone.

So here I was, again awaiting another trial, another load of mental pain. There seemed to be no end. And maybe there isn't.

CHAPTER TWELVE

I realised that I had been waging a war, a war that had gone on now for 20 years.

During this war I had gained a reputation, but nothing more. In fact I had lost almost everything – not just my wife and son, my home and my liberty. I was now not just a Category A convict. And I was not just Category A and in solitary confinement. I had now been branded the worst of the worst. A man held in a Hannibal Cage.

Prison and the asylums had made me worse, not better. I had truly become a hostage of my past, condemned by my reputation and my fucked-up mind.

But one day in that cage at Wakefield there was a glimmer of hope. Apart from trying to build the pond at Parkhurst, when I'd been stabbed, I'd never tried to do anything positive or creative with my life. Some cons become born-again Christians. I became a born-again cartoonist!

I've actually met some good screws on my journey, and if more were like Prison Officer Mick O'Hagan I might have had a fighting chance of a relatively normal life. PO O'Hagan ran the seg unit in Wakefield. He's in his late 50s, 6ft tall and 200lb – a man's man. He's no soft touch. But he's the fairest screw you could ever meet. If you're OK, he's OK, and you will get what you're entitled to. No more, no less. He was a good boxer in his day, but I like him because he doesn't take life too seriously. He has time to laugh and sees the funny side of it all. He doesn't look down on us cons. PO O'Hagan has always taken the time to come to my cage door and ask how I am. He's shown me humanity.

One day, Mr O'Hagan came to my cage door and told me his true opinion. He told me I wasn't stupid; I should start boxing it clever. Why didn't I start studying, learning about art, poetry and writing?

Why not?

I had nothing to lose, and potentially a lot to gain. Not freedom, not parole even, but a feeling of self-worth for the first time in many years. Sure, I was hard, I was strong – but where was my life going?

He got me pens, pencils, rubbers, rulers and loads of paper. It was the best thing that ever happened to me. I sat alone at my cardboard table, went inside myself, and created. I taught myself how to draw, and I got better and better. Mr O'Hagan always encouraged me.

I've since won seven major prison prizes – in the

Koestler Awards – for my writing, art and poetry. Seven in eight years, and one year I didn't even enter (I got two awards the next year). The Koestler scheme was the brainchild of the famous author Arthur Koestler. He believed passionately in social reform, and in 1961 he agreed the details of the scheme with the then Home Secretary, Rab Butler. One art critic described my paintings and drawings as the 'work of a madman'. But how closely linked are insanity and genius? Van Gogh cut his ear off, after all!

So I take my hat off to Mr O'Hagan, and to another decent screw in Wakefield, Mr Maguire. He's also a man I've got nothing but respect for. I'd buy him a pint any time. They couldn't do a lot to make my time in the cage better, but what they did do was show me some respect and humanity. They'd come to my door to chat about boxing, soccer, what was going on in the world. Even if it was only ten minutes a day, they made the effort. There are other screws – and they know it – who I'd lay out given half the chance. They are nothing but bully boys with peanut brains. They are just power-crazed, faceless hobbits. They know to steer clear of me, and I don't talk to them.

A nun called Sister Carmel used to see me most days. She'd sit outside my door and talk. Now let's get this straight; I've normally got no time for sky-pilots in jail. Most strike me as hypocrites. I remember one in another seg unit years earlier. He saw the screws kicking nine bells out of me. He actually turned around and walked away. A few days later when he was doing his rounds, I put it on him. 'Oi!' I said. 'I saw you. You're a fucking disgrace, a coward. Jesus would have seen you walk away, too, so he knows the strength of you! Now fuck off before I chin you.'

But Sister Carmel was a gentle soul, a wonderful lady with an angelic smile. I'd sit on my cardboard chair and talk to her through the steel gate. It's not easy to see out, because of the cage welded to it. Lord Longford also came to see me. His eyes filled up; he said in 50 years of visiting prisons he had never seen anything like it.

I trained alone in that cage. I would pace up and down, stop, and do 50 press-ups. Some days I'd get through 3,000. I had to have a routine. It's the only way of dealing with solitary. There are some days when you can't motivate yourself, just like in normal life. Depression sets in. That's when I know I am lucky to be caged ... when I know I can get dangerous.

It was a little over a month after I landed in Wakefield when they came mob-handed for me. The body-belt went on and I was taken to Bullingdon in Oxfordshire where I was held for a little over a week so I could appear at Luton magistrates over the Hull siege. On the way back to Wakefield, all hell broke loose. The van got a puncture and ended up on the motorway hard shoulder. There were cop cars, sirens, the lot. I was whizzed off in a police van to Leicester, where I spent the night in the seg unit. Then, on 18 May 1994, I was back home in my cage at Wakefield.

It wasn't to last. Governor Parry came up to me. He explained there was going to be a lot of noise over the next few months with workmen in the seg unit. After years in isolation, noise and sudden movements affect me badly. I had a choice. I could stay and they would give me ear-plugs, or I could go back on the circuit, the rounds of Cat A blocks. I thought it over. I knew I would get headaches and possibly snap with all the noise. I said simply, 'Move me.'

Strangeways seg had changed since the massive riot there. It was June 1994 and there were new rules and new ideas. I had a big reception committee waiting, but the seg screws were decent to me. They got me a running machine and locked me in an empty cell to exercise. The food was great and my cell was clean. But I knew I would never get on with Governor Munn. I told him straight; if I had an axe, I'd hit him with it. At least he knew where he stood.

After a week, some silly fucker moved next door. He kept knocking on my wall.

'Oi, mate. Got any burn?'

No, I don't smoke pal. Sorry.

'Got any drugs?'

'Nope, I don't touch them.' This guy was bugging me.

'You fucking southerners are all the same!' he shouted. 'Tight c--ts!'

The next day I took a quick look through his spyhole before I went out on exercise. I memorised his face. You never know … one day.

Later, I wrapped up some of my shit in a little piece of cellophane and stuck it in a matchbox I'd found. I hid it in the shower room, and that night I banged on his wall. I told him where to find his 'drugs'. The next day he picked up the parcel. Try and smoke that, sonny! I often play tricks like that on rats. I like to hear them shout out 'I'll fucking kill you!' People like that make me feel unwell. They're a waste to humanity.

A few weeks later, the van pulled up and I was off to my old hunting ground, Walton Jail and the seg unit. I know Walton's dirty and tough, but it's a man's jail. You know where you are. The sad thing is there is always a mob of screws waiting for me, lined up with their sticks. Walton seg block can be the cruellest place on earth. But there are some older screws who treat me well and don't harbour a grudge about me ripping the roof off in '85.

Exactly a month later, I was in High Down, Surrey, a strange seg to me, with a load of muggy, loud-mouthed cons. I was edgy and getting violent again. I could feel myself going and I had to do thousands of press-ups to release the tension. I knew I was like a walking bomb, and it seems they did, too. I lasted 11 days before, on 15 August, I was transported to Belmarsh Special Secure Unit on the outskirts of London. That was where I would see my dear old dad for the last time.

I knew that bunch of screws well, and they set up the visit with my dad like no other jail could. Even the governors helped to make it special. I was judged too dangerous to mix with other cons, but the screws knew my old man was dying of cancer. They let me, my dad and my brother Mark out on to the seg where they'd set up a table. There was a carton of orange juice and some cups for us. I helped them make it look nice for Dad.

When Dad came in with Mark, he looked weak and very tired. But he still had that spark, the fire in his eyes. He was a fighter until the end. I took him into my cell and Mark stayed outside. It was only a seg cell, but it was clean and I had a toilet and a sink as well as a window and a few bits and bobs lying around.

'Bloody hell, son! It looks more like a flat!'

'Yeah, Dad. I'm doing well now!'

We hugged and both started to fill up with tears. I told him how sorry I was that I was not out there to be with him. I told him I loved him. We went back out on to the landing and sat with Mark. Fuck me. It broke my heart to see my dad this way. But he was a brave man.

We both knew we would never see one another again.

When it was time for him to go, I felt myself getting a bit dangerous. I was upset, wound up. But I fought my urges – not for me, but for the sake of my dear old dad. Mick Reagan helped me a lot, although he may not know how much. He was on duty that day, and

whenever he was on duty, he made me feel calmer.
He's a good man who cares about good people.

As Dad walked out, I watched every single step he
made. I knew that would be the last I would ever see
of my father.

They went through the bullet-proof, electronic door.
And then Dad turned, winked at me, and put his fists
up in a fighting pose. That's the last memory I have of
the greatest man I've ever known. Mick Reagan put
his hand on my shoulder and asked, 'You OK, Chaz?' I
could only nod. I was too fucking cut up to speak. I
managed to say thanks to all the screws – they'd been
such a wonderful bunch that day. Then I banged up
and cried my fucking heart out. Yeah, big men do cry.

The next day it was back to the old routine. It had
to be to survive. I worked out. Press-ups, sit-ups, and I
used my medicine ball. I call her 'Bertha'. She's seen
me through a good few hours, has Bertha. I could
never forget those last few moments with my dad. But
for the moment I had to concentrate on my routine,
otherwise I would have been completely destroyed.
Within four weeks that routine was ruined. Someone
in headquarters was having a laugh. I was off to
Lincoln, a shit move that made no sense. I was being
fucked around once more. I was there only three days.
Then it was back in the van and off to the Scrubs.

I will never, ever, forget those maggots. By now you
will most likely have heard or read a lot about
brutality at Wormwood Scrubs. It's a London jail with
a bad reputation. Screws have now been suspended
for beating cons. Whether they're the guilty ones is
anyone's guess, but I can well remember the bastards
who beat me within an inch of my life. The other
allegations came years after I made my statement –
against my nature, I have to say – to the cops in
October 1994. Fuck-all happened as a result.

For me, it happened the week of my dear old dad's

funeral. I arrived at the Scrubs on 16 September 1994. It was a tense start, so many eyes staring as I came in. Those faceless idiots took me out of my body-belt and led me to a cell to strip-search me. But there was one decent screw I remember from some time back. He winked at me as if to say, 'Get your head down, Charlie!' I said to him, 'You still here, gaffer? Working in this piss-hole?' He laughed and said, 'It's a job!'

'Some fucking job,' I said. 'Why not work in an abattoir?'

The door slammed shut on my cell and I was alone once more. I searched it as I always do. You never know what you might find. Tools may come in handy later; drugs always get slung down the toilet. I remember once finding a £50 note in the hollow of the bed in a new cell.

Frank Fraser had sent me his book *Mad Frank,* so I settled down to read it. Then I tried to get into a routine with my press-ups. But every time the door opened I got the eye-ball treatment. It simply doesn't work with me. I've seen it all before.

Then one cold September morning the call came that I had been fearing. They led me to the office and handed me the phone. It was Loraine. Dad was dead. He was only 70.

'Charlie … you OK? Speak to me.'

'Yeah, Loraine. Thanks for telling me. Keep an eye on Mum. Pull together, eh. And stay strong.' Click.

A week later it was my father's funeral. I desperately wanted to go, of course, but my request was blocked. I visited the prison church and sat there thinking about my dad, my family and about my treatment in prison. I wrote a message for the screws on a piece of paper:

I've had enough. I'm not playing games any

> more. I'm going in the box. I want to be in
> silence − I don't want to talk to anybody. I
> want no legal or social visits, no newspapers,
> no letters, no canteen, no clothes, no exercise.

I wanted to go in the strong box the next day, a
Thursday morning.

I woke early and the door opened for slop out at
about 7.30am. I walked out naked with my bucket
and, as I was walking back to my cell, I saw there
were about ten screws by my door. I went inside and
picked up a jug of water and a toilet roll and said, 'I'm
off to the box.'

'No you're not,' one of them said.

No. I was shunted from pillar to post. In fewer than
five months, I was moved from seg unit to seg unit
seven times − Wandsworth; Winson Green; Lincoln;
Bullingdon; then to Luton Crown Court where I got
another seven years for the Hull and Woodhill sieges;
back to Bullingdon; to Full Sutton; to Strangeways;
and, in February 1995, to Frankland, way up in
County Durham.

I went on hunger-strike in Frankland soon after I
arrived. I was sick of life, sick of their lies; sick of the
constant moves, and of being banged up like some
beast in solitary. I lasted 18 days without food. I was
weak, tired, and I was a problem they didn't want. In
mid-May they moved me back to High Down in Surrey.

I was exhausted and depressed. Then the Governor
came into my cell with all his boys. This Governor
became a nuisance, always popping in over the next
week. I couldn't stand it. I'd been wasting away on
hunger-strike and now I wanted some peace and quiet
to recuperate. I told the senior officer I was sick of this
guy coming around, and if he wanted to see me, he
should just look through my spy-hole.

I'd just eaten a huge Sunday dinner − lovely after

starving for so long – when I heard footsteps coming closer. They stopped outside my door and I heard the key in my lock. I thought this was strange. One set of footsteps, but it was always a mob that came to open my door. It was the Governor, on his own, obviously calling my bluff.

Smack! You c--t! Smack! I jumped on him and then tried to stab him in the eye with my toothbrush. I heard bells, screws running, and I was soon slung in the strong box. It wasn't long before a screw came to my spy-hole and explained they had told the Governor to stay away from me. 'We told him,' he said. 'But he said, "I know Charlie, he's okay with me!"'

Well, he mugged himself off, didn't he? I've never seen him since, but if I do I'll chin him again, just for the fun of it.

I was on the road again – Winson Green; Lincoln; Frankland; Winson Green; Belmarsh; Full Sutton; Walton; Bullingdon; and, on 4 April 1996, back to Belmarsh. It was a bloody merry-go-round and it was making me dizzy.

But Lincoln had shown me another side to life, a side that I loved. I was given some trust, and I helped disadvantaged, backward kids. It happened after I was told in no uncertain terms to behave, and in return I'd get a bit of gym. I was also allowed out of the seg. I went straight into the gym for my first hour's exercise on equipment for over a year. I bench-pressed 150 kilos, ten times. Not bad for a guy who'd been surviving on stodge and porridge!

Then the physical training instructor asked if I'd like to help out with the special needs kids. Yeah, I'd go for that! I love kids. They're so innocent. When I've won prizes for my poetry and art, the money has gone straight to a hospice for kids up north. I've raised hundreds of pounds for them. Now I was being given another chance to help.

Hand-picked cons looked after these special needs youngsters once a week when they came into the prison. I was so pleased; I almost felt human again. It was brilliant!

These lovely people, Downs Syndrome and the like, were like little children ... laughing, happy! We played ball games and they all loved me. I put one lad on my shoulders and ran around the gym. He enjoyed it so much, and so did I. Some were kids, some were adults with kids' minds. But they were all lovely, and I had them laughing! There were about 30 of them, and eight cons. At the start of the second session some ran up to me and hugged me. I devised games for them. Just simple stuff, but it kept them entertained. In one I'd get them to sling footballs at me and I'd head them back. Whoever caught the most was the champion.

It was great, and I did so well that I went up on the wing. I lasted just a day – then I fucked it up. Nothing ever lasts with me.

I met a good guy there called 'Mozz'. We went out for our hour's walk, but after 30 minutes we were called in. Fuck that! I get an hour. It's the only hour of fresh air I get in the day. I turned to my pal and said, 'Go in, son.' All went in apart from me. I wanted my hour, and I got my hour. But when I went in, there were 20 of them waiting for me. I was on my way to Frankland the next day, and, within a month, back to Winson Green.

Within weeks I was buzzing. It was my second stay in Winson Green in less than four months. I arrived in September 1995 and by December I was getting my head sorted. They were even letting me out on the yard with the other Cat A cons. There were two Asian brothers up for murder and robbery, only young and never been in jail before. I was doing press-ups with them both on my back. We had lots of laughs during our hour a day. I'd pick them up and run with them on my back. I was as high as a kite on adrenalin. Full of madness.

But one day I just didn't feel right. I felt a bit disturbed, a bit dangerous. We did our work-out in the yard and then I saw the security door unlock. In walked Dr Wilson. I grabbed him in a neck-hold. 'You're coming with me, c--t!' Then I whispered slowly in his ear, 'Your lucky day, Doc. You've won the raffle. You've won me.'

I walked backwards with him towards my cell. The bells were ringing, there were shouts and boots running. But when I got to my door, I discovered I was locked out. You'd have thought I'd have my own key by now!

All hell broke loose and they steamed us. Fair play to them, they were pros. They saved him. But I could smell a whiff of something unpleasant in the air.

I was off on my travels ... again!

CHAPTER THIRTEEN

Sure, I said I'd eat one of the Iraqis, but in my heart of hearts I never really meant it. I've got a rule of thumb that says I should never attempt to eat anything that disagrees with me. Plus, I'd had a big breakfast that morning.

I'd been shipped out of Belmarsh after taking Dr Wilson hostage. I was ghosted to Full Sutton, to Walton and then to Bullingdon. By April 1996, I was back at Belmarsh.

I was in mental turmoil, confused by all the moves. There had been well over 100 since I first came inside.

I was unsettled and, let's face it, a bit paranoid. I
needed my solitary. They had helped create me, now
they had to deal with me. My vision was going after
years of darkness and artificial light. Eyes troubled
me – other people's eyes. People staring, people
invading my space. People breathing near me. They
had kept me alone for so long, and alone was all that
I really knew – my routine; my solitary. I was
plugging my ears and blocking out the noise, blocking
out the world.

Belmarsh had been good to me. But my dangerous
spells were returning and one day in September 1996
I snapped big style. The day before, an Iraqi on
remand had bumped into me while I was collecting
my meal. He stared at me.

No 'Sorry, pal.' No respect. He probably didn't know
the lingo. But it just wound me up. Jabber, jabber,
jabber. Fucking Iraqi. I brooded all day and all night. I
should have just slapped him there and then. But the
next day, a Saturday, I flipped.

This guy was one of the six Iraqis who'd hijacked a
Sudanese Airways plane and forced it to land at
Stansted a few weeks before. It turns out they were
trying to get asylum here. But I was getting angrier
and angrier about this ignorant fucker who'd bumped
into me.

I despise ignorance. Plus, I'd torn a muscle in my
back weight-lifting. I was in agony, and my mind and
my routine were in pieces. I need my routine to keep
me sane. I was also sick of most of the other cons
whingeing about their lot. When I started off, it was
one hot meal a day if you were lucky, a shower a week
and a bit of exercise. I was fed up with this new breed
of cons. Three square meals a day, satellite telly, pool
tables and they still fucking moaned and groaned.

I was sweeping the corridor when I spotted two of
the Iraqis. Their eyes were boring into me, and my

eyes turned black with pure hatred and rage. The Iraqi siege was starting!

I belted another con called Jason Greasley over the head with my metal bucket and dragged him into the Iraqis' cell. Within seconds, I had not two but three hostages on the floor. There was soapy water all over the place. I smashed off the toilet door and barricaded the cell with broken furniture – a table, chair, mattress and bed.

'Don't fucking move! Keep still you c--ts!'

I ripped out the laces from my trainers and tied the Iraqis' hands. One of them was jabbering on in his own language, so I slung him under a bed. He might have been out of the way, but I could smell him soon enough when he messed his pants.

Screws started towards the cell. I was ranting and raving. My head had completely gone.

'If my demands are not met within an hour, you'll bring in four body bags! I've got a blade; I'll cut them up.'

A Welsh screw by the name of Emyr Lewis, who I knew quite well, came to the door.

'Charlie,' he said. 'Talk to me. What do you want?'

'Is that Taff?'

I didn't have my glasses on and could hardly see through the gap in the door.

'Taff ... I want political asylum. If these Iraqis can have it, I want it. I want a helicopter to Cuba. It's got to land on the sports field. I'm taking Greasley with me.'

I let Taff speak to the hostages, then other screws came to negotiate and I started belting out 'O Come All Ye Faithful'. I was losing it badly, saying I wanted to join my dead dad. I was quite prepared to die that day.

'Don't treat me like a muppet! This is not a game. If I hear any funny business on the landing I'll start snapping necks! There could be a fucking blood-bath up here today if you don't take me seriously.'

Greasley had told me his missus was about to have a baby. I told the screws I was thinking of letting him go – I'd swap him for someone in the Home Office who'd been shunting me round the system all my life. I was getting wilder, madder.

'I haven't had a cup of tea! Get me a cup of tea or else I'm going to eat one of the Iraqis!'

I started pacing up and down, brooding, and then I burst into song! 'He's got the whole world in his hands …' I was laughing out loud, crazily. I took my trainers off and shouted at the Iraqis.

'Right you c--ts. Tickle my feet. I haven't had my feet tickled in years!' They did what they were told, because by this stage they'd learnt to address me as General. They were the Lieutenants. They tickled me for a minute or so. I laughed my head off! Then I was fed up.

'Stop!'

They didn't.

'Fucking stop! When I say stop I mean stop straight away, or I'll snap your scrawny fucking necks.'

I told the screws, 'There's been a change of plan. We're not going to Cuba any more. Listen to me. This is what I want.

'I want a van at the end of the unit, a helicopter on the sports field and a jet at Heathrow ready to fly to Libya. I want political asylum and I want two Uzis, 5,000 rounds and an axe. There are four other Iraqis and they're coming with us. We need seven medium-sized, black suits – and one large, double-breasted, for me. I want white shirts and smart hats for the lot of us. These three will be cuffed to me with ropes around their necks. The other Iraqis will be in the van.

'The van will take us to the helicopter and the

helicopter to Heathrow. Arrange us safe passage through Libyan airspace.'

A screw negotiator said he couldn't agree to my demands, but he'd pass them on.

'No, I know mate,' I told him. 'But it has to go all the way to the top. You're doing all right actually – not a bad job.'

I calmed down a bit and let Greasley go out of compassion, and untied the Iraqis. But the rest of my demands still stood. By this time I was a bit peckish. I began chanting loudly, 'I want ice-cream! I want ice-cream!'

I told the two Iraqis, 'When we get to Libya you two can fuck off. I'm going to go and live in the mountains. I just need a motorbike and an axe.'

Another screw was looking at me through the hatch and spotted a bent metal food tray on the floor of the cell. He asked the Iraqi who wasn't under the bed – the one who could speak a bit of English – what had happened. He said I'd smacked him over the nut with the tray, which I had. The screw asked me why.

Why? Why? I don't know why. It's just fucking madness. I sat down and thought long and hard. Then I gave the tray to the English-speaking Iraqi.

'Hit me over the fucking head!'

He did – four times. Then I smacked myself over the crust another four times. Right! Quits! I told the screws to fuck off and demanded an hour's silence to think some more. I did some squat thrusts and star jumps.

Then I started to talk to this screw Colin Pollard. I knew Col. He'd helped do the time-keeping on one of my world-record attempts for sit-ups. He pointed out that the Iraqis would not be wanted in Libya. I was pissed off, but I still had my blade, which I'd taken out of a safety razor. I said I was still going to Libya – and I wouldn't be getting hurt because I didn't feel pain.

I showed them; I slashed deep into my left shoulder half-a-dozen times. Blood began pissing out.

Col urged me to wash my wounds, which I did. Then he promised me he would personally walk me out and down to the seg unit if I stepped out of the cell.

I pushed back the barricade and found that he was a man of his word. But I felt a huge black cloud enveloping me once more.

★ ★ ★

The aftermath of a siege is actually as disturbing to me as it is to my hostages.

These guys went through seven hours of uncertainty; I got a seven-year sentence, reduced to five on appeal. I'm not asking for sympathy over this – I don't deserve it. But let's face it, in a situation like the Belmarsh siege, *all of us* were locked in that cell, and all tried to find a solution to what started out as a moment of madness on my part, and escalated into sheer insanity.

You take a hostage and you think you're suddenly in a position of power. In a way you are – but right from the start you're on a loser. You just can't fucking win. Free them or eat them, you're facing more years in jail, more years in solitary, more years in the concrete womb.

A lot of physical and mental pain accompanies a siege. It rips you apart; it drains you. You're building your own gallows and bringing your own noose. People want to see you die; you actually become a victim.

When the siege is over, the pain begins. The hostages get pampered in a hospital bed, but you're the beast, the madman, the rabid dog. You become friendless, feared and de-humanised. Stuck in isolation, in a cage, and fed under the door just like a dog.

Belmarsh had been good to me, especially Governor Outram. This man had allowed me some space and had given me a break from solitary. He let me use the gym and allowed me to smash a world record with my medicine ball sit-ups. He treated me like a human, and I felt bad after the siege. I felt I'd let him down, abused his trust. I'd actually signed a contract with him, promising to behave. I felt low and depressed about all the good screws who had also given me a break. Now it was back to emptiness once more.

As the Cat A van sped up the M1, I was locked in a steel 'sweat box', cuffed and confused. I stared out of the window at the passing countryside; I knew it would be a long time before I was ever allowed to walk on grass or stroke an animal.

The Cage at Wakefield was ready. It was time to reflect. Was there any future for me at all? Was I mad, or just bad? I didn't know the answers, but I knew that I was as sorry as hell for the whole incident. No man is as sorry as me when these things blow up. I can't really say why it happened, but I know I seriously lost the plot that day.

The shit goes on; the hole I'm in just seems to get bigger. My problems escalate and my mind deteriorates. It is as if I am nomadic – jail to jail, asylum to asylum. Nobody seems to want me anywhere, so my frustration and anger grows. My only real contact with people is yelling through the cell door. I rarely see fellow cons; most only hear of me arriving and leaving. Some I shout to. A solitary voice, a voice in the wilderness.

Even when I see the opticians I am surrounded by screws. Not one, two, three or four, but as many as a dozen. I remember going when I was at Bullingdon. The lights went out and the letters lit up for me to read. The poor man must have thought I was

Hannibal the Cannibal and about to rush him. I actually felt really sorry for him.

My eyes are bad due to the years of unnatural light I have had. My vision is terrible; I have to wear shaded glasses even to read. Years of solitary have left me unable to face the light for more than a few minutes. It gives me terrible headaches if I do.

My life is illuminated by one dim 40-Watt bulb during the daytime. A red bulb in the ceiling casts a strange, eerie light during the night. Because I have to shout to be heard by the other cons, ordinary people are often, apparently, alarmed by the loud way I sometimes talk. Years of silence, and intermittent shouting, distorts your hearing, your perception of normality. You are about as in control of your speech as those unfortunate people who are partially deaf.

Occasionally, at night, you hear a grown man crying – or screaming. You learn to recognise people not just by their voices, but by their screams. It is truly haunting.

Solitary eats away at a man's soul.

Solitary means you cannot reach out and touch your fellow human beings. Years of loneliness in small cells have left me paranoid about people invading my space. I now can't stand people getting too close, crowding me. I hate people breathing on me and I hate smelly bodies coming near me. Mouths to me are simply for eating – never for kissing.

Prison time is dead time, and being in isolation is like being in a coffin. Twenty-three hours a day of nothing but loneliness, fading memories and vague dreams. Then one hour's exercise – again in solitary.

A man needs a routine to cope with such an extreme situation. For me it is my push-ups and sit-ups. I also pace the room and count each step. Some I know lie down on their beds for three hours on their left side, three hours on their right, and three on their back. Anything to break the day, to make time pass. Sometimes breaking the monotony by counting the stains on the ceiling, turning them into patterns by joining them with imaginary lines. Sometimes by counting the metal strips in the air vent above the door ... in ones, twos and threes. Taking each minute, each hour, each day as it comes.

I personally sleep in the foetal position. It is pure solitude, peace and protection. I try to blank my mind, but often I see the faces of those I love. I see their caring, loving eyes. It's as if they were real.

A routine means survival in solitary. But, in a way, routine can break a man as well. How can you ever mix properly ... even in prison? How can you accept the unexpected?

As with anyone who has lived the solitary life for so many years, I long at times to retreat to it. It's a place of safety. Yes, the Wakefield Cage is gruesome, cold and empty, but at times it has been a sanctuary to me. A place of peace where I can search myself and go inside myself – where I can ask the question, 'Why am I like I am?'

It is institutionalisation at its most extreme. That extreme, to me, has become normality.

Madness is a strange brew. Seven weeks after being shipped off to Wakefield I was transferred, at the end of October 1996, to Bullingdon in Oxfordshire – and within days I grabbed my next hostage.

I should never have been in the same room as Robert Taylor.

My lawyer at this time was Lucy Scott-Moncrieff. I couldn't have asked for a better brief. I'd known her for years and she'd done a tribunal for me in Broadmoor in the 1980s. We lost that one, but she was brilliant anyway.

Unfortunately, Lucy accidentally let me down at Bullingdon.

When Lucy visited me, she always confirmed in advance. But this day I was in for a shock. My door unlocked and ten screws stood there – all friendly, no tension.

'Visit, Charlie! Your lawyer.'

I was a bit unsettled. I had been doing my cell work-out and had no idea I had a visit. I was unprepared and taken aback. My head was not quite right anyway – it was only a few months since the Iraqi siege and I had been sent there because they were doing building work in Wakefield. I should really have been in The Cage at Wakefield, where I was safe.

I had a quick wash and then all other movement stopped as I was escorted the 30 yards from the seg unit to the area for legal visits. In all my years, I'd never had a serious problem with solicitors. Most are good. They advise me, work for me, help me. Some are prats, but I sack them.

So there I am, walking into this room. Two doors, a table and two chairs – and glass in the walls. It's like a Hannibal room, and there's this geezer in it who I don't know.

Who the fuck was it? Where was Lucy? Why had she not told me she was not coming? Was this guy a cop – was it all a set-up? I started to sweat. I tried to fight my urges but the room began to squeeze me. The guy looked relatively calm. He tried to shake my hand, but I refused. I felt that I could hardly breathe. I couldn't stand this any more. I should have shouted to the screws outside: 'Get me out of here!'

This guy, Robert Taylor, was in serious danger.

He said he was a brief and had come instead of Lucy. As he spoke, I felt sick.

I grabbed his pen out of his hand.

'Move, c--t, and this pen is going in your ear at 300 miles per hour. I'll stab a hole in your brain – and if that doesn't kill you, it will vegetabalise you!'

The siege had started.

I told him to sit still and spread his hands on the table. I slung him against a door, then picked up the table and smashed it. Nobody was coming in and nobody was going out. In seconds the office was swarming with screws, staring in through the glass divide. I shouted at them to fuck off, then put this Robert Taylor on the floor where I wrapped him up with his shoe-laces and his tie.

It was all over in half-an-hour, and Robert Taylor has my utmost respect. He was no fool; he kept calm and talked sense to me. I realised very soon that he was not the problem – I was.

I was a very unwell man. I let him go.

Back in the seg unit I buried myself under my blanket and wept. I felt for the man. He'd come in to see me, to help me, to do his job. And I could have ended up wasting him – all because of my paranoia. Would I have done it? Could I have served him up? Sadly, the answer is 'yes'. That day I could have wasted the whole planet.

Robert Taylor wouldn't press charges and refused to make a statement. I admire the man's bottle, and I can only thank him. He may hate me for what I did, but I sent him a nice pen as a mark of my respect.

I was in the van to Walton the next day – back to my old cell in the segregation unit, with a feeding flap in the bottom of the steel door. Just a lodger, just a number passing through. I was destined to stay there eight weeks. I trained hard in solitary and was content. Some of the older screws came to my door for a chat.

Opposite my cell was a smashing lad called Les Cromer, a typical Scouser – all heart. Les sent me over magazines and papers and when he won his case and got out we wrote for a while. He had a lovely daughter who I idolised. The next thing I heard, he had died in a car crash. He was only in his late twenties.

Another con on remand was my mate Badger, a big solid man who worked on the club doors. They breed them tough up there. Sadly, a lot of useless pricks are now pushing drugs on kids. It really is a fucking disgrace. I may be Britain's maddest man, but I don't take drugs, and I don't kill kids. I despise drugs and the strangle-hold they've got on people. A lot of cons today would bend over and take a length for a bag of drugs. They'd even kill. It's so fucking evil.

It was May 1997 and I was back to the shit-hole of Durham seg. I hate Durham – too far up north for people to visit me for a start. But I was pleased about one thing – I was in a cell next to Bob Maudsley. Bob's a funny fucker, genuinely witty. He's got a high IQ. But he has to live for today, as there's no future for him. He's a Scouser, 6ft tall, with long hair and a beard. Now, Bob is the *real* Hannibal Lecter of the system. He's been in solitary over 20 years – he's got no hope and he knows it. I like him because he's a true survivor.

Above me was Big Ashy and Rob Webber, both on remand for violence and gang warfare in the Newcastle area. They are both major faces in the north, feared and respected. But they got badly turned over and got heavy bird – Ashy 32 years and Rob 20 years. I've known Ashy since he was a youngster, serving six years. He does his bird like a man. Just don't fuck with him, and he's sweet. Rattle his cage and your head comes off!

There was another con, by the name of Fontane, who remembered me from over 20 years ago in Hull. He was a big, bald guy, Cat A and in escape patches. On my way out to the caged exercise yard, he stopped me. We had a good chat and got on well. He said he was on remand for robbery, in court the following week. Next week came and a local paper arrived on the seg unit. Fontane's face was staring out at me. He'd got life for multiple rape; one of his victims was just 16. I screamed though his door, 'Fontane, you're a dirty fucking beast! You filthy nonce! A big hard man? You're a big ugly bully who rapes women!'

I'd love a straightener with him. Later, maybe.

No con ever sees me enter Full Sutton – I always arrive at the back door of the seg unit, just as I did a little over a month after being ghosted into Durham. But within half-an-hour, the whole jail knows I'm there – first and foremost the screws. I'm put in a cell on a ten-guard unlock – ten screws standing ready when they open the door. Every morning before breakfast I have to leave my cell so I can be searched, metal detected and put in an empty cell while they search mine. Nobody else has to put up with that shit. It sort of spoils the start of the day.

But there are always good lads in Full Sutton block. This time I met up with Pepi Davis, who was serving a life sentence. Deep down he's a lovely guy, but fuck with Pepi and you fuck with Hell! Then there was Steve Gillen, an armed robber from East London. It was a good ten years since I'd heard from or seen Steve. There was also Chris Brand, a lifer who killed a con in Norwich more than 20 years ago. Chris has got serious problems and I feel sad for him. He was in Broadmoor but they moved him back to prison. He's tried to expose stuff about paedophiles – and good luck to him for that – but the authorities just deny it. Maybe his time will come. Last thing I heard though, Chris had set fire to his own hair.

There was one real fucking low-life in the block – John Steed. This beast was a steroid freak who'd lost the plot in King's Cross and blew away a prostitute in his car. He was also a serial rapist. He'd served ten years of a life, but as soon as I was in Full Sutton I was on his case. I wanted so much to get at him, but it was almost impossible. It's always done one-by-one with cons in the seg.

I thought about jumping a screw to get him to unlock the scumbag's door, but I was surrounded by ten of them every time I came out of my own cell. Steed was on Rule 43 protection. He knew we were not going to meet. He was all mouth through his cell window – pure bravado. He upset me. I told him he was no good to man nor beast, and he might as well die now, rather than spend the rest of his life in jail. I told him it would save a lot of problems, and save someone else getting a life for killing him later!

I left for Belmarsh once more – for a court appearance – and two days later I arrived back to take up bed and board in Wakefield Cage. It was only a few days later that I switched on my radio and heard that John Steed had been found dead in Full Sutton seg unit. The beast had hanged himself and done us all a favour. I was made up!

Reg Wilson was in the next cage to me. Reg is a fitness fanatic – not a man of many words, but a man of action who I admire. And he's a brilliant artist. Reg is serving natural life, like Bob Maudsley. In fact, the Prison Service is now saying Bob, Reg and I might be banged up together – the three most 'difficult' cons in the country. They're talking about a special unit for us. But it's not an answer to my problems, and not an answer to theirs.

My visitors in Wakefield only saw me through the cage door. They shook my hand through the flap in the bottom of the cage. They may not have seen much of me, but they saw the dullness, the emptiness, the raw reality of life in a 12ft by 6ft cage.

Apart from my loyal friends from years back, there were two wonderful visitors to my cage. Firstly, Rosemary Kingsland. Rosemary is a talented author who lived among the natives of a forgotten tribe in South America for a year to research a book. These natives were generally peaceful, but would think little of eating human beings. She not only survived them, she survived me! Rosemary is one of the nicest people I have ever met. Secondly, there was the singer Terri Vasillion. She came in with Rosemary. Terri's eyes filled up when she saw me, and I felt a bit bad about that. But then I asked her to sing.

She did, too! Terri sang 'Hurt' by the great singer Timi Yuro. The whole seg went silent; cons put their ears to the doors, and screws stood still. I got a lump in my throat. It was like a dream; this song was for me. Then she sang 'Unchained Melody', another favourite of mine. What a visit, what a singer! It blew Wakefield away. In 100 years that jail had never seen or heard the like before. When it was over and when the outer door had shut, I lay in the darkness and I felt blessed.

My other visitors up there were my loyal friends Ed Clinton, Chris Reid, Lyn Jameson and, of course, big Ray Williams. Ray's from Ellesmere Port and has been an unflinching pal since I was in my teens. I asked him a big favour. 'Ray,' I said, 'please help me find my son.'

It was 22 years since I'd seen Michael. I knew I was asking a lot, but Ray did me proud. A week later he found Mike. He was a 26-year-old chef. It looked like I would soon be meeting my son for the first time since 1975, when he came into Hull Jail with his mum Irene. I'd seen neither of them since then.

The committal on the Iraqi case was coming up, so they moved me to Belmarsh seg in September 1997. Tony Steel was there. Tony's serving four lifes – he is probably one of Britain's top-five most dangerous men. But I love him (we all do) because he's fearless.

I was sad to hear that the prison officer in the gym,

Mr Murgatroid, had had a heart-attack, but I was glad he survived. He's a lovely man. I also got to see Governor Outram and we discussed my life. In spite of the Iraqi siege, he never washed his hands of me. He told me to believe in myself.

Ten days later, I was back in the Wakefield Cage with a big smile on my face. I had a letter in my hands from my son! Ray was going to bring him in to see his old dad. I felt I had found myself as well as him. I was overjoyed.

Governor Parry and PO O'Hagan set up the visit in a room in the seg. I was being let out of the cage so that I could hug my boy! The seg staff were all brilliant. Even though I'm on a massive security unlock, they all stayed back and there was no tension. I came out of The Cage and put my shoes on (shoes are always kept outside). I had my monkey suit on – the green-and-yellow check boiler suit they make me wear. And then they walked me 20ft to a room where my lad was waiting with Ray. Hell! I filled up. It was like walking into a room filled with light and hope. My little boy was now a grown man. We hugged. It was like looking at myself 20 years earlier. Even Ray had tears. I hugged him, too. Then we sat down and looked at photos Mike had brought me – photos of his childhood, the years I had missed.

That night I felt bad, sick. I had a pain in my chest, and I mean big-time. I was sweating and felt like I could hardly breathe. I thought I was having a fucking heart-attack. I tried to shout to Reg Wilson, but I couldn't, so I rang the bell. A night screw came and looked through the Judas hole. I gasped that I thought I was dying. The medics came and opened my outer door, but they wouldn't open the cage door itself. I had to put my arm through the feeding flap at the bottom while they took my pulse and blood pressure. Then they pushed some pills through the flap and shut the door. I was alone. I could have died. Who would have given a shit?

The next day the doctor said it was stress, an anxiety attack, down to all my problems and the excitement of the previous day meeting my son.

In October I was back at Belmarsh ready for my trial at the Old Bailey. I pleaded guilty to all charges over the Iraqi siege, because I was expecting a concurrent sentence. I told the judge, 'I'm as guilty as Adolf Hitler and OJ Simpson ... I was on a mission of madness, but now I'm on a mission of peace. All I want to do now is go home and have a pint with my son.'

Prison Officer O'Hagan was one of the guards in the dock. He was prepared to speak up for me, but they never asked him. However, my barrister Isabella Forshall explained that years of isolation had left me phobic with other people. She added, 'With his human warmth, he has a great potential to do good.' The prosecutor called me 'probably the most disruptive inmate in this country' and pointed out, 'He has been known to bend cell doors with his bare hands.'

It was a bad result – I got a full seven years added on. I felt shafted.

I was back to the Wakefield Cage. Where was my life going? I had no answers. I simply knew that I needed to block out the bad and concentrate on the good. I still had my pencils, my ruler and rubber and my art card, and I focused on creating some of my best drawings. I saw no particular future. Then they came to my door and said a new unit was opening at Woodhill in Milton Keynes. The Close Supervision Centre would house the worst of the worst. At the very least I'd be back with some of my pals once more! I left for Woodhill on 18 February 1998.

That particular unit is max secure, a jail within a jail. It would be incomprehensible to most cons, let alone ordinary people. It's a totally structured life. For instance, I was told I could have only eight photos. Why eight? Why not nine ... why not seven or – fuck me – *ten*! I couldn't have cassette tapes, and I could only have so many pens. Silly things like that.

There were four wings – A, B, C and D. You go on to B at first, then C and, if you behave ... up to the Hull unit. It's meant to be a progressive system. If you fuck up on B you are put on A. This is real punishment; no radio, no window to open in your cell, and only two half-hour visits.

D wing is the seg unit – make it there, and you're back to 'normal' life going from punishment block to punishment block. All the cons in the special unit are fed through the cell door.

So I went up on B. I was the fourth to arrive, and there was my old pal Fred Low. Tony McCulloch, a double-lifer, was also there (he's now doing triple-life after a prison siege). Tony's a big con with a big heart who I last saw in Hull.

And then there was old peg-leg himself, Michael Sams. None of us spoke to Sams. He'd earlier grabbed a woman probation officer in Monster Mansion – Wakefield Prison. Sams was jailed for life for murdering an 18-year-old Leeds girl and imprisoning another young woman, an estate agent from Birmingham, in a makeshift coffin for eight days. He's got one leg, but he managed to get away with the ransom money for the kidnap of the estate agent, Stephanie Slater. He was on a little moped, dodging down an old railway track with the loot. But he left so many clues.

Fred and I would play chess. He's bloody good, but sometimes I won. (Sorry, Fred, I nicked a few pieces!) He'd help me train. Sometimes I got him on my back and we'd run in the yard. There was no gym in this unit, so I used Fred as my 'human gym'. I'd get him on my back and do push-ups. And then others arrived.

One was Joe Purkiss, a lifer who'd just held a con hostage and cut his throat. I used Joe as a weight. He's thirteen-and-a-half stone. One day I got Joe on my feet and pushed him up in the air! I blew a muscle in my back. It took months to heal and I still get bad pain from it – but life is pain.

I joined many of the others on C wing about a month after them. Fred was there, so was Tony, and Sams. I was progressing – me of all people. Sure, I had bad days. But overall I felt in control of my life, and I felt good. I'd also got two years off my seven stretch for the Iraqi business. I'd wanted more off, of course. I told the three judges at the Appeal Court to enjoy their Christmas lunch ... and choke on their chicken. I don't have to bow down to them. What do I fucking care?

Sadly, about this time I fell out with my soul-sister Loraine. I wrote to her to try to patch it up, but maybe she didn't like my sense of humour on this occasion.

> *Dearest Loraine.*
>
> *Look! What's it gonna take to have you laugh again – and light up my world? Why are you being so cruel: I've said 'sorry' – what more can I do?*
>
> *I want to confess.*
>
> *It was me who strangled your rabbits all those years ago! (Yes, me!) It's been on my mind for nearly 40 years. Me, me, me. I don't know why I did it. I just did. I hate rabbits – all they're good for is eating.*
>
> *And yes, it was me also who jumped out and smashed your boyfriend's legs. Guess you always knew it was me. I did it 'coz you were 16 and in love with the goon. He never loved you. Plus, he was an Elvis fan (a prat). I only*

wanted the best for my sister. I done his legs 'coz he was a toss-pot.

Look, when I nicked that horse for you on your 17th birthday and took you riding across the fields – look how we laughed. Look, when I took you to Brighton and I slung that muppet Hell's Angel over the pier. What a laugh we had! (Lucky he could swim – shame his bike couldn't!)

Look sis, we are now drifting away. Don't allow us to. I know I was nasty to you, but I was in a hole. I'd lost my way. I was under so much pressure, babe. Hell, I had lost my soul – I was in a Hannibal Cage. It's taken me years to get out of that hole. I guess I took one too many hostages. Now I'm a hostage of my past. But I'm still me. Look! I still see your beautiful face in my head. I still love and adore you (we all love you).

The planet sucks, but you're my angel – a lovely, wonderful sister who I love. Come back to me! I've not seen you since the Iraqi siege! Hell, Loraine, am I so bad?

I know I called you a fat little porky midget (but I never meant it). I was upset when I said it. I don't ever blame you for when you hit me with Mum's rolling pin, or when you pushed me in front of the bus. Look, when you set fire to my bed (with me in it), I laugh it off – only 'coz I love you. We are Lutonians, sis. 'Proud'. You were the Luton beauty, and still are to me!

So get your fat arse up to see me, and give your brother a big hug!

Miss you so much Loraine. (Hey, I'm doing well! I'm free in five-and-a-half years!) Love and respect – Charles Bronson.

Loraine and I are now in touch again. And, to everybody's amazement, Charles Bronson made it to the Hull special unit on 6 August 1998. The last time I was there I left in a body-belt with a smashed jaw after taking the Deputy Governor hostage. He was lucky he had so many screws surrounding me. Because once you've got me angry, I just don't stop. I can't be beaten while I'm conscious. I keep coming and coming; the more I'm hit, the more violent I become. That's why I'm a good fighter.

It's almost a challenge to see how much pain I can take. I get a buzz off it. It's not a sexual thing, it's a test of endurance. In the Hull special unit, big Freddy Low used to whip me across the back with a skipping rope while I held on to the punch bag.

I once hit that bag so hard it came off the chain. I'd wrap my arms around it and Fred would lash out. Six hard strokes! Then he would go on to the weight-lifting belt, a six-inch-wide leather strap!

Fred would enjoy it, because he's a raving psycho. Fred's got little or no feelings – Fred's just Fred. You could play chess with him one moment and he'd stab you the next. He's 19 stone, shoulders like a bear and hands like shovels. He's not the brightest of guys, but he's my all-time best buddy. I've trained with Fred as my 'human gym' – he gets on my back and I do press-ups. At times, we had to mop the landing at Hull. I'd grab a rag in my fists and lie down. Fred would lift up my legs and hold me in a 'wheel-barrow' position. Then we'd race around, cleaning the floor as we went. But Fred would never pass his driving test! He smashed me into concrete walls and pillars a few too many times!

When we were in Woodhill, I used to lift Fred up in the yard and run with him on my shoulders. Once I tripped and 34 stone smashed into the wall. I hurt my back and head and Fred caught his leg, but we were back on our feet in no time. At other times I'd get Fred to punch my body about to see how much I could take.

That's what madness does to a man. At times, I've wanted to be beaten to punish me for my life.

He once caught me a blinder in the ribs. I buckled up and thought the end had come! He's caught me on the head, the chin ... all over. I guess he likes it. Helps him to release a bit of madness.

Funny thing is, Fred could serve up any human being no problem – but he loves animals and creepy crawlies! You wouldn't believe it, but when we were in the Hull special unit he had a little pet spider. Normally with Fred it's mice he finds running about his cell. But here he was, doting on this hairy little spider he called Harry the Hornet. He taught it to do tricks, like jumping over match-sticks. One day it died and Fred was really low. We actually had a funeral for Harry in the prison yard! We put the little bugger in a big match-box with hundreds of match heads, then cremated him as we all sang hymns. At least it cheered Fred up a bit.

The majority of folk will never understand Fred – I doubt he even understands himself. Fred's mad on *Star Trek* and all those funny little creatures from outer space. He's really on another planet himself sometimes, but I love him like a brother!

He's not that good with words, but he was so upset over his spider dying that he wrote about it to a pal of mine:

I was relley down in the dumps. But when I banged up Charly had got me a new littil spider. I've called him Wendy Bendy – he's got a mad name cos he's a right mad little bugger. Well, you know me – I like littil anamels and I never did like persons.
I only liked persons when I use't to berry them

*when I was an undertaker. Then when I was a
butcher that was OK to. Iv told the Govenor
hear that no-one better upset my pet spider
(Wendy Bendy) or I'll slice and dice them then
berry them.*

*I'm feeding my Wendy Bendy milk and I catch
flys for him. I will teach him some tricks when
he gets a bit bigger. I was so happy with my
new pet that I byed every lad on the unit two
or three oz's of tobacko each for comeing to the
frunule. Wendy Bendys looking lonly so Im off
to play with him.*

That's our Fred!

More joined us, making seven in total. We were all
men with short fuses, all with psychological problems.
All were violent. Two had killed in jail before, and
probably all of us had nearly killed. It was a powder
keg, a potential war zone, so it was important to make
an effort to get on.

Some screws were brainless, so I spoke to those I
liked and blanked the rest. I just got on with my
'bird' like a normal con. I did my cleaning job, went
to the gym, cooked meals and did my art. Fred and I
played a lot of chess. It was generally peaceful, but
some people are never happy. They have to play their
little games, like nicking our chess pieces. Ha, ha.
Very funny. But it's not very funny when I lose my
head, is it? The only problem was, we never found
out who it was.

Soon enough there was a rift between the cons. I
won't say why, but it happens on units like this. I
blanked three of them, walking past them without
seeing them just as I do with some screws.

Tension was building. All the others could have a
photo taken with their visitors, but I couldn't because
I was 'high profile'. They could all record cassette

tapes for family and friends. Again, I couldn't. Then they came to me for a piss test. Everyone knows I despise drugs. I told them, 'Suck my dick. I'm not fucking doing it. Do all of us, or none of us.'

One day, shortly before Christmas 1998, I was told I would be on the Hull unit for the next five years up to my release date, and would never come off Cat A.

Fair enough, sweet. I accepted it.

Then in January, just a few weeks later, I was called into the office again. They told me the Hull unit was closing down! I'd be moved to a seg unit until a new special unit was opened at Durham in April or May. I was in shock. To say I was upset is an understatement. I was being told one thing one moment, and another the next. I felt cheated. Next, my granny – my mum's mum, Martha, up in Ellesmere Port – died. I loved her. She'd had a good long life – she was 89 – but I knew I wouldn't be allowed to her funeral, just like I couldn't go to my dad's. To top it all a teacher who came into the prison upset me by criticising one of my cartoons. I was a bomb about to explode. Everyone and everything was in danger.

I hated the planet. All my hard work was fucked – why should I go back to isolation? I felt betrayed. They were playing games with a madman. They know how I am; they know how I get. Were they deliberately trying to set me off to shut the Hull unit down?

I'd wanted words with Phil Danielson, the teacher who I thought had insulted one of my cartoons, since December. Everyone else had praised it. Who was he to slag it off? I've won awards for my art. It was a big health and safety poster. I'd spent hours on it. It basically pointed out the risks of smoking, drugs, being over-weight, and having unprotected gay sex. I'm not homophobic. But it's a fact: if you're gay and sleep around without using a condom you're more likely to get AIDS. It's just common sense. Smoke and you're likely to get cancer; eat too many pies and you're going to get fat and risk a heart-attack; take drugs and you're a mug who's going to an early grave. I wasn't fucking happy.

So, Hull special unit was to close? Well, let's close it in style. Let's destroy the godforsaken hole once and for all.

What you see is what you get with me. When I'm good, I'm the best. When I'm bad, I'm the baddest, meanest motherfucker on this planet. My art is my one joy in life, and this teacher slagged it off. It was time to show them who was who.

I'd been on the rowing machine and my adrenalin was pumping. I was bare-chested like a warrior. My leather weight-lifting belt was tight around my waist. I was in my jogging bottoms and lace-up training boots. I was ready for action.

Then Danielson stuck his head round the door. He was on the unit – and he was mine. I rushed him by the classroom door. Smack! One slap to the side of his face and he was down. His glasses went flying. I stood over him with a knife I'd got out of the unit kitchen. I told him quite simply that it was his day to die.

The computer equipment went flying. Ray Gilbert and Freddy Low wisely left the classroom. I yanked the cables out and, with the blade between my teeth, wrapped up Danielson's wrists and ankles. A huge volcano of rage was exploding within me.

I shouted to the screws, 'I've started!'

The unit was evacuated, the cons were banged up, and I was scaring the hell out of my hostage. He went over my shoulders as easy as a shepherd carries a sick lamb … and then – bang – down on the snooker table. His belt and loop of keys came off in a flash.

'If you don't keep quiet, I'm going to let Fred out.'

Fred had banged up. Fred liked Phil Danielson. He

also wouldn't bat an eyelid about plunging him with a blade.

Danielson did as he was told.

I trashed the unit. The noise reverberated as I picked up the deep freezer, held it above my head, and slung it down the staircase. The cooker and other bits of furniture went the same way. The barricade was built. I doused it with cooking oil and soap in case I needed to fire it.

Dumb-bells from the gym went flying. I slapped a blob of butter over the lens of one of the security cameras to stop the screws prying. This was my unit now.

Danielson was squirming. He said it wasn't him who'd slagged off my cartoon.

'Charlie, it's fine. We are waiting to get it framed up. The only thing I privately did wonder about ... I just wonder if it smacked of all gay people spreading AIDS.'

I tied him to a chair.

Then I made a big mistake, one that almost killed me. I wrenched the washing machine off the wall in the utility room. Water spewed all over. The wires tore off. There was a bang and an almighty blue flash. I was thrown across the room as electricity surged through me.

I screamed and groaned. I thought I'd had a heart-attack. I was knocked out for several minutes. When I came to my face was as white as the driven snow. My hands were trembling.

I allowed Danielson to put his feet up on another chair. They were still tied. Then he said he was desperate for a cigarette.

'I hate fucking smokers.'

'All right, Charlie. I take it back. I'll manage.'

'OK. We'll get you some. But I'm not talking to the fuckers.'

Later he got his wish. A cigarette was thrown down from the landing. And I threw something up, too. A note in a boxing glove to my girl Joyce Conner. She's a Canadian serving a sentence at a women's jail in Derbyshire. Joyce and I have never met, but she stands by me and writes me lovely letters. She's a great artist, too. It's obviously more platonic than anything, but she's my princess.

I told Danielson to write a letter to his partner.

Then I told him to cut my ear off.

'I can't go to my grandma's funeral, so cut the fucking thing off and bury it with her when you get out of here. I want a part of me alongside my granny in her grave.'

I still had my knife. I wanted the teacher to cut me with it. But then I got a blinding headache. The fucking fluorescent lights were doing my head in. I smashed them all with the point of a snooker cue. I calmed down a bit.

'Phil, I believe you about the cartoon. I'll make you a cup of tea soon. I know you're cold. Don't worry. You're in shock – it will pass.'

I made my spear out of the knife and the snooker cue, and made Phil a cup of tea. Well, it was a plastic jug of tea and I had mine out of a coke bottle; I'd smashed all the cups earlier.

I was getting more anxious, more upset. I found an empty Newcastle Brown Ale bottle, held the neck and smashed the base off. I ripped open Danielson's shirt and stood over him. I was in control – barely.

Charlie made no sound. He was just staring. I was absolutely petrified. I was as scared then as I had been at the beginning when I had the knife held at my ribs. The bottle was held at me for a few seconds and then Charlie stepped back. My hands were shaking. Charlie was still holding the bottle. He then, without making any sound, put the bottle to his head and scraped the jagged edge down his bald head. Blood gushed from the cut down his face and on to his shoulders, chest and then the floor. I sat there, too terrified and too shocked to say or do anything.

'I'm going to untie you now and we are going for a little walk.'

He tied one end of the skipping rope around my neck and held on to the other end. I felt very much Charlie's slave – his puppet – and that he had full control over me. I felt total humiliation. This went on for about an hour. Then Charlie re-tied me.

This was a fucking long siege. I talked to the negotiators through the bars of the gate at the end of the unit and I let Phil chat to them. I tried to show him some compassion. I gave him blankets and made him cups of tea. But this was a siege that was to last 44 hours and we had to sleep at some point. I threw a mattress down on to a steel suicide net between the walkways of the landing and told Phil to jump on to it. The rope around his neck was tied to the netting. Awake or asleep, he was still my hostage.

The negotiators stood at the gate while we supped our tea. I could hardly keep my eyes open. They promised I could see my solicitor if I gave up peacefully. I decided to make a deal. Phil Danielson would stay another night, then we would walk out. My word was my bond.

I had a shower. I knew it would be my only chance for weeks. I opened a window. The YPs – the under-21 inmates – were shouting, 'Charlie, Charlie! Have you done him? Is he dead?'

Charlie then shouted back a most unusual reply. 'Look, you lot, do you realise what a good man this is, because I've just had a heart-attack and Phil has brought me around and given me the kiss of life?'

Some shouted back, 'Ooooh!'

Charlie collapsed on the floor in fits of laughter. I

*stuck my head out of the window. I heard shouts of,
'Are you all right, Phil?' and 'Phil, you're gonna get it.
You'll get your throat slit.'*

I released Phil Danielson at 10.00am precisely. I
walked out myself at just before 10.30am.

The van must have been using rocket fuel! They
whisked me away and caged me up in record time.
There were so many screws in the van with me that
some were sitting on the floor on pillows. I was in the
locked-up steel box in the back of the van, cuffed-up
and in my monkey suit. I didn't have a clue where I
was going, but I sensed trouble. One of the screws was
reading the Hull paper. I could see him through the
box window. I was on the front page, and there were
two more pages on the siege inside. I was shagged out,
tired and fed up, so I closed my eyes and nodded off. I
awoke when my head smashed against the inside of
the steel box – there are no seat belts in those things.
We were rolling through the gates of Whitemoor
Prison in Cambridgeshire. We drove up to the back of
the seg unit. Boy, were they in for a shock!

There were a good 20 of them waiting for me, most
in riot gear. Hey! Tough guys! But I tell you what,
they couldn't even manage to open the lock on the box
I was in! The lock was stuck. They brought in
workmen with a grinder.

The noise, the sparks and the smoke were giving
me a headache. I hate smoke. They still couldn't get
in. They were pissing me off.

'Oi,' I shouted. 'Stand back!'

I gave the door a dozen good kicks, putting all my
weight behind them. The door flew off!

They grabbed my arms and led me into the block
where a cell was ready. Then all the shit started. I
wasn't allowed a toothbrush, it had to be kept outside
my door. I had to stand up when the door unlocked. I
couldn't have my property. I said, 'Hold up! Are you

saying I can't do my cartoons?' They said I could have one pen ... no pencils, no rubber, no ruler.

Bollocks.

I made an official complaint but they overruled me. What was I to do? Sit and look at four tiny walls all day and every day. My art is my life. My one enjoyment. Why couldn't I do it? What harm was there? Was it not bad enough being caged up?

Fuck it! I decided – no art, no life. I went on hunger-strike. For 30 days I took only water and tea, and throughout it all I was on a riot unlock. I was seriously weakening, but they would come in with helmets and shields and search me and my cell. They put food in, and then came to take it away again.

I was dying, slowly. This was not my way. My body is my temple; I've worked on it all my life, built it strong. Forget booze, fags, drugs.

I felt like I was blowing myself away.

My hunger-strike carried on another ten days.

I went 40 days, the same as Jesus had done. But he did it in the wilderness, not inside a concrete tomb. (Also, I reckon he ate shrubs, berries, plants, even the odd rabbit!) Me? I lost three-and-a-half stone. My muscles were wasting away.

But I survived and I've got to thank all the cons who gave me support – Tony Crabb, Richie Halliday, Barry Cheetham, Little Ali, Yellow and Fergie.

On April 23 1999, I was transferred back to Woodhill's special secure unit – and that's from where I'm telling you this story, the story of my life. I was a success here before, but they have put me on A wing. No privileges – nothing but the warehousing of a human being. They will not let me progress through the system, however well I behave. There are disturbed killers on better wings in the unit, yet I'm in a cell with no fresh air, no window to open. My bed is a concrete plinth six inches off the floor and I have only two half-hour visits a month. Why should my old mum travel 250 miles for half-an-hour with me?

If I were Irish or black I could complain of racial prejudice. But I'm not. I'm Charles Bronson. I'm a dead man in a concrete coffin, caged up 23 hours a day. I've dug my own hole and they now seem determined to bury me in it.

EPILOGUE

I am like a fly in a spider's web. I'm trapped. I can't get out.

Will I have the life sucked from me? Will I be left as just an empty shell? Will I ever be trusted again? Would you trust a man who has spent almost all his adult life in cages and dungeons?

I doubt it.

I've lost almost everything, even the right to breathe fresh air. But I will still fight on. They can throw away the key – they probably did years ago. But I will go on. I'm a survivor, see.

Sometimes I think there is no way out, that I'm gonna destroy myself. They're making me sick in the nut. And when I get bad heads, I'm unsafe, unstable. But I know I'm not a psychopath. I've lived with psychos; I know what makes them tick. I do have a conscience, and I do feel guilt. I'm deeper than any psycho. There are two sides to me. If I like a person, I'd die for them. If I hate them, they may die for me. Just pray you never get on my bad side. My bad side is your worst enemy.

But some days I get doubt, depression, anger. I feel isolated beyond anything you can imagine. HQ says I'm too dangerous to mix. Maybe I'll end up like Rasputin, or Rudolph Hess.

Some nights I switch off, plug my ears and sit at my cardboard table under the security light ... creating my art. I smile, I laugh, I feel happy. It may take one hour or ten hours. Who cares? But when I finish I feel drained, emotionally, physically, spiritually. It's like giving birth to life. It is the one release I have from my inner self.

I've come a long way over the last five years and I am going to climb out of this stinking hole. I'm going to win. I owe it to my family and friends – and, most of all, to myself.

I don't care if I face another 20 stinking years. I'll do it. I'm a solitary fitness survivor. Once I've overcome my urges to tie people up, I'll be a nice man on a mission of peace.

I'm going to walk out of whichever prison I'm in, in my black suit and shades, clean-shaven and ready for the start of my life on the outside.

I'll walk away from that jail and not look back. And then all my loyal pals and I will go for a nice slice of apple pie and a cup of tea. We might have a sing-song. We'll probably have a beer.

Then I'll go to the coast and, if my bones are not too

creaky, I'll run along the sea-front like I did during my 69 days of freedom back in 1987. They bet then that I would last only seven days. I proved them wrong.

I'll prove them wrong again. Sooner or later I'm coming home. I am the ultimate survivor. One day the cell door and the gates will swing open and I'll breathe again.

It'll be a lovely day for a spot of bowls or a game of croquet!

Right now, I've gotta dash. Lots to do and only 20 years to do it in.

Stay lucky. And God bless!

Charles Bronson appeared at Luton Crown Court on February 14, 2000 and defended himself over the Hull siege. During a four-day trial he was found not guilty, on the judge's direction, of causing Phil Danielson actual bodily harm, and also of a threat to kill. In evidence, Mr Danielson said Charlie had been 'compassionate' during the siege, making him cups of tea and giving him blankets.

Charlie pleaded not guilty to damaging prison property and false imprisonment, but on February 17 he was convicted unanimously by the jury. He'd argued he had been 'under duress' at the time of the hostage-taking, and gave an impassioned speech to the jury about his years of isolation. 'When I wake up every morning I wake up with a headache from lack of air. Unnatural light. My eyes hurt. The first thing I do every morning when I wake up is go over to that window and stick my lips on the grille and suck in air. That's how I get my air. Even the birds don't come to Woodhill. The birds are frightened by Woodhill.'

After the guilty verdict, he was asked by the judge if he wanted to offer any mitigation. 'Just crack on, give me some more porridge,' he said.

Charlie was jailed for life. His earliest parole date is 2010. Before being led away to face more years of confinement, he said, 'Why don't you just shoot me?'